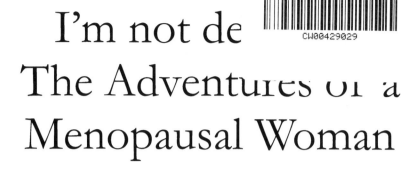

I'm not de
The Adventures of a
Menopausal Woman

Jan Coulson

ISBN:9798673749371

DEDICATION

For Peter and Maureen who made everything possible.

And for my new Vietnamese family - Anna, Greenie, Eric, Sunny, Helen, Misa, Kayla, Toby, Ethan, Enly & Linh.

Many thanks to Peter for all the technical help with the computer and getting this book onto Amazon.

Special thanks to my friend Kirsty Scarratt for designing the front cover for me.

Thanks to all the people I met along the way, nice ones and irritating ones, they were all great characters to observe. Some of them have had their names changed, but I assure you that everything written actually happened apart from one thing, I will leave you to guess as to whatever that might be.

CONTENTS

1 THE BIG IDEA

It all started in the March of 2018. Peter, my husband of 18 years (more about him later) and I went on holiday to Hoi An in Vietnam. This was our fifth visit and we love the place. Unfortunately the weather wasn't great whilst we were there so when it came for the time to go home I had only just started to relax and felt a bit disappointed that we hadn't really done very much .

You know what going on holiday is like for any woman. You do all the organising, all the packing, work like a trojan to get everything in the office up to date and then for some strange reason you clean the house from top to bottom, change the beds, empty the fridge and cut the grass. Why do we do it? Who's benefit is it all for? We are supposed to be having a relaxing holiday, a break from it all. If a burglar breaks in to your house, he isn't going to worry that the sink has got toothpaste around it or the pillowcases are not freshly ironed, and I happen to know that it is much easier for police dogs to track an intruder through long grass. Anyway, going on holiday, I am usually worn out before I even get to the airport.

I also hate flying. It is the one thing (apart from rats) that truly terrifies me. I have absolutely no problem with any other type of transport. I think that is because it would ultimately be your choice to get off, you can jump off of a train or ship, leap out of a car or bus, in a plane you have no other option than to sit there. I estimate that I have been on at least 170 flights in my lifetime time so far. I read a self help book years ago, Feel the fear but do it anyway - by Louise Hay, and I have never let my fear of flying get the better of me nor has it ever stopped me travelling, but contrary to popular belief it does not get any easier. The week before I go away I get myself into a complete lather, I convince myself that this time the plane will definitely crash, so by the time I eventually arrive at my destination I am bouncing off of the walls with agitation and hysteria.

Getting to Vietnam is not a straight forward process. It takes at least an hour and a half to get to the airport from our house. You then have a three hour debacle at Heathrow, then spend 12 hours squashed into a metal can in the sky with shrink wrapped food and half a glass of water. This is then followed by a three hour stopover in Singapore, by which time I am so disorientated I have real trouble negotiating the enormous Changi Airport where you have to change terminals for your onward flight. You then have to spend another three hours in an even smaller tin can to fly onwards to Danang with even worse food.

By the time I reach my hotel I am so tired and dehydrated I cannot sleep. It takes me at least a week to come down to earth and adapt to my new environment. Also at the age of 54 I now have a further problem : my body has to cope with the heat and humidity of South East Asia. Menopausal women get hot in the middle of January in the UK, so coping with 90% humidity and 30C heat is yet another thing we have to contend with. Meanwhile my husband is having a wonderful time, thoroughly relaxed and sleeping like a baby.

Let me explain what the menopause is all about. Imagine you have been kidnapped by aliens and have been taken back to their planet. Once there they cut open your head, remove your brain and replace it with a pink fluffy marshmallow. Whilst you are on their operating table, they fiddle around with your internal thermostat by jamming it onto VERY HOT. They then delve around with your personality by removing most of the good bits and fill you up with a load of emotional trash. They then stitch you back up and send you back to resume your former life whilst laughing uproariously at their great joke as you descend down to earth. You still look like you on the outside but you feel very different internally. When you arrive back on planet earth, because you now have a very small piece of confectionary where you once had a brain, nothing works properly.

You start to ache in places you didn't even know existed. You have trouble doing any sort of exercise as all of your joints hurt. You cannot get off of the sofa in one swift movement anymore. You put on weight when you eat one crisp. The smallest stupidest little things get magnified out of all proportion. You get really grumpy and furiously angry, then the next day you start sobbing whilst watching a film about a family who inherit a Christmas tree farm??? You can't find anything in the house and you put things in very strange places (I once found a whole pack of smoked salmon in the cutlery drawer) You retain absolutely no information whatsoever, if an event is not written in my diary or is not on the calendar it will not be happening. Your sex drive takes a complete nose dive, and all you really want to do is sleep but you can't because you have vicious night sweats that keep you awake all night. When eventually you do get some sleep it wipes clean any memory of the previous day and you can't remember what you were doing before you went to bed.

Then to top it all, your husband begins to give you funny looks and starts avoiding you because he no longer recognises the strange woman he is living with. To help him cope with it he then starts going out all the time, leaving you alone in the house which is NOT RECOMMENDED.

When it first started in 2014 - I can almost pinpoint it to the day, I went to the Doctors three or four times out of pure desperation. A particular incident where I had completely lost my rag with Peter in the garden over a tent prompted the first Dr's visit. (I hope the neighbours all enjoyed the screaming, hysterical, mad woman entertainment). First of all they tried to fob me off with anti-depressants which I declined, then one Doctor (a female would you believe) actually said I wasn't that bad so she could not recommend HRT and I would just learn to work my way through it. Well Doctor I am 5 years in and IT STILL ISN'T ANY EASIER!

The only useful help I did receive from one GP was a prescription for some sleeping tablets. They will only give you 14 at a time, and I have to use them sparingly. But after a few weeks of sleepless nights I occasionally take one on a Friday night. They send you into total oblivion, I don't even feel the night sweats, and can easily understand how people get addicted to them, I can sleep for 10 hours straight after taking one. It is certainly not a solution to the sleep problem but I always feel better for a few days after a decent nights rest.

Those of you who have been through all of the above will recognise all of this, nod and sympathise. DO NOT BELIEVE any of the media hype about how the menopause is empowering to women, it's a load of crap, it makes you feel like SHIT. For those of you not yet there, it really is something to look forward to as you get older - NOT.

Anyway I digress, as I said I love Hoi An and I felt a bit cheated that we did not get out and about as much as usual.

At that time I was working for a Recruitment agency (money for old rope, a bit like Estate Agents). The group of people I worked with were an eclectic bunch. Probably the most foul mouthed and racist people you could ever wish to meet, and I hated working there. The office I was in had no windows, the kitchen and toilets were disgusting. The management were so mean they would not even pay for a pint of milk, so you had to provide all of your own beverages including drinking water. I was 53 years old at the time, going through what I think has been the most difficult period of my life so far. I felt completely exhausted all the time as I never slept properly, tearful, anxious and my hot flushes were off the scale, I certainly had no confidence at that time to go out and try to get another job.

Technology, don't get me started on it. My husband says I am an analogue woman in a digital world. If I can write something down on a piece of paper I am happy. Don't get me wrong, I can work a computer, send an email, I have an iPad, iPhone and I am on Instagram and I use WhatsApp all the time. I just do not understand how to use all of these gadgets to their full capability and the big thing is I AM NOT INTERESTED! Just turning the TV on in our house is a complicated procedure. I do not kid you but the TV in our lounge has four different remote controls. One to switch it on, one to turn the sound bar on and the other two are still a complete mystery to me and sit on the sideboard covered in dust.
And don't get me started on Facebook and Twitter. The rubbish that people put on there, don't some of these stupid people realise that the whole world can see what they are posting (Donald Trump take note). I have a friend whose wife literally lives out her entire life on there. She slags off her husband, moans about her children, family, employer and everyone else she knows. Then she wonders why we all try and avoid her like the plague. And the time that people spend on there everyday liking things, not liking things, being in a relationship, being single, being gay, posting photos of their dinner and their pets, WHO CARES?
Well somebody obviously does because they are sitting there reading all this Crap.

To apply for most jobs now it is all done online, gone are the days when you applied for a job in the local newspaper on a piece of paper with actual handwriting. I have a CV which I emailed out to dozens of agencies, but I got absolutely nowhere, not even one reply came back. I have since learned that it is the way you word your CV not what experience or qualifications you actually have. Apparently you have to 'Big' yourself up. So instead of saying you are 'reliable, methodical and are looking for a new position' you have to say 'I am dynamic and performance driven and I am looking for the opportunity to utilise key transferable skills and expertise to a new challenge.'
Over the last few years I have seen some amazing CV's, all typed up on a computer. They teach them at school how to sell themselves nowadays and their self confidence on screen is staggering. Unfortunately sometimes when the person has been appointed to do the job they can't spell or do basic mathematical calculations in their head. But if you do not have the correct buzz words in the CV, you will never be picked up online as a suitable candidate. I have a friend who employed a girl with an amazing CV but who could not work out 10% of any figure in her head OR even work it out on a calculator!

My friend Carlos eventually rewrote my entire CV for me. I hardly recognised myself on paper when he was finished, he made me sound like some sort of super executive who could take on the Marks and Sparks Clothing department and turn it around into something amazing (which of course I couldn't do but at least I would ensure that the sizes fitted properly).

So there I am in this recruitment office for the last 2.5 years, working with a woman who made Cruella De Vil look like Baby Spice. A woman who was always cold and had to have the radiator on at full blast at all times throughout every season. Our office was so hot you could fry an egg on the desk and grow crops of orchids or pineapples, I felt really ill some days with the heat. Winter work wear consisted of a thin skirt and a strappy vest top to be able to cope with the tropical temperature. This was a woman who wouldn't let us have the radio on to break the awkward silence that lay between us nearly every day. A woman who flitted between behaving like a sweet little girl one minute and Godzilla the next, who would literally snarl at you if you said one word out of place. I never knew what I was walking into on a Monday morning which made Sunday evenings in our house a bit tense. This woman could sulk for England, if it was an Olympic Sport she would win a Gold medal for it. She had been particularly vile to everyone for the past three weeks and I had had enough. I had my own menopausal and health problems and I had reached the end, I didn't have the patience to put up with the Queen Diva or the crappy office anymore. I had an excuse for my madness, she didn't.

Over the weekend of my birthday in April, Peter and I discussed my total misery and we decided I should just leave. I have a condition called Graves Disease and it can be set off by stress, the last thing I wanted was for that to kick in again. So on that Monday morning I went into work with my handwritten notice in my handbag. Strangely enough on that particular morning my miserable colleague decided to go into one and verbally attacked me, accusing me of talking about her behind her back and scheming to take her job, which was about as far from the truth as could be possible, so in the end I did not work my notice and just left.

Oh the amazing feeling of freedom!! The Liberation! The wonderful comprehension of knowing I would never have to go back to that shit hole ever again, then the downside of being hit by sudden blind panic of not having any income. Since I left school at sixteen I have always worked and feeling a bit washed up at 54 I was not sure what would happen now and I had a few sleepless nights I can tell you.

Fortunately the boss paid me up to the end of the month which was the least he could do as I was instrumental in helping to save his companies arse in January when he and his partner got into a financial mess, so at least I had one full months salary in the bank.

Before I met Peter, I lived on my own for four years, working three jobs to pay for my mortgage & car and to ensure that I always had a holiday, so I am very good with managing money. I figured out that I could last for possibly three months before the cash ran out. After that I would have to use my savings or sub off Peter.

During the next week I bumbled around, just trying to catch my breath, feeling oddly relieved one minute and then a bit frantic the next. What had I done? What was I thinking of? Was anyone ever going to employ a 54 year old mad menopausal woman to work for them?

My sister, knowing how down I was, whisked me off to the cinema in the middle of the day, which I felt was very decadent. We spent a pleasant few hours ogling Hugh Jackman in 'The Greatest Showman' which somehow lifted my spirits and during that week I slowly started to emerge from the gloom. I was beginning to have an idea in my head of something I really wanted to do but dared not actually voice it out loud or put it into words. In the end Peter just asked me outright what I really wanted and it all came tumbling out. I wanted to go travelling in South East Asia for three months, ending up spending some quality time in Vietnam.

It is strange how you think someone will react and when it actually happens it's never as bad as you imagined it would be.

Peter said it was something that he felt I needed to do and I should go for it!

"Go" he said, "it's important to you, get it out of your system".

So I did and this is the tale of my big adventure.

2 PREPARATION

In the meantime I had landed a job with a charity on a temporary contract which would end in January 2019. The money wasn't very good but it fitted in with my plan and I was quite up front about it when they employed me. I was already a volunteer with them and knew most of the people in the office. I had always said that I would never work for them as I was so heavily involved with the volunteering side but I discovered that I really enjoyed it. The money eventually didn't seem so important, I felt part of a team, everyone got on well, no-one had an ego and we had such a laugh in that office. We talked about everything, there was nothing that we didn't discuss. The males in that office were well educated during that time, they know all about smear tests, giving birth, the menopause & women's underwear. Hopefully it will stand some of them in good stead for the future!

I think that they were all as surprised as me how well we all got on. I have a bit of a reputation for being a bit stand offish and intolerant, I admit that I certainly take no prisoners, and I say it as it is, but I think they realised it's all a bit of an act and bit by bit they broke me down. I still scare a few people now and again but I feel it never hurts to keep a bit of a guard up and keep people guessing.

Everyone was very kind and always helped me when I couldn't do anything regarding the dreaded IT/technology. No-one looked down on me or rolled their eyes every time I locked myself out of the system or lost the spread sheet I was using. And they got me a fan for my desk, so each time I had a hot flush I could give myself a quick blast. The office also had air conditioning and windows that actually opened. It was pure heaven after my previous experience in the shitty greenhouse office.

All in all I felt very grateful for that job, it lifted my spirits in a way I cannot describe and I was really contributing to something worthwhile and felt all my efforts were valued. Everyone was in awe and wonder of my plan and I even managed to talk one of the girls into coming out to Vietnam to join me whilst I was there.

I decided to embark on my trip in February 2019, so throughout the long hot summer of 2018 a plan started to come together. Peter had stipulated from the start that there was to be no back packing and to be honest I am way past that, the thought of bunking down in a dormitory with a load of sweaty strangers really didn't do it for me. I decided to do it in a bit of style, I needed clean sheets, a working hot shower, a good breakfast and most essentially air con everywhere I was to stay.

I told my mother who just shrugged in a vague sort of way which is quite normal for her. When I told Maureen, Peters mum, I got a different reaction all together. She was so encouraging and interested and said yes I must go. And then the cherry on the cake was that she said she would give me a sizeable cheque towards it (My mother also gave me a donation). Maureen is an amazing woman and I love her to bits but I secretly think she quite fancied having her little boy to herself for three months without me around.
 I decided to use a portion of my savings and altogether had a budget of £10,000, all I had to do was to decide where and how I was going to spend it.

I knew I wanted to go to Burma or Myanmar as it's now called. It's certainly not an easy place to get to. There are no direct flights from the UK and the tourist infrastructure outside the main cities is still a work in progress. I found one tour which was reasonably priced and covered a lot of the rural side of Burma. When I actually read the itinerary properly, I would be sleeping in huts with no running water let alone aircon or cotton sheets, and don't laugh but one of the days I would have to cycle 30 KM in temperatures of 80C. As my husband knows only too well, last time I went on a bicycle (strangely enough in Vietnam), I fell off and went head first into a paddy field clonking my shin on the pedal. On the return flight, two days later, my leg swelled up, went black and blue and I could hardly walk when we landed. I had to go straight to the Drs when we got home as we thought I may have developed a DVT on the long flight. Fortunately it was only a chipped bone but I have not been on a bicycle since. The thought of coming off in rural Burma with no hospitals for hundreds of miles didn't really do it for me.
The only way I could see to do it safely was by boat sailing down the Irrawaddy River, stopping at the rural villages and ending up in the city of Bagan. There are numerous companies that run vessels up and down the river between there and Mandalay.

I now came across something that always does my head in: Single person Supplement. What is that all about? I only cause one amount of mess, only eat one breakfast, only use 1 towel, only use 1 toilet roll, only drink 1 in house beverage and yet you can be charged hundreds, in some cases thousands of pounds over the top.

I thought I would start the trip in style but these cruises were not cheap and I knew that, but once you factored in the SPS they were mega expensive. One company wanted £6000 for 10 days, which was over half of my total budget for the whole three months. Battling on through the heat of the best British summer for years, I spent hours in front of the computer, researching flights & hotels and pricing up tours.

I had worked out the rest of my itinerary and decided the easiest and safest way to put it together was to get an independent travel company to help me with part of it. I am not a backpacker who can just move around on a whim, I needed something organised in advance. So many thanks to Kay from Travelbag who helped me put it all together.

I still had not got the Burma bit worked out but in the meantime Kay looked at all the tours through Laos for me. I had also booked two 3 star hotels in Hoi An for two months on the internet. I booked two because I just could not decide where I wanted to be. One was between the beach and the town and the other was right in the centre. Hotels are incredibly cheap in Vietnam and in the end I chose a three star between the town & the beach which worked out at £22 per night for a double room with breakfast & aircon. The hotel even had a pool, it had 5 star reviews on Trip Advisor and seemed perfect. I just had to figure out my route and how I was going to end up there.

I found a slightly cheaper cruise on the Irrawaddy which with SPS worked out £3799 which was still way over my budget. I was beginning to think I would never get to Burma when during one lunch time I was browsing the Internet and ended up back on the holiday website where I had originally seen the cruise. That morning they had reduced the price to £1999 and removed the SPS and that included the flights. Kerching! It was absolutely perfect. I sneaked off to an empty office, rang them and booked it immediately. The trip also included the return flights to the UK but a quick search on the internet showed me the difference between a one way trip and a return was £108. I would only lose £108 booking the whole thing with them and they could put me as a no show on the return journey so I could just fly off somewhere else. As I had just saved £1799 I did not feel that this was a problem. It meant for the first leg of my trip, when I would be at my most vulnerable, I would be with other people and get looked after by the tour company. So I was booked onto the RV Kindat Pandaw sailing down the Irrawaddy River on 1st February.

Once this was confirmed everything else then started to fall into place. I would fly to Singapore, change planes and fly onto Mandalay with the tour company and pick up the Pandaw cruise. The return flight to Heathrow then went from Mandalay to Yangon to Singapore and I was to leave the tour group at Yangon which all was included in the price.

Kay booked me a hotel in Yangon (5 star, it was very cheap) and a private tour with my own guide and driver for 3 days. From Yangon I would fly on to Bangkok, transfer to the beach and then return to Bangkok for six days in another 5 star hotel (a bit more expensive). I would then fly out to Vientiane, the capital city of Laos, and pick up the tour which also encompassed Luang Prabang. From there I would head out to Hanoi, onwards to Danang eventually ending up in Hoi An.

I decided to pay extra at each airport for a private pick up, as I felt it would be safer and easier than having to deal with taxi drivers. I know I could have done it a lot cheaper on the bus or train but as the money was in the budget it meant I would not have to contend with dragging my luggage around, someone else could do it of me.

By the end of July everything was confirmed and booked. I would fly out from the UK on 1st February and return on 29th April.

Shopping, well most women love it, I am no exception.

What did I need to buy? How much sun cream would I need? How much insect repellant can you fit in one suitcase? (I am particularly susceptible to the mosquito, they love me). Would there be any reason to wear something smart? And the very important question of how many pairs of shoes should I take?

It was August, Britain was still in the grip of a heatwave and the shops were full of Christmas cards. All the clothes for sale were black, grey or sparkly party dresses. Not a pair of shorts or flip flops were in sight.

Trawling through many shopping centres I managed to get some flip flops that had been reduced to clear (and after wearing them I know why). I could not get any decent female shorts anywhere so I ended up buying three pairs of mens cargo shorts, which made me look like Eric Morecambe in his famous sketches when he wore baggy shorts. It was hopeless trying to get any sun dresses but I did manage to get a very short skimpy sundress from Dorothy Perkins which I was very unsure of. I even bought a cotton jump suit from House of Fraser that Peter said made me look like Andy Pandy. Coming from a man who thinks the skater boy look is De Rigueur, what did he know? M&S Outlet provided the microfibre knickers which I planned to wash myself and knew would dry overnight, and Matalan supplied some cheap bras as I did not want to take any of my decent underwear.

Everything else would have to come out of my current wardrobe as it was hopeless out on the high street. Even the Internet was a bit of a let down, everything in my size was out of stock, but I did manage to get a decent bag and some vest tops.

Clothes shopping all sorted, I now turned my attention to the medical side. I had two large sandwich boxes which I stuffed full of every kind of tablet and concoction known to man. Diarrhoea tablets to stop you going, laxatives to make you go, pain killers of every description, creams, lotions and potions for every ache and pain. My Doctor even let me have two lots of antibiotics on a private prescription which only cost £14.00 (work that one out!). One of these was for any water infection that may come on and boy can they come on quickly, and the other was for any other general infection. I knew I could get most other serious drugs in Vietnam but felt I needed to take something in case I went down with anything early on. I stuffed an old wash bag full of out of date bandages, swabs, eyewash and plasters that I had to make up a first aid kit.

Fortunately as I have travelled in South East Asia numerous times I did not need any more vaccinations as I was already covered. I was advised to take malaria tablets but as I was not actually going to any high risk area it was not considered mandatory, so I didn't bother. Last time I took them the ground kept moving up and down and it was most disconcerting.

I find it is the toiletries that weigh your luggage down the most. Shampoo, conditioner, hair wax, sun cream, face cream, aftersun, foot cream, toothpaste, hand wash & hand gel (very important in Asia), I wanted to take all my usual brands with me as I knew I would probably only get anything decent in Thailand and that was 13 days into the trip. They weighed a tonne.

I also had to buy a separate travel insurance which ended up costing me £156.00, something else to come out of the budget. If you travelled abroad for more than 45 days on our existing policy it would not cover me. I was more worried about the medical side than losing my luggage or a delayed departure. I wanted full Evac from Burma, Laos or Vietnam should I get seriously ill or be in an accident and flown to a Bangkok or Singapore hospital for treatment. Surprisingly Saga came up with the best plan and as I was over 50 I could have one of their policies.

Other things to consider: where was I going to get my hair cut? Now this may not seem very important in the scheme of things but it was still something to think about. I was currently rocking a very short layered style as I had recently decided to let my hair go grey. Fortunately it had gone an amazing platinum colour that my hairdresser says cannot be replicated from a bottle, but she did say I had to have a funky style or it would age me. It had to be cut every six weeks to keep this look and with images of little grey haired ladies in my head this was bothering me a bit.

Back on the internet to research hairdressers in Hoi An. In the Old Town was a beauty parlour ran by a Viet married to a Scot who did her training in the UK, a good result. I would book an appointment with her as soon as I got there.

Another thing to think about was laundry services, I knew I could get it done fairly cheaply in all of the destinations outside of the hotels. In the hotels they can charge as much as £2 to wash one pair of knickers! I also needed to remember not to take any decent clothes with me if I was planning on taking them home again. What with the sweat, sun cream, the boiling heat and the various ways of Asian washing, nothing would be fit for purpose by the end of the trip.

Getting my nails gelled or eyebrows waxed would never be a problem as every other shop in Vietnam and Thailand was a beauty parlour, and it would also be really cheap. Maybe I could also get my cellulite massaged away at one of these parlours?

After Christmas we put our house up for sale. I know it wasn't the best time to try and sell up but encouraged by the estate agent (who over priced it, now there's a surprise) we decided to give it a go. I really wanted to downsize to something smaller and clear our remaining mortgage, I was excited by the thought of maybe moving house when I got home from the trip. More about this later.

In December the next thing to tackle were the Visas. I needed a Burmese and Laotian tourist visa, which allegedly would be easy, but for Vietnam I needed a special visa. You can enter Vietnam for 14 days without one but for anything longer you needed an individual one and it would not come cheap.

Peter had to help me with all of the online forms of course. Burma first as I thought it would be the trickiest, but I was completely wrong, not only was it the quickest, it was also the cheapest at only £35. I got a 90 day Visa through the Vietnamese embassy in London online, which cost me a whopping £122.

The most awkward one was the Laotian visa. You could not apply online and had to go to their embassy in person. They also wanted a lot more details of where you were going and where I would be staying than the other countries had asked for. I did not have all the information at this point and Kay from Travelbag had to email the Laos travel company to find out. A visit to London was now called for. The Laos embassy has to be the cutest embassy in London. It looks like someones private house, there are no security guards with guns or any metal detectors. You step inside into a room that looks like your grannies parlour. Completely cluttered, full of boxes and sofas, all very ordinary looking. I handed over my passport and

£55 cash and then had to kill 4 hours in Kensington before I could return to pick it up.

By mid January I was correctly documented. Peter bought a huge map of South East Asia and marked out my route in pink highlighter pen so he could follow me and stuck it on the kitchen wall. I wrote out my whole itinerary for him, including flight numbers, times and all the hotels I would be staying in. I had to give my emergency contact and insurance details to all of the companies I was using to tour with, but I also needed Peter to know where I was at all times in case of any emergency.

He also created a blog for me so I could keep in touch with my family and friends and they could follow me everywhere. Technology again. I would have to log onto Google each time, which meant more log ins and passwords. For a woman who could barely remember if she had had breakfast this was more than I really could cope with. I practiced using it in the months leading up to the trip and I did get the hang of it eventually and could even post photographs. I did have a few tricky moments with it now and again but I just deleted those postings and restarted . I thought I was the bees knees that I actually mastered it, I think Peter thought it was a small miracle as well. He also gave me a long and boring lecture about switching off my data and only using Whats App to send messages or make phone calls. Yeah, Yeah whatever. I knew Thailand and Vietnam would have good Wifi everywhere but Burma and Laos might be tricky and it could be a while before I could make contact with Planet Peter.

The weekend before D day, I started the mammoth job of packing for three months. I was planning on travelling with one suitcase, a small piece of hand luggage and a handbag. When I laid everything out on the spare bed I realised I would need a 38 tonne articulated lorry to convey all of my stuff. I am an expert packer and I did try very hard to cram everything into a normal sized suitcase but it was absolutely hopeless, so I ended up getting a bigger one out of the loft. Peter guffawed when he counted up 14 pairs of shoes lined up. God, I was going away for three months I wanted a change now and again, but shoe by shoe I sensibly put 8 pairs back in the wardrobe along with half of the clothes I had laid out. After I had added my medicine boxes, first aid kit, guide books, some boxes of cereal bars, underwear, shoes and toiletries, I had nearly filled the whole of the bottom part of the case. That meant I had to cut down on even more clothes. As Peter was coming out to visit Vietnam whilst I was there, I packed him up a little parcel of extras to bring me should I need them.

The Airline allowed 30 kg in the hold and my case weighed 24.5kg. I packed all of my camera gear and several changes of clothes into my hand luggage. A few years ago we lost all of our luggage in Abu Dhabi (a complete nightmare) for two whole days and had to wear what we stood up in, so now I always pack a change of clothes in my carry on bag. I also spread my cash (sterling, US dollars & and Thai Baht) around my luggage, of course I then forgot where I had put it which set me into a panic until my brain kicked in and I remembered where it was.

By the end of that weekend I felt that I was ready. I was also extremely hungover as the guys from work had come round for the evening and it had all got a bit loud and hysterical, or at least I had. We spent all evening trying to leave messages on Steve's answer phone (our boss) in a Chinese/Vietnamese accent which made us all howl with laughter. They bought me a framed picture of George Ezra which they had all written little messages on. 'Shotgun' was played on the radio at least ten times a day in our office and it drove me mad, so they all thought it was hilarious. (The picture now hangs on the wall in our study).

I had been so busy what with Christmas and then all the planning I had not really had much time to think about what I was actually doing and had been feeling excited, intrepid and daring. Suddenly I was seized with massive panic and doubt. What the hell was I thinking of? I was going 8,000 miles away on my own for three months, I must be out of my mind. What if Peter had an accident whilst I was away? As he casually pointed out in that annoyingly sensible voice of his, he doesn't normally have an accident whenever I am not at home. What if the plane crashes into the jungle in Laos? How long will it take to recover my body and inform my relatives? What if all my teeth fall out and I need a dentist? What happens if I am in an accident in a taxi in Bangkok, how will they ever know who I am at the hospital?
These rantings in my mind were of a mad woman. I felt really sick and would have felt really relieved if someone had cancelled it all and I could have gone to bed for a week.

The only good thing that happened during that last week was that the Office manager and the big boss (Steve) called me in for interview for a permanent job beginning on the 1st of May, so I would have a job and salary to come home to. At least he didn't hold it against me about the strange messages I had left on his phone whilst we were all drunk. That was very good news and one less thing to worry about.

One of the warmest British Winters on record and the day before the trip it decided to snow. Two flakes of snow in the UK brings the country to it's knees and OMG, according to the weather forecast it was going to snow all night at Heathrow. The plan was originally for Peter to drive me down there early on the Friday morning, have some breakfast with me and then go to work. I was now getting frantic that I would not get to the airport on time, we would get stuck in the snow on the M25 and I would miss my flight and thereby the connection to Mandalay, everything would then fall apart like a pack of cards

I left work at lunchtime in tears, I didn't know if I would ever see anyone ever again as I was beginning to think I might die on the trip, I was being so irrational.

When I got home I threw up and had to lay on the sofa all afternoon. What a state to get into! Watching the weather like a trained meteorologist I was panicking big time. In the end Peter took control and booked me into a hotel at Heathrow, drove me down there that evening and left me there, promising to come back early in the morning, (he couldn't stay overnight as we hadn't had time to make arrangements for Missy, our dog). Once settled in my room I calmed down a bit, had a bath and took a precious sleeping tablet. It was essential that I had a decent nights sleep, it was going be a long journey the following day. It was still snowing when I finally succumbed to sleep and I had no idea whether Peter would actually get to me in the morning or not, and whether our last goodbye was me waving at him as he waltzed off down the hotel corridor.

3 BURMA

Day 1

Having slept surprisingly well for me in a strange room, I awoke to a cold dark Winter Wonderland called Heathrow Airport. Actually on closer inspection the roads looked OK outside. As promised Peter turned up at 6.45am to drive me to the airport, apparently the snow was nowhere as bad as had been predicted, typical. By this time I was not panicking anymore, I was still terrified but I now had a steely determination to accept whatever fate might meet me along the way. I knew I could still drop out and go home, however Peter would have been so disappointed, he was planning on three months of football, riding his motorbike and eating Chinese takeaways.

The airline check in was all a bit of a faff. It is all computerised now, you even have to print out your own luggage tags. Unfortunately the check in machine would not accept the Burmese visa so we still had to queue up and speak to a real person - a bit of a novelty really - the computer said no. Eventually, after a lot of messing around, I was checked in all the way through to Mandalay. I waved goodbye to my bright orange suitcase unsure whether we would ever meet again and wandered off with Peter to Costa for a bit of breakfast.

I managed to get two pieces of toast and a cappuccino inside me which I really thought might reappear at any given moment. Heathrow was surprisingly quiet and void of people, it's normally heaving. Peter and I made small talk across the table. I then made my way to the point of no return, Airport Security, where we said our final goodbyes.

There are just two of us in this marriage, we have no children and we have both been married before (me twice before - I know shocking isn't it?). My friend Julie says she understands why we never had children because Peter behaves like a 10 year old. I often say he is like Peter Pan and has never grown up, which is actually part of his charm. The loves of his life (in no particular order) are: Luton Town Football Club (probably first), his Indian Motorbikes, Missy the dog, the pop star Toyah (if you don't know who she is look her up), his business, his volunteering work, and possibly me. He works in the shoe industry and owns 66 pairs of beautifully crafted shoes. If our house burnt down we would have to put in a massive claim just for his footwear. He is slightly younger than me and dresses either like a skater boy or Hells Angel depending on what mood he is in. Because he is such a joker and has a deadpan sense of humour, you never quite know whether he is being serious or not. When I first met him I never knew quite how to take him but now I generally assume he is talking crap most of the time. He is also the cleverest person I know. I have watched people get caught out by his quick brain and intelligence because he acts a bit vague and dopey. Underestimate him at your peril, he could run rings around most people if he so chooses.

We have our own individual interests, we do not live in each others pockets and are not joined at the hip. Peter goes away a lot on business and I often go on holiday on my own (he hates travelling), yet we still spend a lot of time together volunteering.

Marriage is really hard. Having a bad marriage in some respects is relatively easy because you give up trying to make it work and you just don't care anymore. Having a good marriage takes time, commitment, selflessness and lots of ongoing work. If you don't do the maintenance it will fall apart and break down like a worn out car. It needs an MOT, a good service and a full overhaul now and again. Our married life may not be everyones idea of perfect wedlock but by allowing each other to be their own person it has seemed to work for us. I know some couples who have never had one night apart from each other since they were married and I am sure some of our friends secretly felt something was wrong with our relationship for me to want to go away on my own for three months. The truth is that I would have only been too glad for Peter to have come with me but he admits he would have hated all the moving around. He likes going on holiday to a resort for a fortnight but hates sightseeing or changing hotels, he would not have enjoyed this trip and would have ruined it for me.

I can honestly say this was the most generously spirited thing that any man could have done for his restless wife. To be given three months complete freedom to go off and 'find' myself. I know some husbands who wouldn't even like their wife to go away for even a long weekend and there are very few men who would have allowed their wife to do what I had got planned, so I will always be very grateful to him for his love, trust and support.

Our goodbye this time felt very different. I burst into tears, great big sobs, I could hardly breathe I was crying so hard. What if we never saw each other again? What if I died on the trip? Peter also welled up a bit and I am sure we looked a pathetic sight clinging to each other by the glass partition next to Security with all the travellers wheeling their cases around us.
I eventually managed to peel myself off of him and snivelled my way into the queue. Another wave, a cheeky grin and then he was gone. It would be 8 weeks until we saw each other again. I now needed to pull myself together and get my marshmallow brain to work. I unloaded my IPad and IPhone, took off my shoes and belt but of course I still set off all the alarms and had to be frisked. Then they wanted to look through the contents of my carry on bag, I hope they enjoyed fondling my clean underwear. At last the indignity was over, with my shoes back on, I escaped into the vast departure lounge.

Because I cannot bear to think about what I am about to endure, I tend to wander aimlessly around at airports looking in all the shops. The shops in this terminal were all boringly high end designer and out of my price bracket so I lost interest after five minutes, I plonked myself down in front of a screen, so I could keep an eye out for my departure gate.
People watching at any airport now is so boring. Pretty much 99% of people are on their laptops or their phones and the other 1% are asleep. What am I missing out on? What is so fascinating about looking at a tiny screen for hours on end? I can't even see mine properly without my glasses. And why do they have to shout down the phone so that you can hear their whole private conversation? I had already switched my Ipad and phone off and I wasn't planning on turning them back on until I got to Singapore.
I also think that small suitcases on wheels should be banned at all airports as hand luggage. The amount of times I have been taken out around the ankles by someone totally oblivious to their mobile lethal weapon that they are dragging through the departure lounge! If you have hand luggage it should be carried by hand - the clue is in the name, that would then stop people trying to cram oversize suitcases into the overhead lockers. If they had to carry it through the airport it would make most peoples luggage considerably smaller and lighter and therefore would leave room for other peoples luggage. Voila - easy isn't it?

Aha the departure gate popped up on the screen and I set off on the 20 minute hike to find the plane. I found a seat in the lounge and started looking around trying to guess who might be on my trip, it was a big plane and their were hundreds of people to choose from. I started to eavesdrop on a chap on the phone who was sitting behind me. He was telling someone he was off to Burma for a week, so I guessed he must be one of them. When he got off the phone we started chatting and yes he was on the same trip as me. Contact made, I had a name and a face to travel with. An announcement was made over the tannoy that due to the bad weather the Captain and crew had been delayed on the motorway: funny how all the passengers had managed to get there on time. So we were now running an hour late and I had already been at Heathrow for 5 long hours.

At last we started boarding, it was an A380 aircraft with 470 passengers and it took forever. First and Business class passengers went straight in, the airlines loyalty passengers second, Premium third and cattle class last. I had an aisle seat in economy on the back row of one of the sections. A friendly couple on their way to see their son in Australia were next to me as I nervously took my seat. The cabin was rammed full and there were no spare seats. How the hell was this thing going to get off the ground? The doors were closed and armed : we were at last ready to go. I think I was the only passenger remotely interested in the safety briefing which I paid close attention to, noting all of my emergency exits. This was the absolute point of no return, I could not get off now even if I had wanted to. Trying to hold back complete panic, we roared off down the runway. Goodbye England, see you in three months.

With tears rolling down my face I looked around me, no-one else was freaking out, well not that you could see. The plane was climbing and the stewardesses were out of their seats and starting to do their jobs. The seatbelt sign pinged off which is always a good thing as it means nothing is going wrong in the cockpit. I went on a plane once on the way home from Florida which developed a fault on take off and instead of turning around and going back we carried on to see if it rectified itself. The captain made us all keep our seat belts on for the whole 4 hour journey until he then decided we needed to emergency land at JFK airport in New York in the middle of the night. That was an interesting situation, as most of us were still wearing Summer clothes and flip flops and it was snowing in New York. So now I work out that if the seatbelt sign doesn't go off within 20 minutes of take off, there must be something wrong!

I was offered a drink, yes please double gin and tonic all round. Looking around some of the passengers were already asleep. How do they do that? It has to be drugs. I can only ever sleep for a nano second, I am too busy flying the plane in my head, keeping an eye out in case the pilot misses something. Peter went on a business trip to Germany last year. He doesn't remember taxiing or take off and the stewardess had to shake him awake after they had landed in Dusseldorf as all the other passengers were getting off and he was still fast asleep.

Lunch arrived. Would I like wine with it, you bet I would. The food was passable but I always wonder where it has been sitting for the last two weeks in its shrink wrapped containers. We got given ice-cream for dessert that was so frozen that it broke my plastic spoon in half. Would I like another glass of wine? Yes please that would be very nice.

Three hours in, the stewardesses cleared everything away, made us pull the blinds down so it was pitch dark in the cabin and then all disappeared up the back of the plane, not to be seen again for several hours. It was only 3pm in the afternoon and there I am sitting bolt upright in the dark and expected to go to sleep.

I had decided not to take any decent jewellery with me. Searching the house for a cheaper watch which was actually working, revealed that the only one with a functioning battery was my £2.50 green fob watch of off my volunteer uniform. I stuffed it into the cubby hole in the back of the seat in front of me so I could keep an eye on the time and settled back to another 9 hours of complete hell. Thank God for Mama Mia and Bohemian Rhapsody, they killed four hours and occupied my mind so that I nearly forgot where I was (only nearly). I fell asleep for a full three minutes and then watched Johnny English followed by Oceans 8 and Papillon. I can't say that I followed the plots religiously as I kept drifting off and then waking up with a start every few minutes. I was also really thirsty by now and grabbed any non alcoholic drink that the cabin crew came through with.

Day 2

Slowly the cabin lights came back on, people started to stir and open up their window shades. There was a glimmer of light outside as the sun started to come up, we must be nearly there. Breakfast was served. What exactly is chicken sausage? Mine looked anaemic as if it had not been cooked, the baked beans were luke warm and served in one solid lump. I did eat the muffin, the yoghurt and drank two cups of the airlines unique tasting black coffee to make me more alert.

Breakfast was tidied away and the crew prepared the cabin for landing, which as far as I can see is just tying up the curtains, collecting the rubbish and wandering up and down the cabin in an imperious manner.

Seatbelt on, headrest upright, wheels down, we landed very smoothly and very quietly into Singapore. Hurrah, we didn't crash on landing and the captain got us onto the exit ramp exactly 12 hours after takeoff, not bad. There was the usual rugby scrum to get off and I was then out on the ramp waiting for my new chum. He appeared with another chap who had sat next to him and was also on our tour, so with my new friends Derek and Ivan, we set off to navigate Changi airport and change terminals.

The airport is enormous and has three terminals. There are two ways to change, go on the monorail or by internal bus. As we seemed to be nearer to the bus stop we went for that option. Whilst waiting we picked up a very posh couple with very plummy voices who were also on our trip, so three became five. We had two hours to make our connection, we arrived at the gate a little early and it wasn't yet open, so we plonked ourselves down on a row of seats to wait, we had made it.

Looking around I noticed a small elderly woman who was wearing the strangest outfit. Dressed like a hippy in a long black baggy vest and leggings with loads of leather bracelets and dangly things hanging from her. From her face you would think she was about 150 years old, but common sense told me no-one alive was that old or would be travelling on their own. She seemed to sort of float around the departure gate like a bit of a spectre. I wondered where she was going?

A huge group of Burmese arrived: mums, dads, grandmas, grandpas, children with all their hand luggage and pushchairs. I don't know how people get away with it but they always seem to. All of us British had the one smallish bag each but these people had about five pieces each. If my hand luggage was 1cm too long or weighed 1ounce too much I am pretty sure I would be arrested, imprisoned and have to pay a massive fine.

The gate eventually opened and we queued up and trundled in. Of course the Burmese family held up everything as they argued vociferously about their luggage with the staff at the desk. Finally at last with everyone through they started to load the plane. This was a 737 and much older, tattier and smaller with only one narrow aisle. I was on the aisle near the front so got absolutely battered by all the luggage that was then dragged through the cabin.

Seatbelt on we roared off down the runway. And I mean roared. This small plane was so noisy compared to the enormous A380 we had arrived on. It felt so small and was really bumping around as it went upwards, on the bigger plane we had been lucky as we had hit no turbulence. I was in pure purgatory, 3.5 hours of this, I could not wait for it to end. My body clock was reading 2am but we were now on Singapore time which was 10am, 8 hours ahead of the UK. All I wanted to do was sleep, but I was flying the plane in my head so had to keep alert!

We bumped along through the clouds and they served lunch (no alcohol). You had a choice of noodles or noodles so I opted for noodles. At some point I was so knackered that I must have actually dozed off, so that killed at least another 20 minutes. Eventually we arrived in Mandalay, the old plane banged down onto the runway, the noise was deafening as they reversed the thrust of the engines to slow us down. We had another time change, going backwards by one hour this time, it was now officially 12.30pm.

I can honestly say I have never been more grateful to get off an aircraft than that one, 22.5 hours since I left the hotel at Heathrow and I was in BURMA.

Actually I wasn't officially there yet as we had to get through the immigration process.

Welcome to Burma! The immigration process took 2 hours. There must have been over 40 people in the queue ahead of me. There were 12 desks but only four were open as is normal in most immigration halls the world over. I calculated that it was taking three minutes to process each person, and there was nothing you could do about it. If you kicked off they would probably shoot you, so you just have to grin and bear it like we British do, we are gold medal experts in queuing. Shuffling along inch by inch I was thirsty, tired and emotionally overwrought. What am I doing here? I really want to go home.

In the luggage hall I reconnected with my heavy suitcase. Well that was an added bonus to have my luggage. Out through the customs hall, I instantly spotted the tour company sign sign and the guide and yes, I was on their list. I counted 22 people in the group as we made our way to the bus, 8 men and 14 women and I was definitely the youngest (by a long way). I also noticed the funny old bird I had seen at Singapore airport in the group. On the drive down to the boat we went on a bit of a detour to see the Jade Pagoda. Now I am all for getting my monies worth but I really was not interested in looking at anything at this point except the inside of my eye balls. But of course there were people in the group who wanted to get off the bus to look at this pagoda and take photographs. I made a mental note of the ones who I thought were going to be the most irritating on this trip and dozed off for a whole 10 minutes whilst they all faffed around getting back on board.

Eventually we arrived at the boat. It was everything I had expected and more. A two tier wooden 'Death on the Nile' boat where you open your cabin door straight onto the deck and the river is just on the other side of the railing. The staff and captain were all lined up on the river bank to greet us and there were welcome cold drinks handed around. There were only 16 cabins on the boat so it was fairly quick to get the key and find my cabin, my luggage was delivered almost immediately.

What a sheer delight! I had two wooden cabin beds with storage underneath made up with spotless white bedlinen. A wardrobe, dressing table, safe, aircon and fully tiled shower with L'Occitane toiletries (which I know are posh). They provided a cotton waffle dressing gown with matching slippers and under the sink was an enormous can of insect repellant. I was just about to lay on the bed when someone walked past my door banging a gong announcing that lunch was ready on the upper deck. Not even having had a chance to change my shoes I went off in search of the dining area. On the upper deck there were 4 dining tables laid out, some comfy sofa's and loungers dotted around in the sun and shade and there was a salon with glass sliding doors, which I presumed was for the evenings.

Derek and Ivan waved me over and I went and sat with them. I have to say the food was amazing as was the service. All the alcoholic drinks were included in the price but I did not dare imbibe at this time of day as I would probably pass out with exhaustion, probably not a good way to introduce myself to the group. It was all very civil and colonial sitting in our wicker chairs with potted palms dotted around the deck. I have to say we all felt knackered but strangely exhilarated to be there. It had been quite a journey. After lunch just when I thought I could escape to my cabin for a lie down, the two guides (Sen and Yen) appeared to inform us that we would be leaving on our first coach trip in 20 minutes. WHAT?ARE YOU MAD? I can't go sightseeing, I need to lay down on a sun lounger and catch my breath.
No-one else seemed to be kicking off about it, so I rushed back to my cabin to quickly get changed. I only had time for a hasty spray of insect repellent, which I knew I would pay for later on. The weather was sunny and warm so I pulled on a pair of shorts, slipped flip flops on my feet and made my way off the boat and climbed up the steep sandbank to get on the Bangla bus. The bus had electric blue and lime green satin curtains and was decorated with swags of bright yellow tassels, it gave me a headache just looking at it. Everyone on board we set off for our first proper look at Burma.

The roads here were very narrow and twisty but were tarmac so the journey wasn't too bumpy. When the bus stopped we had to get out and transfer to, I'd like to say jeeps but I think they were in fact adapted animal trucks. It was a bit of an effort to climb aboard and you needed a bit of a bunk up to get on but once loaded we trundled off to go up Sagaing Hill. The scenery along the way was really green and lush, there were temples literally everywhere and hundreds of golden spires were peeking up through the trees. There were children playing in the roads and we saw several monks ambling along in their dark red robes. We unloaded at the top of the hill and had to remove any shoes and socks as we entered the Sun-U-Ponnya-Shin Pagoda. 89% of Burmese are Buddhist and unlike most of us heathen Westerners their religion is of upmost importance to them, removing your footwear is a sign of respect. Judging by some of the dodgy feet, I can see some people in our group needed a good pedicure, my feet looked quite pretty with their pale blue gel. After climbing several sets of steps we emerged at the top where there was the most amazing view of the Irrawaddy River and the surrounding hills, I had an almost spiritual moment but I think it was just the jet lag.

Back to the bus to go to the U Bein bridge. Now I had read up about this and it didn't look that exciting, just a 1 km long wooden teak bridge, what could be so special about it? From the busy car park we were directed to a small jetty where some very small and fragile shallow boats were waiting for us. In England Health and Safety would have condemned these boats to be used as firewood, but we were expected to get in them and sail out into the middle of the lake. It was by now about 5.15pm and the sun was starting to go down and the insects were starting to come out. Out on the lake I could see what the fuss was all about. There was the most amazing sunset which went down behind the bridge, it was a really beautiful sight. As we were sitting in our little boats admiring the view, another boat pulled up next to us with a member of the Pandaw crew handing out champagne flutes containing the cocktail of the day. Real glasses mind you, no plastic rubbish. What a dignified way to see the sunset. Unfortunately the boat in front of us, which was full of Chinese tourists, developed a leak and literally sunk in front of us which was a bit worrying. Fortunately the lake was only three foot deep so the soaked occupants managed to wade back to the pier.
Back on land we piled back on the bus and headed off to a silk factory. REALLY, WHAT NOW? The last thing I wanted to do was go shopping. So I stayed on the bus and fell into such a deep sleep that I did not feel us drive off and had to be woken up at the other end by Sen or it could have been Yen.
When we arrive back at the boat we are given a cold drink and a blob of hand gel. We were instructed to remove our shoes which were then cleaned and left outside of our cabins later on. This happened every time we went ashore.

Back in my cabin I had just started to unpack and get organised when the dinner gong sounded. We all had to attend a staff and safety briefing in the salon during cocktail hour. The internet router was in the salon and I sat right next to it but could not get any connection, so I gave up trying to contact home. For the staff briefing we were introduced to all the crew and the purser explained how everything functioned on board. He was a gorgeous young man with a real twinkle in his eye and a funny sense of humour (I found out later he was 38 years old and wasn't as young as I thought). We were also instructed to use the metal water canisters for drinking water on the boat as they did not supply bottles of water as Burma is trying to cut down on plastic waste. Well it's certainly a good way to start. With a few gin and tonics inside me I was having a right old time, getting to know everyone and the jet lag temporarily disappeared during the very jolly dinner.

By the time dessert arrived most of us could hardly keep our eyes open and we all retired to our cabins straight afterwards. It had been 31.5 hours since I had last slept and I crawled into my comfy bed with the aircon on full blast and unusually for me went out like a light.

Day 3

I was awoken at 5.30am by the sound of someone performing their ablutions outside my cabin, splashing around and gargling. I climbed out of my lovely bed and had a peek outside the door, it was only one of the crew having a wash in the river, like you do. It was also really cold so I climbed back into my lovely warm bed and nodded off again. I woke up again as the engines cranked up and we started to move, and so the adventure began.

I was the last person to make breakfast, this is quite normal for me, I am not a morning person. It was really cold early on and I was clad in my jeans and a thick cardigan. Apparently there had been coffee on deck for the early risers at 6am, sod that for a game of soldiers.

After breakfast we moored up and are informed we were going on a walking tour of Mingun. I already had three mosquito bites on my right leg which were the result of not applying the repellent properly in the rush the day before, so I was completely creamed up and smelt strongly of lemons. We walked into the village where there were a few traders hanging around. There was no hard sell like in other Asian countries and all they really wanted to do was practice their English with you. There were lots of gorgeous children all covered in Thanaka which is a yellow cosmetic that they all wear on their faces. It is the Burmese equivalent of Creme de la Mer. Some of the women in our group bought some but in my opinion it was a bit too late to start worrying about their skin.

On our walk we came across the biggest pile of bricks in the world, Mingun Temple. It was supposed to be the base of what was going to be the largest pagoda in the world, higher even than the Pyramids, but it was never finished. It was ruined by an earthquake in 1838 and subsequent quakes have rendered it unsafe. The cracks were metres wide and it looked like it was about to fall down. You used to be able to climb to the top but it is banned now as it is in such a precarious state.

Around the corner we were confronted by what looked like a frosted Christmas cake, the Hsinbyume pagoda. It was pure white and with the sun reflecting off of it you needed to be wearing sunglasses just to look at it. It was full of courting couples, so every time you went around a corner you bumped into a young couple having a crafty snog.

All around the monuments were groups of monks and nuns. In Burma the monks wear dark red as opposed to the saffron robes they wear in other parts of Asia, the nuns wear pink and have shaven heads. They had no problem with us taking photos of them (always ask permission first) and likewise the children would all pose for you and I took some really good pictures.

By now I was feeling a bit jaded and could have easily gone back to bed. There were a couple of women on the trip who were travelling together and who were complete shopaholics. They kept stopping at every trader and stall on the way back to the boat and held everyone up whilst they tried on clothes and practised their bartering. It was only day one, give it a rest ladies, plenty of time for shopping later on.
Back on board lunch was served. Yet another delicious meal with good company, me sitting with Derek and Ivan again. Another lady sat with us who was travelling with her husband but he did not feel very well after the journey and was still in bed. I wished I was. The old dear that I had first spotted at Singapore floated silently around the boat wafting her hippy kaftan around. Glasses clinking we cast off for Mandalay City.

Back on board the Bangla bus, which I was beginning to love, the first place we visited was the Mahamuni Temple, the second most revered shrine in the whole of Burma. Now this might upset some people but women are not allowed into the inner sanctum !!!! Shock!!Horror!! This did not bother me at all, this is Burma, they have different traditions and none of the local women were complaining or waving signs about equal rights. They just looked on proudly as their menfolk adorned the Buddha with sheets of gold leaf, there was a camera inside so all the ladies could watch the religious ritual on a big screen outside. All the men on our trip went in for a look whilst us girls watched the proceedings through an open window.
By now the sun was very hot and I was trying to stay in the shade. Because we had had to remove our shoes, the tiled floors were red hot to walk on and your feet got absolutely filthy. Fortunately every time you went to put your shoes back on a crew member would pop up with a wet wipe to clean your feet and hands.
To get back to the boat they drove us through the centre of Mandalay City. All the streets are set out on grid system, a bit like Milton Keynes. It seemed a pleasant enough place, no tall high rise buildings or modern shops and the traffic was almost non existent compared to other Asian cities I have visited, the sun was starting to go down and it was starting to turn a bit chilly.

Back on the boat the dinner gong went. There was absolutely no point in dressing up as it was so chilly at night, so I wore my jeans and cardigan to dinner again. The two shopaholics were already in the salon, all glammed up wearing full make up, jewellery, glittery dresses and sparkly sandals. I just looked like Worzel Gummidge.

I sat on a table of six with my two new chums, the two shopaholics and a lovely lady from Wales. Dinner was another fantastic affair, with lots of laughs and good conversation as we got to know each other. I had 4 G & T's and then thought it might be a good idea to try and ring Peter. Result, the internet was actually working. He was as shocked to hear me as I was to hear him, as we knew Burma might have dodgy connections, it was like he was in the room with me, clear as a bell. I then rang Maureen and my best friend Julie. With 4 drinks inside me I enthused over the boat, the crew and Burma in general. I could not update my blog as every time I logged on to Google it kept coming up in Burmese. I later found out that I just had to change it to English. I am such a technological thicko!

Dinner finished they bought some very petite and beautiful dancers onto the boat for our entertainment. Their costumes were very colourful and their intricate hand and feet movements were fascinating to watch. Apparently they start learning when they are about 5 years old and it takes around 20 years to get to this standard. When they had finished their performance, of course they invited some of us to join in and have a go. Ivan and myself had purposely sat in the middle of the back row so we wouldn't get picked on but Derek had sat right at the front and was a prime target. He is a really big bloke and about 6ft 4 in height. It was really hilarious watching him dancing with this tiny dot of a girl trying to do the hand movements with his enormous shovels. Seriously heckling from the back, Ivan and were shouting 'Disaster daaarling' and other Strictly insults. He took it all in his stride and was a really good sport.

It had been a really good day and I had managed to stay awake until just before midnight. Knowing everything at home was ok, I retired to my cabin and passed out.

Day 4

I woke up at 5 am to the sounds of the crew gargling and washing and gently drifted off to sleep again. I got a panicky message from Peter during breakfast that I had not turned my roaming off on my phone and he was being charged for Singapore & Burma Internet. He's the most generous person in the world but hates paying for things like that and Oh God I thought I had switched it off.

Technology drama over, we set sail for Yandabo pottery village. I must say I was looking forward to this with about as much enthusiasm as I had had for the silk factory. We dropped anchor and set off at a snails pace on the walking tour to the village. There were two elderly ladies on the trip who both used walking sticks and they were each given their own member of the crew to assist them. These delightful young men were so polite and respectful towards them, it was really sweet to watch. The two ladies were obviously loving having a gorgeous young man on their arm and were enjoying all the attention. Good for them. So would I.

Arriving at the village we could see thousands of large terracotta pots laying around. Our guide, it could have been Sen or Yen, got one lady to show us how they were made. The whole thing was totally manufactured by hand and it was very interesting to watch how they were crafted and designed. There are 25 families living together in the village and they each have their own individual pattern to adorn their pots. The Burmese do not like ice cold drinks, neither do I unless it's a G&T or fizz, so they use these pots to keep their drinking water at room temperature. It was a real cottage industry and everyone in the village was involved somewhere in the process. The pots are exported all over Burma and I did see some in Yangon when I was there. She then did the most amazing juggling act and carried three pots on her head whilst she paraded in front of us.

After a well deserved round of applause we slowly made our way back through the undergrowth to the boat. That's when Gordon sidled up to me. I had not really spoken to him yet but I had heard him: everyone had. He had the most timid little wife called Helen who gazed doe eyed at him all day long and who I had not actually heard say one word so far.

"Come along darling keep up"

"You don't really want one of those do you darling?"

"You're not really going to have another drink are you darling?"

"Darling I think it's time for bed"

You know the type. He had the same camera as me and wanted to know if I would like to use his zoom lens. Now I do not know if that was his usual chat up line or if it was a euphemism for something else but I politely declined his most generous offer and dived into the salon for a cold beer where I related the story to Ivan and Derek, who found it very funny.

After lunch we were given some free time. Yippee! I sprawled out on a sun lounger to read my book. The scenery was serene and beautiful, the water calm and still as we glided through it. The old woman was floating around in another voluminous kaftan jiggling her jewellery and feathers. I was joined by a few of the others and we made light conversation as one by one we all nodded off. I only woke up as the sun started to go down and it felt considerably chilly, but the scarlet sunset out the back of the boat was one of the best I have ever seen, it was a truly glorious spectacle.

At dinner that evening we had some nocturnal visitors and were inundated by millions of lake moths. They were in my hair, my dinner and my drink. The crew put up fly paper everywhere and turned the lights down low as it was the light that was attracting them. It didn't really help, if you do not like flying insects it was like hell on earth. Some of the women were squealing and flapping around, I went and got a scarf from my cabin and wrapped it around my head like a Hijab and just got on with my meal, no screaming from me. After dinner we all retired to the salon, shut all the doors and pulled the curtains closed but the flies still managed to get in. God knows how many flies I consumed that evening but I expect they were a rich source of protein.

In my guide book it says never to start a conversation with anyone about Burmese politics unless they bought the subject up first. Well tonight the guides did a presentation regarding the current political situation in Burma. It was very interesting and informative. Aung San Suu Kyi is the leader of the National League for Democracy, she can never be president as the Burmese constitution forbids this as she has children that are foreign nationals. She has recently lost a lot of International support outside Burma due to the issues with the Rohingya Muslims. The Burmese absolutely adore her and are seriously worried about what will happen when she dies (she is 74) as they say there is no-one to replace her. They are terrified that the military will get back in power, and both the guides cited experiences of friends and family who suffered under the former military rule. It was a thought provoking talk and showed that there are always two sides to any argument.

Day 5

Waking in the morning, there were dead flies everywhere. In the shower, toilet, all over the floor and on my bed. Out on deck there were huge piles of insect corpses stacked up which were quickly swept up by the staff.

Another solitary breakfast for me, Billy no mates, doesn't anyone else on this boat sleep in late?

After breakfast we were all given a 1000 Kyat note (about 70 pence) and a piece of paper with Burmese word on it. Each of us had to go to Pakokku local market and buy whatever vegetable was written on their piece of paper.

Well this turned into a hilarious outing. We piled into Tuk Tuks and zipped off to the market. These are not like the Thai vehicle of the same name. These have a cabin on the back and are attached to a motorbike with three wheels and seat up to allegedly 8 people, that is 8 Burmese people. We had real trouble trying to squeeze four big Westerners bums into one and then we had to ensure that our weight was evenly distributed. They are quite unstable and every time we went around a bend it felt like it was going to tip over.

The market was huge and of course total chaos, with motorbikes zipping between all the shoppers and huge lorries unloading their veg in the middle of the road. You had to have eyes in the back of your head to avoid getting run over or being hit with a load of cauliflowers. Derek, Ivan and myself set about our task with great gusto, I even had a Harrods carrier bag to put it all in. What IT was we did not know. Showing our little bits of paper to the stall holders they pointed us all in different directions. It turned out my veg was Okra and Ivan had a small pumpkin but Derek had a huge bunch of something green. I had no idea what is was, let alone how you would go about cooking it. It was nearly as big as me and we had to cart this huge bunch of whatever back to the Tuk Tuk. I am sure it was alive with something as we were all scratching and itching by the time we got back to the boat. Handing all our produce over to the chef we were told it would all be cooked for dinner that evening, judging by the size of this mysterious green veg we would be having it every evening for the rest of the cruise.

After another tasty lunch we walked back up the bank and headed for the local orphanage which was run by some monks. I was a bit dubious about this visit as I thought the children might be very sad and I would want to take them all home with me. Pleasingly I could not have been more wrong about the place. There was a lovely feel to it and all the children were smiling, if a little shy, and came out to talk to us. They looked clean, well fed and cared for and were all learning English as part of their education. Some of them wanted to be policemen, teachers and doctors. I really hope they get to achieve their dreams.

The head monk then brought all of the novices out of the monastery to meet us and we presented the children with pencils and notepads that we had all bought at the market. We then had our photos taken with all the children, monks and staff. It was a very special moment, something I will always remember.

On the way back to the boat we visited the Ayartaw clinic. There are no hospitals or doctors surgeries around here for miles. This was one of eight clinics set up and supported by Pandaw where the local villagers get a chance to see a medical professional without a long and expensive journey to the big city involved. There was also an ancient Toyota people carrier that had been donated as an ambulance to take people to hospital if it was needed. This battered old vehicle would never have passed an MOT in the UK, let alone pass a CQC inspection but it was a lifeline to the nearby villagers. Big gangs of children came over to see us and posed happily for photos. They were all gorgeous, with their yellow stripes of thanaka smeared across their little faces and I could have kidnapped all of them.

Back on board we were treated to a 'Vegetable presentation' by the Head Chef. It was a bit like 'Guess my vegetable', some of the stuff was completely unrecognisable. It turned out that Derek's bunch of greenery was spinach, but not as we know it in the UK. The chef whipped up a ginger salad out of some of the ingredients we had purchased, it was delicious but fiery as it was full of red chilli. The Burmese love spicy food, the hotter the better, so do I and demolished two bowls full.

After dinner that evening a few people retired to bed early, not feeling very well: Derek and one of the glamorous shopaholics were amongst them. Strangely enough the missing husband that had gone to bed for three days had arisen and it was the first time any of us had seen him to speak to. After a few drinks most of us decided to turn in early as we wanted to get up to see the balloons over Bagan at dawn. The internet was completely off and I could not speak to Peter, imagining accidents and catastrophes galore at home I did not sleep very well that night.

Day 6

At 2am I ended up sitting in bed reading, so when my alarm went off at 5.45am it was a real struggle to get out of bed. Was this really going to be worth the effort of getting up at this hour? I pulled on my jeans, donned my Pandaw waffle dressing gown and headed up on deck with my camera. It was absolutely freezing and there were piles of dead flies everywhere, especially underneath the lights. Up on deck everyone had had the same idea and were all wearing their robes and shivering in the early morning mist. The sun started to poke its head above the horizon and as it did there must have been 40 balloons that slowly started to rise up with it, it was quite a sight against the back drop of all the temple spires and it was definitely worth getting up for.
As I was up so early I actually had company for breakfast on this morning and I sat with the two older ladies. They were a great pair of girls, both

widows who travel together each year. They were 80 and 82 respectively and had been everywhere on the planet, they were off to slum it in Singapore for a few days when they got off the boat.

We had another casualty today who was not feeling well and was staying in their cabin. Both Derek and the shopaholic had V & D during the night. I know it was cool at night and early morning, but it was very hot during the day. Now I am no medical professional but I had not seen either of them drink any water, only alcohol, and I was pretty sure that that had something to do with it, it definitely was not the food. I have eaten in a Luton kebab shop on a Saturday night, I know rank food when I see it and this was good quality. And on the boat everything was so clean and hygienic, every time we came back on board someone would give us a squirt of gel to clean our hands and it was available all around the ship.

So it was three people less that climbed aboard the little mini bus to take us to Tankyi Taung Mountain. The roads were terrible, full of pot holes and it was a really rough ride, if you were not feeling ill when you got on board, you were by the time we came to a stop. Once there we had to climb a lot of steps in bare feet. There were a lot of pigeons around and you can imagine what we were walking through. At the top was a huge and beautiful pagoda entirely covered in gold leaf, glistening in the sunshine. There were lots of Burmese families up there worshipping together on a day out and they kept stopping us to have their photos taken together. Take note, they were photos taken with actual cameras not mobile phones. They were particularly interested in me with my platinum hair and the blonder ladies in our group.

Before we got back on the boat the local villagers put on a performance of the Elephant Dance on the river bank. This involved two grown men getting inside a heavy ornate costume, a bit like a pantomime horse. They then danced around and did amazing tricks. It must have taken amazing strength as the one at the back took all the weight of the other man whilst they pranced and twirled around. I was otherwise occupied by three adorable little girls who came and sat with me, they were so cute, clapping and dancing along, they had obviously seen it all before and knew the whole routine.

After lunch we had a bit of free time so I sat on a lounger to read my book but nodded off as soon as I opened it. By now there were five sick people in the group. Oh God, I prayed, please don't let me go down with it, I am having such a good time.

This was day 5 of the trip and by now I had had a conversation with all of the passengers on board and there were a few that I was trying to avoid. Some people are just so annoying and such know it alls, if I can hear their voice before I can actually see them I generally steer well clear. Gordon was like that, he had an opinion on just about everything and one of the ladies on board suggested we start a 'Save Helen' group to rescue his very dull but sweet wife. Ivan took great exception to him and they had had a couple of heated debates, so I was trying to ensure they were kept apart so he could avoid him too. The other really irritating person was the floaty old woman, she was full of new age nonsenses and dressed like a hippy in her tie dyed clothes and flowery adornments, another one to stay well clear of.

We arrived at the village of Salay. I liked it here, it would have made an amazing film set. It was full of ghostly Colonial buildings which were all slowly decaying in the sunshine covered in moss and lichen. There were some beautiful houses here with wrought iron balconies, not quite what you would expect in the middle of nowhere. They used to belong to the British who were working for the Burma Oil Company but have now been empty for years. A local village has built up around them and as we walked around we were invited into one of the villagers houses to meet his family. It is experiences like this that make Burma different from other Asian countries, it is like a dip back in time. The houses are all wooden with interesting outside toilets on stilts with small ladders which must be a nightmare to navigate if you are caught short during the night. I really feel that with some investment this could be a beautiful place to stay. Someone had already bought and restored a trading company warehouse and turned it into a small hotel and restaurant. It was on the banks of the river surrounded by flowers and tropical plants and we went there for a drink before heading back to the boat. Whilst we were there the sun went down for another extraordinary sunset over the Irrawaddy turning the water and sky vivid red and orange, absolutely beautiful.

After dinner we all headed for the salon as the lake moths were out again in their zillions. I noticed a couple of the other ladies had adopted the headscarf approach to dealing with them whilst eating their dinner. There was a film show this evening of 'The Lady'. If you know nothing about Burmas political past and the story of Aung San Suu Kyi and her father, then watch this film. It stars Michelle Yeo and it is very good, if very sad. I would be seeing the actual house where Suu was under house arrest for 22 years when I got to Yangon.
As I was so tired that evening I took one of my treasured sleeping tablets and slept for 11 hours solid, a minor miracle. I did not wake up until 10 am and missed breakfast completely.

Day 7

We had a free morning today as we set sail for Bagan. I managed to get on the internet and updated my Blog and rang Peter. Knowing he was still alive and the house was still standing, though not selling, I relaxed on deck watching the world go by. Everything happens along the river. I watched a group of women doing their laundry, banging their clothes against the rocks, it made me thank God for my washing machine and tumble dryer at home. There were gangs of workmen building new river boats as big as ours completely by hand. Another group of ladies were taking their bath and I felt a bit intrusive watching them as they were really going for it with the soap. The children were ever present jumping around in the water and showing off for us tourists.
The weather was glorious, everything in the world felt right.

After lunch we boarded another bus to take us in to the Bagan Archeological zone. There are around 3000 religious buildings here spread over 50 SQ KM and it was like a lost city. You would think it comes under UNESCO but due to the massive renovation programme that the military government pursued of rebuilding the monuments using modern bricks and cement, it has currently been denied World Heritage Status. Therefore some of the buildings look new, basically because they are. The government also relocated all of the villagers to New Bagan so there are very few locals around except outside the Bigger Temples where they do a bit of tourist trade. So apart from the odd tourist wandering around the place is deserted. Even so what a place! I just adored it. I have been to Angkor Wat in Cambodia and amazing as it was there must have been a million people there. Here there was no-one, we had the place entirely to ourselves to stroll around and just take it all in.

The first place we went to was the Shwezigon Pagoda which was covered in gold leaf and had ornate enamel panels all around the edges. Whilst here I was approached by a young woman selling pretty clothes. Now I had not bought anything so far on this trip as I would have plenty of time for shopping later, but from her bag she produced the most beautiful blue Burmese traditional costume, consisting of a long skirt and a short blouse with a mandarin collar. I knew they would never fit a 5ft 7 size 16 Westerner so I declined. She then announced (in a very loud voice) that she could do big lady sizes, so I ended up purchasing this beautiful outfit for $12. Back on the bus the shopaholics immediately spied my purchase, somehow they had managed to miss these for sale. Where did I get them and how much did I pay?

We were then driven to a viewing platform to watch the sun go down over the temple spires. It wasn't really a platform, more of a hill and it was full of people of all nationalities awaiting the sunset. Where had they all come from, we had not seen more than a handful all afternoon? I got talking to a Norwegian guy covered in tattoos, he was on a cycling tour, maybe it's the one I originally looked at. I don't mind tattoos, Peter has 8 and even I have 2 but this guy did not have a bit of bare skin on his arms or legs: absolutely hideous. But I do say he was very nice to talk to, I am a sucker for a Scandinavian accent. We witnessed another glorious sunset over the temple spires, bright orange and yellow this time as we traipsed back to the bus. I have to say the sunsets here were out of this world, I have never seen such vivid colours.

Back in my cabin I carefully unpacked my new outfit only to find the top was missing. I went to find our guide and he rang the bus driver to see if I had left it on the bus, but no such luck. So myself and one of the crew got a huge torch and we ambled back along the sand bank to see if I had dropped it somewhere. This particular crew member was the one who always came ashore with us and he knew exactly what I was looking for and how much I had paid for it. It was pitch black by now, thank god for the torch as I am sure the riverside was covered in rats. We found nothing so I went back to the boat a bit dejected. The first thing I had bought and I had lost half of it! What a dopey tart!
At cocktail time I was relating the story to the two shopaholics, when one of them exclaimed that she had managed to buy an outfit just like mine at the viewing point and when she got back to the boat it had two blouses with it. Dappy woman, she had taken mine when she was examining it on the bus and put it in her bag. Drama over I was happily reconciled with my blouse (it all fitted as well - result). I then imbibed in a cocktail or two, Derek was feeling much better and we headed out onto the deck for dinner. It was decidedly warmer in Bagan in the evening and also the moths had disappeared so there was no extra protein with our meals tonight. After dinner some locals put on a colourful puppet show with music. It was a little bit repetitive and I could not keep my eyes open so I sneaked off to bed early to do a bit of packing and sorting out in my cabin.

Day 8

All of a sudden it was our last day on the cruise and we were off to the city of Bagan again to explore more temples. One of the ladies was feeling really ill but decided to come with us, she had come all this way and wanted to at least see some of Bagan. I did feel for her, it was very hot and she just kept sitting down in the shade every time we stopped and was obviously having a thoroughly miserable time.

First stop today was the enormous Ananda Temple. There were four separate entrances, each with an enormous gold Buddha that all had different silhouettes, some looked almost female in shape. The outside had thousands of green glazed tiles running along the bottom of the walls and the rest was plastered in white, it was an imposing site in the morning sunshine. Whilst we were inside one of the other ladies came over all faint so there was a bit of a drama whilst we fanned her down. She came round very quickly and was absolutely OK to carry on after a drink of water. When we left the temple we walked past the stalls selling trinkets and I spotted a lady selling green celadon type vases. They were a very unusual style and I had seen these everywhere and decided I now wanted to buy one. I picked up a medium size one and asked the price. It was only $3, so I decided to buy a bigger one at $4, not even using my tiny brain to think that I now had three months to cart this big piece of pottery around Asia.

After our last lunch on board we ventured out again and took a leisurely walk around some smaller temples and shrines ending up at the tallest building in the whole area, the Thatbyinnyu Temple. Apparently you can see this place from all over Bagan.
There was some serious restoration going on and you could see the workmen crawling like ants all over the roof just wearing flip flops on their feet, no hi-vis or safety helmets here. The whole building was held up by bamboo scaffolding. One last group photo and it was back to the boat for our last evening together.

With all my packing done I decided to glam up a bit for our last night and donned my new Andy Pandy jump suit and put on a bit of makeup for a change. We had anchored up in the middle of the river and the crew were busy moving furniture off of the boat and building a bar complete with twinkling fairy lights up on the sandbank. They were holding a special goodbye party for us. There were even fire torches to light the way up the steps they had carved out of the sand and a huge camp fire was burning to take off the evening chill. Leaving the boat I made my way up the steps and was instantly handed a G&T by the barman, he knew exactly what I wanted by now without asking. I found Ivan and Derek and plonked myself down between them on a rattan armchair.
We were all chatting away when Gordon and his wife appeared at the top of the steps wearing matching red outfits. They had obviously decided to dress up for the party as well and looked like they were on the set of 'Strictly' and about to perform a tango. For some reason Ivan and myself found this hilarious and I nearly fell off of my chair laughing.
The party kicked off to a noisy start with all the crew singing a couple of songs around the camp fire whilst one of them played guitar. They were all

wearing their official uniforms this evening and the Captain and First Officer looked really smart in their white uniforms and caps with their gold epaulettes. The crew then lit a couple of huge paper lanterns and let them off up into the sky. This was a bit worrying as most of the houses around here were made of wood and so was the boat! The lanterns drifted off over the boat, phew it did not catch fire. There is very little light pollution here and you could see millions of stars as we watched the lanterns disappear over the horizon. They then let off some very dodgy fireworks which either fizzled out really quickly or exploded like a cannon. Pyrotechnics over it was time to get up and dance. So to the sounds of ABBA, Queen and Adele we all boogied on a sandbank in the middle of the Irrawaddy. At some point I ended up dancing with the First mate wearing his officers hat and then I danced with one of the waiters. He was 18 years old and said I was a really good dancer, Ha I always knew it!

By now Gordon and his wife were draped all over each other and one of the shopaholics was draped all over one of the guides, was it Sen or Yen? I went back to my seat next to Ivan whilst Derek was gallantly dancing with one of the single ladies. As I sat down, Ivan put his hand on my thigh in a very suggestive manner and said something along the lines of 'you look really beautiful tonight, I like what you have done with your makeup'. Now did I imagine it? Was a 75 year old man really making a pass at me? It had to be the sex on the beach cocktails that he had been consuming at an alarming rate, either that or it was the Andy Pandy suit that was driving him wild. I was so gob smacked I was lost for words for a few seconds which doesn't happen very often. I was saved from speaking by the dinner gong which broke up the awkward moment and we all made our way back to the boat for the last supper.

That party was something I will never forget. I did not take my camera with me purposely so I have no photos of the event. I wanted to just absorb the whole thing, it is all etched on my brain and I will remember it forever. Even the strange incident with Ivan.

Tonight was a buffet and we all tucked in. It was strangely subdued during dinner, I think we all knew the adventure was over, except for me. Mine was only just starting. I said my goodbyes to a group of six who were heading off very early in the morning extending their trip with a few days at Inle Lake. The rest of us had a few more drinks and then made our way to our cabins as we all had an early start the next day as well. I left a hefty tip for the staff, tips are included on the trip but I could not thank or rate the staff highly enough and felt they deserved so much more. It doesn't matter how luxurious the boat is if there isn't a decent crew. Ours had made this cruise truly special, watching gently over each and every one of us and I was truly sad to be leaving the boat. I felt like I could have gone round again.

<u>**Day 9**</u>

I had a bit of a weird night. I had strange dreams and felt a bit disorientated, like I was having an out of body experience. I awoke at 6.30 feeling slightly sick. I knew this was nothing to do with the mystery bug that had gone round the ship but it was because I had to get on another aeroplane today and I then would be on my own. I wish I could control my body but my irrational brain always takes over.

I couldn't stomach anything for breakfast and just had a cup of tea. We had to meet the coach at 8am to transfer us the 4 hour journey by road to Mandalay airport, back to where it had all started. The others had left at 7am for Heho airport so we were now reduced to 16 passengers. The suitcases were all lined up by the coach, you just pointed at yours and the driver loaded it in to the hold for you. The staff all came ashore to wave us off and there was a lot of faffing around with the luggage etc before we were all on and could set off. The roads were atrocious, little more than dirt tracks as we bumped and bounced along. We had gone about three miles when the woman in front of me (the one with the sick husband) suddenly exclaimed that she had not seen her suitcase loaded onto the bus. So we pulled up and she and the driver got out and unloaded the luggage to find her case. Of course it was there, right at the back. The luggage was reloaded and back on board we set off again. We were another couple of miles down the road when the floaty old hippy woman (the one with the jangly jewellery) suddenly started kicking up that her case wasn't on the bus either. So again we went through the whole process and yes of course it was in the hold. I was not feeling great at that point and my patience had totally run out, what a stupid bloody woman.

Back on the road we got a really good close up view of 25 balloons floating above the temples. The bus pulled up again as everyone wanted to take photos. By now we had been going for about an hour and had got literally nowhere, we hadn't even left Bagan. I settled back trying to fight my increasing nausea but the terrain was terrible and the bus was lurching about all over the place, I even put my seat belt on to help keep me in my seat.

After about 2 hours into the journey my piddly cup of tea decided it wanted to come out and I was dying to go to for a wee. It is never easy for a woman to pee by the roadside. When I went to India, I invested in a Shewee in case of emergency. If you have never seen one it consists of an oval shaped plastic saucer which you attach to a tube, they come in different colours. You are supposed to be able to discreetly have a wee without having to pull your knickers down. You slip the saucer into your underwear through the flies of your trousers underneath your ladies bits. The pipe then clips on and takes the overflow, so you end up peeing like a man with his trousers still on and can point the tube wherever you wish.

Warning: You need to practice this before you ever attempt to use it in public.

The trouble is that you need to be really desperate in the first place to contemplate using this contraption. As you are now dying to go for a wee you cannot control the speed with which you empty your bladder and you end up filling the saucer far too quickly. Because you can't stop once you start (unless you have an amazing pelvic floor) it then overflows and your hands and clothes get covered in wee, which is defeating the object entirely. I gave up with mine after practicing and having one too many accidents all over the pedestal mat in the En-Suite! Fortunately the toilets in India were not too bad so it wasn't called for.

Anyway with no other option I now had to struggle to the front of the roller coaster bus to ask the driver if he could stop somewhere. I would have been quite happy to have squat down behind a bush but no the driver pulls up outside a private house in the middle of nowhere. He asks the owner if I can use her toilet and she waves me into the back of her modest house watched amusedly by a coach load of people.

 I was confronted by a room full of buckets of water and cannot see a toilet anywhere. The floor was soaking wet and very slippery and I stuck my head around the corner to ask where the loo actually was, she waved her hand past the buckets. I spied a concrete block about a foot and a half high with a hole in the middle: this was it. There was absolutely nothing to hold onto and everything was soaking wet so I decided to take off my trousers and knickers before I climbed up on the plinth or attempted to squat down. Business done and feeling highly relieved, I climbed gingerly down off the plinth, as I did I went sliding across the wet floor and then nearly broke my neck trying to put my trousers back on. My mad mind went into overdrive as to what would have happened if I had really hurt myself in that toilet. I made a mental note to be more careful from now on, I could not risk injuring myself. Back on the bus I felt more comfortable and settled back for the rest of the rough journey. Fortunately an hour later we hit tarmac, it was the Road to Mandalay.

We arrived shaken and stirred at the airport and were directed to check in. I felt quite relieved that the airline knew I was not going to Singapore with the others and I was checked in to get off in Yangon. My suitcase weighed 26 kilos, it was that damn celadon vase weighing it down, fortunately I am still allowed 30 kilos at this point.

Immigration was another nightmare. This time there were only two desks open and it took just as long to get out of Mandalay as it had to get in.

When I got to the desk, 1 hour later, I was informed that I was in the wrong queue and should have gone through the domestic channel. By now my stress levels were quite high and I was worried that the flight would go without me as I relined up in the domestic queue. Once through, I located my chums who were waiting for me as the aircraft had already commenced boarding.

At least the flight was short and smooth, no dramas today. We were given a sandwich and a thimble of water which I scoffed very quickly as by now I was starving and hadn't eaten a thing since last nights buffet. When we landed in Yangon due to security issues, all of the passengers had to get off the plane, go through transit and get back on again at the other end. Fortunately I was getting off here and there was an airport welcoming committee waiting at the top of the ramp for all passengers going into the city. I said my goodbyes with a big hug to Derek and Ivan (making sure I did not press my breasts too hard against him) and promised to email them with tales of my adventures. A wave to everyone else and that's it I was now on my own. The welcoming committee escorted the thirteen passengers that were staying in Yangon down to security and I had to queue to go through immigration yet again. This time there was only one desk open but it only took 25 minutes to get through. Joy of joy my suitcase was already on the carousel and I am out within half an hour. I looked around the arrivals hall, there was a beautiful young man wearing Burmese traditional dress holding up a sign with my name on. Yep it is me: I was in YANGON.

The young man had lovely manners and immediately grabbed my bag and suitcase, he then nearly gave himself a hernia pulling it through arrivals and out to the car. Outside the temperature felt much hotter and I was grateful when the driver pulled up and I could get into the air-conditioned vehicle. I was offered bottles of cold water by my gracious guide and off we set for Yangon City.

I could instantly see that this place was a very different animal to Mandalay. There was a lot more traffic for starters, it was odd but all the cars were white, nothing sapphire blue or flame red. There were international 5 star hotels, skyscrapers and huge shopping malls everywhere. I spied a Gloria Jeans coffee shop and was that really a KFC? Realisation hit me that I was now back in the real world, I had been totally wrapped in cotton wool on the boat, my brain had become more vacant than ever.

At the hotel reception they were expecting me and I was escorted to my bedroom by the concierge. I knew this was supposed to be a five star hotel, but I wasn't sure what to expect in Burma but my room was super stylish and most importantly, it was ice cold. I had a bathroom with separate bath, a shower cubicle, toilet and a sink with a huge vanity mirror. I was just inspecting the quality of the in house toiletries when the phone next to the toilet rang, as it does. A woman called Zara informed me in perfect English that she was to be my guide for three days and would pick me up at 12 noon tomorrow to start our tour. Well, so far so good, I was in the right hotel and my tour was all confirmed.

The internet here was phenomenally good and I managed to have a long conversation with Peter, giving him a guided tour of my luxurious room. Brexit was kicking off at home and I was so glad I was missing it. Right or wrong, in or out, Labour, Tory, or Looney, the British public voted and the government should have been breaking their necks to sort it out. Instead they were too involved in their own party power struggles and personal ego's. It would never had happened if Maggie Thatcher had been in power, she would have spanked them all and sent them to bed with no dinner. Peter had also caught another mouse under our kitchen sink. We had already caught three this year and he had now come up with a cunning plan to stop them. Good luck with that, just get it sorted out before I come home, please. I asked him how he was getting on with the household chores and if he had mastered the washing machine yet. I had been away for 9 days so far and he told me that he hadn't actually done any laundry yet! He was waiting to see if the lovely fairy who normally picks up his dirty pants, washes them and puts them back in his drawer had gone on holiday as well.

I went for a nose around the hotel and found the swimming pool out in the gardens where there was a lot of activity going on as the staff were preparing for a wedding. There must have been tables for around 200 guests and there did not seem to be any expense spared. The wedding cake was at least as tall as me and there were fresh flowers everywhere. I thought Burma was a poor country, someone in this city had some money to be holding their nuptials in this hotel.

I decided to have dinner and a drink in the bar. The staff were delightful and the food was passable, not quite the quality of the boat. Whilst having my meal the bridal party came through. The blushing bride was wearing the most enormous meringue of a dress covered in ice blue lace. She was very pretty but absolutely plastered in make up, you would need a scraper to get it off. She tottered off with her groom to the wedding party through the double doors, only just managing to get her massive dress through the 2 metre gap.

I decided to turn in for the night, I was tired after the early start. I lay in bed watching Donald Trump on CNN and catching up with what had been going on in the world whilst I had been off the grid. I rang my friend Lisa who was looking after my volunteer group, it was still together so that was a bonus.

Day 10

I slept OK but woke up every few hours, the room was absolutely freezing and I had to get out of bed to turn the aircon down!!

I don't normally eat lunch on holiday and I always have a big breakfast. I found the dining room on the ground floor where there was the most enormous International buffet artfully arranged. I filled up with fruit, bacon & eggs and delicious pastries. I had two hours until I had to go out on my tour so I decided to sit by the pool. It was very hot and I chose a shady spot under the trees. There were a few people lounging around and I got talking to a huge bald Swede who was in the city on business. Strangely enough we were reading the same Michael Crichton book. Obviously his was in Swedish, mine was in English. I had a dip in the pool but it was icy cold and I lost all feeling in my feet and had real trouble getting out as for some strange reason there were no handles or rails of any kind to hang onto.

I got changed into a pair of long elephant trousers and vest and stuffed my trusty scarf into my bag. I had been advised to cover up as shorts are not allowed at the temple we were going to visit this later that afternoon. I went down in the lift and sat waiting in the glitzy lobby for Zara who arrived in a chauffeur driven white American car, a brand of which I had never heard of.

We hit it off straight away, she was 38 years old, divorced with one daughter and does freelance work as a guide. The first place we go to is a restaurant on the top floor of the tallest building in downtown Yangon. The weather was beautiful, the view was 360 degrees and you could see for miles. In the distance was the Sule Pagoda and further still the Hlaing River. We were surrounded by Malls and upmarket Hotels, there was a Shangri La, Meridien and a Pullman. After the simplicity of the Burmese countryside I really was not expecting the city to be quite so modern. However in the distance I could just make out some not so smart buildings which is more of how I had imagined it would be. We sat at a table and the waiter brought out the most enormous tray of food. A black lacquer platter with six segments each containing a curry of some sort. Oh my god I should not have had that huge breakfast. Zara doesn't eat and refuses any of mine so I struggled to eat as much as I can. I hate wasting food, I only ever take what I can eat from a buffet and never leave anything whilst critically watching others who pile their plates and discard most of it.

I was a bit worried about the food but the restaurant looked hygienic enough and I am comforted by the cleanliness of the toilets.

My thinking is that if the toilets are filthy then probably so is the kitchen.

After my huge lunch we met up with our car and drove to Bogyoke Market. Zara and the driver constantly complain about the traffic but to be honest it was no worse that Bedford town centre on a weekday.

The market was a maze of over 2000 shops and stalls spread out over two floors, selling clothes, jewellery and souvenirs. We had a good old rummage around and I bought a real jade ring and a bracelet for $1 each. Zara then dragged me off to her favourite stall which sells fabric. They had some fantastic 100% linen and she talked me into having a shirt made. The linen cost me $3 and to have it made another $4. She then decided she wanted to buy her new boyfriend a Longyi. This is a type of traditional wrap round skirt that is worn by men and women. Whilst she was haggling with the stall holder I spotted one in Luton Town colours: blue, white and orange. Knowing my husbands eclectic wardrobe I imagine he would like one of these, so I purchased it for him. Wandering in and around the shops and stalls were monks of all ages collecting alms and food from the locals in small metal pots. The colours, smells and sounds were really vivid and I was really enjoying the whole experience.

We crossed the road, entering a plush modern shopping mall and decided to go for a coffee. It was just like any other mall, I could of been anywhere in the world. There was a huge crowd gathered downstairs and there was a lot of loud music blaring out over the PA. Looking over the railings Zara pointed out Burma's top female pop star signing autographs on a small stage downstairs. She was surrounded by people trying to get to her, the security staff were having a bit of a nightmare trying to keep the mad throng at bay. There was a very bored and tired looking gentleman sitting on a step playing with his phone slightly away from the crowd, Zara told me that he was the pop stars husband. He was being completely ignored by the crowd and looked really fed up with the high glamour of being in this shopping centre.

Zara started to tell me about her life and we discussed Burmese politics. She remembers the military rule and hates what she calls 'the cronies'. These are allegedly Burmas tycoons with shady ties to the former ruling Generals and they are the ones who supposedly own all the money and businesses in Yangon. She says that the weddings at the hotel will all be connected to the families of these people. She has nothing but praise for Aung San Suu Kyi and says it was unfair of the Western world to strip her of her Nobel Peace prize due to the Rohingya problem. According to Zara there are much darker forces still at work within the country that we know little about in the Western world.

Political discussion over, we headed over to the Shewadagon Pagoda which is Burma's most sacred Buddhist shrine. Nowhere else in the whole country is so revered or visited in such large numbers. There are four entrances with massive ornate golden stairways leading to the top. All along the stairs are stalls selling religious paraphernalia such as incense and floral offerings. Emerging at the top we were surrounded on all sides by golden buildings and stupas. It was so overwhelming I did not know what to look at first. There were a lot of people gathered here and we have to go through security to get in: I tried not to imagine the chaos that might ensue if something awful did happen.

We had to leave our shoes in a kiosk and walk around barefoot and I had to cover my arms with my scarf. Even though there were a lot of people here, the place was enormous and there was plenty of room, with no rugby scrums to get the best photos. There were only about four Westerners walking around and I was one of them. It had a very nice feel to it and I was not at all alarmed by the sheer numbers of humanity walking, praying and just generally sitting around absorbing the atmosphere. We stayed for about an hour and as we left, the car park was starting to fill up with coaches of all nationalities. Zara said they were here for the sunset and it was always heaving at this time of the afternoon. Grateful that I had missed the rush I felt privileged to have been able to visit this sacred place. I like the Buddhist religion it is very tranquil, non judgemental and very accepting of other faiths.

Back at the hotel I decided to go to the beauty salon and get my toenails re-gelled. The hot sun has reacted with the blue gel colour I had done in the UK and they had gone a strange mottled nondescript colour. For $17 they stripped off the old gel, gave me a pedicure and foot massage and then painted a new dark red gel on.

Whilst I was sitting there (it took two hours) I got to watch another elaborate wedding. This time there must have been tables set out for at least 500 guests and the cake was another enormous frothy concoction which must have cost a small fortune and would have kept a whole village supplied with cake for a year.

The bridal party arrived to the tune of Pachelbels Canon in D Major. I don't know an awful lot about classical music but this was instantly recognisable. There were 8 bridesmaids all wearing slightly different cream dresses and carrying small posies. A very annoying compere, I suppose it was their equivalent of a toastmaster, announced each of them over a very loud crackly microphone as they stepped forward in turn, you could tell they had been practising their walks.

Then the bride appeared - She was wearing the biggest pink dress I have ever seen, bigger than anything on 'My big fat gypsy wedding'. She struggled down the steps of the hotel towards the swimming pool lugging this huge embroidered dress, which must have weighed a tonne. When she got to the pool she had to cross a small bridge which was beautifully festooned with flowers and twinkling fairy lights. As she stepped onto the bridge the massive dress got caught on the lights and the flowers went everywhere. She was absolutely determined to get across this bridge, she pulled and tugged really hard until the fairy lights pinged off of the side of the bridge and then got entangled around her dress. Fair game to her, I have to give her 10/10 for effort as she arrived demurely on the other side of the bridge wrapped in fairy lights and covered in broken flowers, she looked like a badly decorated Christmas tree. She was rescued on the other side by one of her bridesmaids who gently unwrapped her. Not one guest had batted an eyelid, there would have been massive gasps at a British wedding, but they just carried on as if nothing had happened and was all perfectly normal.

Thinking that the indignity must be over for her, the compere then pulled the couple onto the stage to play a game. I imagine it was a bit like a Burmese version of Mr & Mrs. I have no idea what they were saying but it was cringingly awful and very loud so I decided to leave. I left by the route the bride had come in and made my way up the stairs. At the top of the staircase were two billboard size photos of the bride and groom along with a table laden with presents. A lady standing guard told me that the bride was a famous clothes designer in Yangon. I examined the enormous photos, she was wearing another dress in one picture which looked like it was made completely out of white feathers. In the second one a dark red number with a massive train which made her look like Morticia from the Adams Family. I can't say I would rush to buy anything in her shop.

It had been another good day. I ate in the bar again, I had not really got my bearings and I could not be bothered to venture outside. Back in my room I FaceTimed the girls at work - they were very excited to hear from me and I made a few other phone calls to catch up with some of my friends.

<u>Day 11</u>

I slept in fits and starts again and sensibly ate a decidedly smaller breakfast than the day before. Zara and the driver picked me up and we headed off downtown. The driver dropped us off and we went for a walk around the Colonial quarter. Zara informed me that these 19th & 20th century buildings are all that is left of the time when Yangon was one of Asia's most Cosmopolitan Cities. They are very imposing buildings but sadly most of them are now empty and derelict although one or two seem to be undergoing extensive renovations. With the buildings fully repaired, this imposing road would give any London Street a run for its money. Along here there were hundreds of second hand book stalls lining the pavements. There was everything from maths books to the latest Jackie Collins bonk buster. We ended up in front of the Strand hotel and decided to go in for a coffee.

The Strand has been there since 1901, originally the creation of two Armenian entrepreneurs and it used to be the Cities poshest hotel. It has recently been restored and is very beautiful inside. Modern and slightly contemporary but reeking of money. Zara talked the receptionist in to showing me one of the rooms on the pretence that I would like to stay there on my next visit. Only in my dreams!

The bedrooms are luxurious, opulent and tastefully decorated and we were escorted around one of the suites by the head Concierge. I can't imagine them doing that for me in the best hotel in London if I asked. We sat in the bar and ordered two coffees, the service was classy and dignified as you would expect, even though we only spent a few quid we were treated like royalty. I could have stayed there all day chatting but we had to move on.

We crossed the busy road outside to the waterfront to catch the local ferry across the Hlaing River to the village of Dala. I kid you not I was the only Westerner and had to go through a separate entrance marked 'Foreigners' and pay the sum of around £1.80. Zara got on with everyone else and paid just 10 pence. The journey took about 10 minutes and there must have been at least 1000 people on the ferry, sitting, standing, laying, some with cycles, some with children or chickens and others with huge back packs of food or carrying other merchandise. It was a cacophony of sound and smells. Getting off was a bit tricky, a ramp comes down but doesn't quite reach the shore so you had to wade through thick stinky mud to get on land, some of the locals bypass the queue entirely and leaped from the upper deck directly onto the river bank.

Zara negotiated the going rate with two cyclo riders to take us around the local villages. The cycles had a seat with a cushion set into a wooden frame, I could only just fit my big derriere in, and there was a lop sided parasol tied to a wooden pole to keep the midday sun off of our heads. Once loaded we set off at a very sedate pace.

These villages could not be more different from the modern buildings across the water. The majority of the houses were made up of planks of wood that looked like they had been scavenged and were all different shapes, colours, and sizes that have been roughly nailed together. Some of them had plastic bags stitched together as roofs and that was a luxury. Pretty much most of the houses were hovels and ugh you should have seen the toilets. Very small children were playing in the mud amidst the recognisable human faeces and there were scabby feral dogs everywhere which chased the cyclos, the drivers had to warn them off with a big stick. It was all very eye opening and unfortunately very real.

This place was a complete slum but everywhere we went the locals smiled and waved at us, and the children emerged from the mud to gawp open mouthed at me, a silver haired white woman sitting like Cleopatra in her chariot. We ended the visit at another local orphanage, again with happy smiley children, not quite as well kept as the last one, who I could quite easily have scooped up and taken home with me. Not sure what Peter would have made of it if I had turned up at Heathrow with 6 Burmese orphans in tow.

There was another complete rugby scrum to get back on the ferry, with people jumping off the ramp before it had even gone down properly. Back on board the locals paid not one jot of attention to me, I wonder if it was because I was with a guide? Had I been on my own I might have seemed more interesting. I used to go to Egypt a lot (my ex husband lived there, it's a long story), you would never be on your own there for long before someone sidled up to you to ask you where you were going, were you married, what did you do for a living and how much money your earned. Here no-one was slightly interested in me.

We had lunch in a tiny authentic Rangoon tea house which was heaving with locals and Westerners alike. The whole menu was vegetarian and I had a delicious vegetable curry, this time Zara ate as well - it must have been in the budget for the day. Again we sat chatting for ages, we just got on really well. She told me all about her irresponsible ex husband who was a bit of a gambler and eventually left her and their baby daughter five years ago. He has never paid a penny for their daughter's upkeep and even now she is still paying off his gambling debts. She has a new man in her life now who loves her daughter and helps her with the child care but she doesn't want to get married ever again.
For a Burmese she is very well travelled and has been to USA, UK and all over Europe. I liked her a lot.

After lunch we went to Central station for a ride on the Circle train that goes all around Yangon strangely enough in a loop, hence the name. It is an old fashioned locomotive and we had to walk across a live railway line to get to it. When it pulled up there was at least a three foot gap between the platform and the height of the carriage floor. Luckily there were two handles either side of the door and I managed to pull myself up. Once inside it was like an oven, no Aircon in there. We were the only two people in the carriage and the train pulled out very slowly. We travelled through the outer suburbs of Yangon at a very sedate speed, there are some surprisingly nice properties amongst the less salubrious ones. There was washing hanging out of every window, that must be nice with all the fifth from the railway track floating around in the air. There were adults, kids and various animals wandering about on all the tracks, they always seemed to move out of the way just in time before they were flattened by the heavy locomotive. Getting off the train was interesting, the only way to do it was to jump or get out backwards holding onto the rails. We made our way back across the live track to find our driver waiting for us outside the station. Zara had a mobile with her and she kept in touch with him constantly, which is why he was always in the right place at the right time. On the way back to the hotel they showed me Aung San Suu Kyis house where she was held under house arrest, she lives in Napyitaw now which is the new capital city of Burma. I can picture the news reels I had seen and it still looks just like that. It does have an armed guard on the gate, but now it is to stop anyone getting in to the grounds not to stop her getting out.

After they dropped me off I went for a walk around Kandawgyi Lake which was opposite the hotel. I had a very pleasant walk even though it was still very hot and I felt a bit sticky and sweaty. No-one approached me and I was left alone as I strolled around in the fading afternoon sunshine. I came across a commanding statue of General Aung San, Suu's father, who was murdered by the generals. There were a couple of newly weds having their official photos taken there, he obviously still has great relevance to the Burmese people. As the sun went down over the lake I made my way back to the hotel. I was still stuffed full from my enormous lunch so I just had a piece of cake and a Cappuccino for tea. I took a lovely long bath and laid on the bed all evening wearing my fluffy hotel dressing gown, yakking on the phone to my sister and nephew.

Day 12

For some reason I did not sleep very well at all and dragged myself out of bed just in time for another huge breakfast. I was in for a real treat today (NOT), Zara had decided to take me to the local Chinese food market. I wish I hadn't eaten first, there were bits of dead animal everywhere, plates and trays full of intestines, brains and other unrecognisable organs, the smell was awful, the ground was slippery with blood and mucous and there were flies everywhere. There was lots of pushing and shoving going on as the stall holders jostled with the shoppers for sales. One woman managed to tip a tray of something yellow and slimy all over my right foot splashing blood up my leg, she then scooped it all back onto the plate to sell to the punters, it was really revolting. I am surprised I didn't puke up as I was beginning to feel very queasy at this point and the smell was suffocating. Fortunately the animals are actually dead before they get here, I would certainly not have been able to stomach it if they were being chopped up live in front of me.

We at last escaped the heat, smell and bustle of the market and got back to the cool of the air-conditioned car. Zara handed me a bag with two frozen flannels that she had bought from home, and I put them on the back of my neck, absolute bliss. I also gave my leg a wash to get rid of the dried blood and goo.

For our last adventure together she took me to the Kyauk Htat Gyi Pagoda. There is a spectacular 70 metre long reclining Buddha which Zara tells me has just been renovated and is very different from any other statue in Yangon. The gleaming white Buddha has the most amazing green glass eyes that seem to follow you around and look spookily real, it even has long black eyelashes, like bristles on a broom. She asked me if I would like to sit with her whilst she prayed, so I settled down on my haunches and looked around me, I am sure the Buddha's eyes move in my direction. Considering this was a serious place of worship there were families sitting on the floor eating their lunch and everyone was taking selfies. I contemplated life in general whilst Zara prostrated herself on the floor in the way they do.

Today she took me to lunch at a genuine Shan restaurant. Now the Shan area of Burma is allegedly where all the drugs come from so I was wondering excitedly what we would be having. Boringly it was another huge plate with 6 different portions of Shan cuisine that I again struggled to eat. What is it with the portion sizes here, I had enough to feed three people for a week. I noticed that Zara just had plain chicken and salad, the budget must be running low today.

When we got back to the hotel we gave each other a big hug and I gave her and the driver a generous tip. I am not usually a big tipper but they deserved every penny of it. She had been a knowledgeable and affable guide and I had enjoyed her company immensely.

I spent the afternoon relaxing by the swimming pool and thinking about my time in Burma. I had absolutely fallen in love with the country. The people have had terrible problems (and still have) but they are the most amiable and charming people you could ever wish to meet. I had not met one person who had been rude, unhelpful or unfriendly and no-one had tried to rip me off. The scenery had been amazing, the food good and my accommodations much better than expected and I felt very privileged to have visited all the places I had seen. It had overwhelmingly exceeded all of my expectations and I would be very sad to leave.

After a very light meal in the bar I retired early to my room to pack and prepare myself for more adventures, I was off to THAILAND in the morning.

4 THAILAND

Day 13

I slept much better last night, I have to say I felt exhausted. I had been on the go for 13 days and I was looking forward to a few days relaxing at a Thai beach.

After a light breakfast I waited in reception for my 7am pick up to take me to the airport. Several drivers come and go but none of these are for me. By 7.20 there was just myself and a driver in reception, he was waiting for a Mr & Mrs Angelo. I was beginning to get a bit tense at this point so I asked the receptionist to ring the travel company to see where they were. They tell her that the driver was already there and waiting for me with a big sign, but I could see no-one. In the end it turned out that I am Mr & Mrs Angelo and the driver had picked up the wrong name sign.

Panic over he whisked me off to the airport. The journey did not take long and I was first in the check in queue. For an international airport it was not very big and there were only a few people around. Whilst I was waiting in line I watched a video about poaching and the smuggling of elephant bracelets. Apparently you can buy bracelets there that are made out of elephant skin and there is a serious penalty for just owning one. Why would anyone even want to wear or own such a hideous item? Apparently they change hands for a fortune and are completely illegal.

At check in I waved my frequent flyer card at them and they weighed my case which for some reason now read 25 kilos. Bingo, right on the limit. Kay at Travelbag had advised me to sign up for the frequent flyer programme with this boutique airline so that I could take excess baggage for no charge. It worked like a dream and I was checked in for my 1 hour flight to Bangkok. It took just 30 minutes to get through immigration and I was officially but reluctantly out of Burma.

As usual I was feeling sick and nauseous and I wasn't even on the plane yet, I went back and forth to the loo for several nervous wee's. We were delayed by 20 minutes but eventually we were called and loaded. It was only a small 737 but it looked fairly new. We take off and it was fairly smooth as I gripped my seat arms in my usual terror. We just got served with tea & coffee and a biscuit, nothing very exciting, no booze. As we came in to land at Bangkok, we were obviously flying round and round in circles getting into a stack for landing as it is such a busy airport. I absolutely hate that sensation, I just want to land and get off, not fly around in a spiral. We landed without incident and are off very efficiently. This was a Thai budget airline and it was within their interests to turn the plane around very quickly as they were off somewhere else 30 minutes after us.
Suvarnabhumi airport was very very busy and it was a really long walk from the plane to immigration. Here I could see at least that every desk was open and there were thousands of people queueing up. It looked like total chaos but I was through within half an hour and I could see my luggage going round on the carousal.

 I had very detailed written instructions on where to head to once out of the terminal and I was greeted by a flustered Thai woman with a clip board. Hurrah my name was on her list and she asked me to wait whilst she organised my car. There were lots of other tourists all gathered in the same spot waiting for their transport.
 My vertically challenged driver arrived and grabbed my suitcase, he was so small it was almost the same size as him, and he dragged my case over to the waiting mini bus. I was secretly worried as to whether he could actually touch the pedals or not but he obviously manages it as we set off and pulled out of the car park towards the motorway for the three hour journey to Cha-Am. I was staggered by how much Bangkok has grown since I was last here. 15 years ago it took an hour to clear the suburbs but now it took at least 1.5 hours and when we hit the coastline there were buildings, shops and factories everywhere. I did not recognise a single thing on the journey and I have been along this road six times. I dozed off periodically but keep getting awoken by the driver who took dozens of calls on his mobile whilst he was driving in the fast lane of the motorway.

3 hours after leaving the airport we arrived at the 4 star Hotel in Cha-Am. Actually as it turned out for me, it was more like hell on earth. It was full of Scandinavian families and their children.
After the beautiful hotel in Yangon my room was a complete disappointment. I looked it up on my iPad just to check that I was in the

correct hotel; I was, but it had been very cleverly photographed. All of the furniture and floor were made of dark wood which was scratched to buggery and almost blonde in places. The bed linen was clean but all crumpled and for the life of me I could not work out the lighting system. The bathroom was old, basic and there was limescale along the bottom of the shower. It was totally bog standard and nothing special but hey it was cleanish, the aircon worked and the internet connection was excellent, after all I was only staying here for three nights. I checked in with Peter, he was still alive, hadn't starved to death and the house was still intact.

I was a bit disorientated and it took me a while to get my stuff organised. By the time I had got myself together it was dark outside and I ventured out to the local village for something to eat.

The other downside of my room was that it was on the 11th floor with just three tiny lifts to service all 20 floors. Every time the lift stopped at my floor it was packed full of buggies and pushchairs so I ended up going down the emergency exit stairs. Of course they were not air-conditioned so by the time I got to reception I was like a wet rag and dripping with sweat.

I wandered into the village, there were a few restaurants and shops and I had a delicious sweet and sour prawn dish to eat and a couple of beers. I stocked up on bottled water as there did not appear to be any provided in the room. The shop also sold Haribo jelly teddy bears (a particular favourite of mine) and I bought a few packets to keep me going through the next few days whilst I was lounging by the pool. The prices were a bit of a shock compared to my last visit, it was still cheap in comparison with the UK but at least double to when I was here last time. I also dropped off a huge bag of washing into 'Roses Laundry' which cost me about £3.00, at least that was still cheap. I retired to bed fairly early, it had been a long day. I ended up watching 'Mission Impossible - Rogue Nation' on the TV in complete darkness as I still couldn't figure out the lighting system.

Day 14

I slept well and woke up to the first Valentines Day ever spent on my own. Seriously, I have luckily always had a man around for every 14th February since I was 17 years old. I opened my card which Peter had given me, as is normal for my husband it was not your usual sort of Valentine card. It was a quote from Shakespeare about The World being my Oyster. It made me smile and I wondered what he was doing today, then I realised: it was 2am in the UK: he would still be in bed snuggled up with the dog.

I sweated my way down the 10 flights of emergency stairs to the dining room for breakfast, I gave up totally waiting for the lifts. The restaurant was absolutely heaving, really noisy and all the tables were taken. There were kids everywhere and there was a children's entertainment team already at work doing face painting and playing games.

A lot of people assume I do not like children, they couldn't actually be further from the truth. There is nothing more delightful than a well mannered articulate child but so many children today have no manners and can't hold any sort of conversation unless it is with their phone or pad. I just couldn't eat a whole one and I certainly don't want to share my holidays with a big gang of them.

I got some breakfast and made my way to the end of the restaurant where there was an enormous rectangular table set for 12 with just three people sitting at one end. I perched on the other end and was just about to eat when the freaky blonde woman asked me to leave as she was saving the table for rest of her family who were completely absent and probably still in bed. Oh dear she picked on the wrong person here. After we exchanged a few heated words I got up and moved to sit somewhere else, only because I couldn't stand her huffing and puffing whilst I ate my omelette. I made a mental note to see if she had already put her towels out on 12 beds by the swimming pool.

With the breakfast ordeal over I made my way outside which was actually nicer than the inside of the hotel. There were several pools and I plonked myself down on a sun bed as far away from the family pool as was possible to get. It was really hot and I slapped on factor 30 all over. A child and his father were tossing a ball around and it hit my bed several times, I gave them a Paddington Bear stare and they slunk off back to the family pool.

There was a man and woman on the sun beds next to me and we got chatting. They were from Barnsley and informed me that there was only one other English couple staying in the entire hotel. They too were disappointed with their room and found out that the hotel is having a complete refit starting in March which will take two years to complete, it definitely needs it. Good luck to the guests staying during the renovation: all that dust, banging and drilling! This odd but friendly couple had about 100 mosquito bites between them which they got in Bangkok, they didn't bother with insect repellant because they hadn't seen any mozzies!! It was their first time out of Europe and so far they were disappointed with Thailand as it's not like Spain. Err excuse me that's because you are in South East Asia! She was a paramedic in Rochdale and related some horrendous stories about some of the cases she had recently dealt with, she was thinking of packing it in as it had been so traumatic recently. After about an hour they disappeared, when they came back two hours later they were completely sozzled and passed out on their sun beds. I went for a swim in the pool, the steps were broken and it was very difficult to get in and out. When I got back to my sun bed I glanced down at my bikini bottoms and noticed that they were starting to disintegrate. Sunshine, chlorine and machine washing ruins the fabric, this was an old bikini and it literally started to disappear in front of my eyes. Time to go in I think. The bikini ends up tossed in the bin, the first of many clothing casualties along the way.

I got on the shuttle bus (which I have to pay for) and went to Hua Hin for the evening. This is where Peter and I had enjoyed a lovely holiday 15 years ago. Oh my God what a commercialised dump it was now. It was so built up that I hardly recognised anything but I did remember my way around the town. I ended up in an Italian restaurant complete with pictures of the snowy Dolomites and Venice on the wall. It was run by the sexiest male on the planet and I got all hot and flustered when he came over to talk to me. I have always had a weakness for the Latino type and he was an Adonis and absolutely gorgeous, he was also young enough to be my son, and I know he was just being polite to all of his customers. Strangely enough the whole restaurant appeared to be full of single ladies of a certain age.

After my dinner I ended up in Svensens ice cream parlour having a Valentine treat, I felt I had already had it with the Italian waiter, but the ice cream was nice as well. I had a little meander around the lively night market, which was selling clothes, souvenirs and other tourist tat, but I knew I could get all this stuff cheaper in Bangkok so I did not buy anything.

I managed to find the bus in the dark and got back to the hotel ok. I still could not figure out the weird lighting system in my room so I frustratingly ended up having to ring maintenance, this is all as I was about to go to bed. In their defence they appeared very quickly, fiddled around with a few wires and got everything working. Hurrah it was a miracle! The minute they left the room, it all went off again and I had to get undressed by the light of the TV for the second night running.

Day 15

Next morning I braved the breakfast crowd again. This time I ended up sitting on a table with an American gentleman. He lived in Malaysia and was in Thailand for a climate conference. I also found out every other thing about him and his family in the short time I sat with him. He told me all about his boss, wife, ex wife and children. What is it with Americans that they have to tell their whole life story to a complete stranger within minutes of meeting them?

After breakfast I sat out by the pool again, the chap from Barnsley was already prostrate on his sun bed but this morning there was no sign of the wife. They did not get in until 5 am that morning and he was obviously still pissed as a fart. He reeked of cheap beer and cigarettes which must have been sweating out of his pores.

I then had to listen to his life story and he told me all about his ex wife, his difficult relationship with his son and his messy divorce. Oh God please kill me, I only came here for a rest. Eventually he passed out on his bed and peace reigned.

That evening I walked into the village again for dinner. I had another amazing sweet and sour prawn dish and a few beers, whilst I mulled over the last few days. All in All I have to say it was a probably a mistake coming here, I should have gone straight to Bangkok and lounged around the pool there for a couple of days but I wanted to reminisce about the wonderful holiday that we had had in Hua Hin. In retrospect it would also have saved me around £250.00 as well. Sometimes it is never a good idea to go back is it?
Fortunately this turned out to be the only real mistake of the entire itinerary.

Day 16

Early next morning my driver was waiting for me and I gladly left en route for Bangkok. As I pulled my suitcase off of the luggage rack in my room, all the metal strips slid off and bounced all over the floor. This was absolutely the last straw and I wrote a scathing review (all true to be fair) on Trip Advisor.

The three hour journey to Bangkok was uneventful and I read my book whilst the driver chatted incessantly on his phone all the way there. I had chosen to stay at a Hotel which was basically on top of the MBK shopping centre. It was connected to Siam Square and Central World shopping plaza's by overhead walkways and I thought it would be fairly central to get out and explore without having to walk down at street level or contend with having to cross the perilous roads. It was also next to the Skytrain system and meant I would not have to venture far after dark to eat out.

Yes reception had my booking and I was escorted to my room which was on the 27th Floor. It had a panoramic view of the city, golly the skyline had changed, more skyscrapers than ever. I felt like I could have had a nose bleed I was so high up. My room was modern and funky with a gorgeous bathroom, floor to ceiling windows, flat screen TV and cold aircon - I liked it very much.
I completely emptied my suitcase and hand luggage and had a proper sort out as I hadn't unpacked much at the beach resort. I washed my dirty smalls and left them to dry. I also washed my blue elephant trousers, the water went dark purple. Leaving them dripping blue dye into the pristine white bath I set off for a look around the area.

First of all I had to get to grips with which direction I needed to go in just to get out of the hotel and into the shopping centre. The Mahboonkrong or MBK as it is known is six enormous floors of shopping heaven. Clothes, shoes, jewellery, tourist tat, electronics and a massive food hall. It was very difficult not to get side tracked by all the lovely stuff for sale but I found my way out onto the walkway which is suspended above the notorious traffic of Bangkok.

The reason everything in Bangkok moves so slowly is immediately evident : everybody is on their mobile phone. I am not a fast walker but everyone was dawdling along looking down at their screens and we crawled along at a snails pace as it was difficult to divert around the huge crowds. All the car drivers were also on their mobiles and not concentrating, so it was bedlam on the roads below and every vehicle was snarled up in a traffic jam honking their horns.

After the slowest walk ever, I could have walked over a bed of nails in my bare feet quicker, I finally reached the Erawan shrine. This shrine was built by the Erawan hotel to eliminate bad karma over the laying of the foundations. The bad karma obviously never went away as a bomb went off there in 2015 which killed 20 people and injured 125. It is in a very small congested spot and was heaving with people. I shudder to think of the scenes of carnage when it happened and the difficulty of getting ambulances and medics into such a tight spot.

There was a huge poster up at Central World Plaza advertising a motorbike show the next day and I made a mental note to go and find it the next afternoon. I inched slowly back to the MBK centre behind a throng of people on their mobiles and went into a pizzeria for dinner and a Chang beer. I spoke to Maureen, she was full of it, wanting to know everything I had been doing. I walked back through the massive shopping centre, got a bit lost at the escalators and went back on myself and ended up on entirely the wrong floor resulting in me being back in the same place as I came in. Eventually I reached the correct entrance for the hotel and got in the funky elevator to go up to my floor in the heavens above Bangkok.

The following day I was due to go on a tour that I had organised whilst I was in the UK. As I was on my own I really did not want to have to contend with Bangkok's infamous taxi drivers to get anywhere so I had booked several organised trips. Again it was really annoying that several of the trips I wanted to do needed two people otherwise I had to pay double, so I ended up booked on mini buses with guests from other hotels as it was cheaper, which is not always the best option. I never did get to the Thai Floral Culture museum, they just wanted too much money to take me there as a solo passenger.

Day 17

For some reason I did not sleep well even though the bed was really comfy and I had to get up at 6.30am. Breakfast was another enormous International buffet served by the 8th floor swimming pool and I filled my face. The bus was due to pick me up at 7.30 but it was running 30 minutes late which had been conveyed to reception but not to me, I could have had another half hour in bed. When I got back to my room that afternoon there was a note in a formal white envelope informing me that the bus was going to be late that morning?? Why did they even bother, it was such a waste of paper?

When it at last arrived, already on the mini bus were two Americans and an English couple from Royston who were celebrating their 40th birthdays. We all hit it off straight away and got chatting about our different trips. The Americans did not tell us any of their private business which was highly unusual. I had been told to cover my arms and legs as we were going to visit Buddhist temples and not to wear backless shoes: the English lady was wearing shorts, a vest and flip flops. She informed me that she had a cardigan and wrap to cover herself up with and the guide had said it would be ok. I was wearing long trousers, a long sleeved t-shirt and walking sandals. I was already sweaty and boiling hot, that is what you get when you obey the dress code.

We visited several temples which each got bigger, busier and more elaborate than the one before. We arrived at the Royal Palace and Temple of the Emerald Buddha along with most of the other tourists currently visiting Bangkok. This is the most famous temple in the whole of Thailand and is absolutely stunning, I have been here three times before, and it still blows my mind. The colours and opulence of the place are out of this world, and I do not know what to look at first. It was also massively overcrowded and there was a lot of pushing and shoving going on especially at the bottle neck junctions. This place was never built for mass tourism and the throngs of people are oppressive. It flickers across my mind what would happen if a bomb went off here and how they would deal with the crowds and mayhem. There are tourists of every nationality jostling for the best selfie and it was very hot and sticky. You could smell strong body odour mixed with the sickly smell of incense in the air, it was almost overpowering at times. This was Thailands most important temple and it was being trampled all over by people who have absolutely no respect for their religion and culture. However, the Thai's are charging 500 baht to get in (£11.50) so they are making a huge amount of money out of this attraction every day of the week. Fortunately security was tight and people were soon told off if they attempted to sit on the statues which some of them try to do. What are they thinking of? Do they not realise this is a sacred place? It makes me a bit cross, but then I am always cross about something lately.

After we leave the tourist free for all, we crossed the road to the Temple of the Reclining Buddha. This is similar to the one in Burma but much smaller. It is quieter here, more sedate and there were less tourists. Again it was very colourful and all the buildings were covered in gold and the stupas were decorated with brightly coloured porcelain tiles. It was all very pretty but I was boiling hot and a bit Buddha-d out by now. We slowly made our way back through the traffic to my hotel and joy of joys I can at last can take my sweaty trousers off.

After a shower and a change of clothes and I headed off to find the motorbike show. All the motorbikes on display were draped over by beautiful scantily dressed girls (I think they were girls), Peter would have been in seventh heaven. They all have their ample bosoms hanging out which certainly look genuine enough but you can never tell here. I had my photo taken with one lovely girl, she had small hands and feet and I could not see her Adams apple, so I think she was definitely female. She looked very sweet standing next to me, in her sexy French maids outfit, but she made me feel like an enormous hippo. There was an all round good atmosphere, as there usually is when there are bikers around and I took loads of photos.
There were a group of mini bikers around five years old dressed in full leathers and wearing cool sunglasses. They were all posing for the camera's. They looked really cute but very miserable all at the same time, they must have been so hot and some of the parents were fanning them down whilst they were photographed.

After a delicious spot of late lunch I returned to the hotel for a bit of a rest, another shower and yet another change of clothes. I got slightly distracted on the way back by one of the shops and ended up buying six makeup bags for my friends. I also purchased a few more bags of Haribo teddy bears to keep me going during the day.

I was being picked up at 5.30pm to go on a Dinner cruise on an old rice barge along the Chao Praya River. While I was waiting outside the hotel it started to rain. It was the strangest weather, it was raining on my head but the water never got to my feet, it evaporated in the heat before it got to the ground. My ride arrived and I was driven to a jetty along the riverside where a smartly dressed young man wearing Thai traditional dress escorted me onto the rice barge. It was a proper old wooden barge with an arched roof. It was evident that there were several parties booked on the boat and I was hoping to be able to interact with some other people but I was shown to a solitary table set for one. It felt a bit sad that I was in this exciting, amazing city and there I was on my own, Billy no mates again. However it did have one overwhelming feature in that I had the best view of the river from my table. The old barge lurched about in the water, hitting every bit of swell from all the faster vessels going up and down the river. The food was not very exciting if I was honest. Thai food is normally hot and spicy but this was all a bit tamed down for the tourists, and the tonic water I had cost me a whopping £3, but the scenery was amazing especially as it got dark. There were also some very beautiful Thai dancers on board which again made me feel like the size of a house next to them. The down side of going out on the river as it got dark was that I now had three more mosquito bites which itched like mad throughout the night.

Day 18

The following morning, after yet another restless night, I was booked on another boat trip down the canals or Klongs as they are called there. I ended up on a long tailed James Bond speedboat which whizzes down the main river zipping between the larger boats. It was all very exciting and terrifying at the same time, I had to keep my mouth tightly shut to ensure no spray from the filthy river went in my mouth.
There were 8 of us today and we all spoke different languages which made for an interesting if silent outing. There were two Japanese (they ignored everyone), 3 Nepalese (they could not speak any English but were friendly enough), two Koreans (they knew three English words - better than my Korean though) and me - we could all only communicate by hand gestures. The Koreans were very funny, they snapped photos of anything that moved and took hundreds of selfies. The woman looked like an Asian Sue Pollard with her big glittery spectacles, frilly socks and a knitted beanie hat with a pom pom.

When I got back to the hotel and after yet another change of clothes, I headed out to find the Scala cinema. Who would know that lurking underneath the overhead walkway in Siam Square is a 900 seat Art Deco cinema? It was all original and really beautiful inside the lobby but unfortunately they were only showing one film in five different languages, and one of them was not English.
Disappointed I decided to splash out and go to Jamie Olivers Italian restaurant which was just across the road. What is it with Thailand and all of these Italian restaurants? The place was full of well dressed Thai business people, don't they like their own cuisine? I ordered a pizza, a bottle of Pepsi and splurged out on a glass of Italian red wine. When the bill came I nearly fell off my chair, it came to £25. That was without doubt the most

expensive meal I had in the whole three months and it was in a British restaurant!!!

I ambled back through the disorientating MBK Centre and ended up spending more money, as it turned out I never managed to get through there ever again without buying something.
Back in my room I caught up with my oldest friend Sheryl, we have been friends for 40 years, she was loving my blog and we had a long chat.

Day 19

The following day I embarked on an adventure on my own. I wanted to visit the flower market at Pak Khlong which opened at 2am, obviously I did not go there at that ungodly hour but I left the hotel at 7am which was the middle of the night for me. The bellboys called me a taxi, they have a system there where they record all taxis picking up guests at the hotel, so I felt it was fairly safe to get in one that they had summoned. I got dropped off at the market and had a good old nose around. There was a real business vibe going on and everyone was either buying, selling or arranging flowers.
There were huge bunches of orchids, roses and lilies, bags and bags of shaggy golden marigold heads and buckets of water lilies still in tight bud. Some of it goes to the shops but most of it goes to the temples as offerings. The smell was intoxicating, the colours really vibrant and I appeared to be the only Westerner, the sensible tourists were probably still tucked up in bed.

I took the water taxi to go to Wat Arun which is on the other side of the river, it cost me a whole 20p. So far so good, I ended up there just as it opened and had the whole place to myself. The temple was much simpler than the ones from yesterday and in the early sunshine looked very beautiful. The whole place was decorated with tiny pieces of white and coloured pottery and it was really pretty. It was a stunning morning with not a cloud in the azure blue sky.
I got into conversation with a gorgeous blond air hostess from Lufthansa who was there for a few days before she flew home to Germany. I asked her to take a photo of me by the temple, I don't know why as I was wearing a decidedly dodgy outfit that I would not really want on record. As a return favour she then asked me to take video after video of her running around the temple wafting her floaty dress. Why couldn't she just have a photograph taken like normal people?

Massive tour groups started to arrive and it was time to leave. I spotted another water taxi and leaped on, the boats don't actually stop, they pull up alongside for 20 seconds and you have to jump aboard before it pulls away from the jetty. If you make a crucial timing error you will end up in the filthy river. It was busy with tourists and locals alike and there was standing room only. Off we sailed in the complete opposite direction to where I wanted to go, I know I was heading for outer Bangkok so I was thinking that I would just get off at the next stop. Alas the boat then crosses the river again and we were heading out to sea. Just when I was thinking of abandoning ship we pulled up at a pier and I pushed my way through the sweaty bodies and leaped onto the pier. It was just a floating pontoon and it was bobbing around with the swell from the boat and I nearly end up in the water, but at least I was ashore! I was out in the suburbs and no-one here spoke a word of English so I whipped out my map and was pointed to another jetty where I had to jump onto yet another vessel. I don't have the body or knees for leaping anywhere and I am sure it's not a pretty sight.

Eventually I ended up at the Amulet Market pier and I disembarked. I examined the stuff for sale, it was all small pendants that the locals believe will protect them from misfortune and bring them luck. Some of them were very expensive depending on what they are made of, jade, topaz, amber, silver. It was not very interesting for a non believer and I pondered what to do next, I took my life into my hands and flagged down a metered taxi. As is quite normal in Bangkok the driver cannot speak one word of English, so he handed me his phone and I typed in my destination which he then translated into Thai. Aha he knows exactly where we are going and we accelerate off and instantly come to a standstill in a long traffic jam. Fortunately the car has cold aircon and I at least got a chance to have a rest and cool down whilst he navigated the horrendous traffic.

I arrived at Wat Saket and the Golden Mount which is one of the cities older temples, it was originally used as a crematorium. I climbed the 344 steps in the noon day heat.
The sun must have gone to my head, what a stupid idea to come here at this time of day. Of course there were tourists everywhere on the steps taking selfies and generally stopping you in your tracks. By the time I got to the top I was nearly fit to be cremated myself, I was so hot I could well self combust. There was an amazing view of the Bangkok skyline but there was so much pushing and shoving going on I could not be bothered with it all and made my way straight back down the other side.
I found Wat Saket around the corner and went in, there was a prayer session going on with five chanting monks on a raised platform with a crowd of locals sitting on the floor. It was much more peaceful here and I sat down to absorb the atmosphere. I tried to be respectful and put away the camera. I sat on my feet like they do, you must not point your feet towards Buddha, it is very bad form. I had no idea what was being said but

it all sounded very inspiring and spiritual. I glanced up at the platform, one of the monks had whipped out his Samsung galaxy and was taking photos of me as they chanted away.

I managed to get another taxi back to the hotel without incident, the drivers fortunately all know where the MBK is. I spent a lovely afternoon lounging by the swimming pool doing nothing and then prepared for my big evening out.

I had pre booked a seafood buffet dinner at the tallest building in the city, the Baiyoke Sky Tower. The view was supposed to be amazing. It was about a mile and a half from the hotel and the bellboys hailed me a taxi. The area where the tower is could not be more different from where I was staying. To say it was a bit seedy was a bit of an understatement. The taxi could not get up to the door so I had to get out and walk the rest of the way to the hotel. I was totally surrounded by a Fake market, Chanel handbags, Louboutin shoes, Versace clothes, Gucci watches, designer jewellery, not a genuine article anywhere to be seen. No, I do not want an Yves St Laurent Bag or a pair of Rayban sunglasses. I struggled up the congested street fighting off the army of pushy vendors who all appeared to be Indian. When I got inside the hotel lobby I was informed I needed to go to the 15th floor to pick up my ticket. I don't like lifts at the best of times and they crammed us all in. When I got out I wandered around aimlessly looking for the ticket desk, there were no signs. There was a small queue and I lined up with a massive group of Chinese. When I got to the desk they did not have my booking despite me having a paid receipt which I showed them as proof. I was ushered to a seating area, a bit like a Drs waiting room where there were a group of Dutch tourists who also had a missing booking. My booking was at 7.30, it was now 7.45 and I was seriously beginning to think this might have been a bad idea. The hotel was really busy, gaudy and I did not like the feel of the place.

I eventually got my ticket, there was no apology from the desk staff, and I got in yet another lift to go to the 78th floor. I do not know what I was expecting but when the lift opened I was hit by a wall of sound coming from the restaurant, it was full of people stuffing their faces and the noise was deafening. I was shown to a plastic table for one and waved in the vague direction of the buffet. The lights were on full blast and there was no ambience at all, it was so bright that you had to press your nose against the window to see the view because of the light reflection. I could just see the road and traffic below, we were a long way up and I felt a little bit agitated. My mind instantly switched into menopausal overdrive. What if there is an emergency up here? How will we all get out? Most people would have a heart attack descending the stairs to the ground. Actually, are there any stairs? I hadn't seen any.

There was nothing wrong with the food however just the clientele who were pushing old ladies and children aside to get to the prawns. I ate my meal and decided to leave as it was not the sort of place to relax and I could not see the point in hanging around. There was another complete shambles of a performance getting in and out of the different lifts before I actually reached the ground floor.

I now really wanted to leave but sods law there were no taxi's available. At last the Concierge found me a car and I clambered in, noticing that the driver had thrown a towel over the meter. Now I had read in my guide book that if there is no meter on you must negotiate the fare with the driver before setting off. I tried to speak to the driver but he just ignored me and drives off anyway. The concierge had told him where I wanted to go but it was now dark and I had no idea in which direction we were heading, I recognised nothing. I was very alarmed at this point and all the warning lights were flashing in my head that I may have been kidnapped. I tried to imagine whether Peter would be able to get the ransom together, he might have to sell his motorbike, no that was never going to happen, I realised then that I would never be released. Luckily the shyster driver deposited me at my hotel and then proceeded to ask me for 5 times what it should cost. At this point the bellboy had opened the car door and I asked him to repeat what the driver had just said to me. There was a bit of an argument between them and he told me to only pay twice what it should cost. I throw some notes at the slimy git and I am left standing on the pavement as the taxi drives off where I get a firm telling off by the bellboy for not first negotiating the fare with the driver. When I explained what had happened he got very cross and immediately reported the driver and car to the tourist police. Ha it served the cheating bastard right!

Day 20

I had a bit of a lie in the next morning and later ventured out to get on the Skytrain to visit Chong Nonsi where there is an elaborate Indian temple. When I got there it took all of two minutes to look around and you were not allowed to take any photographs. Whilst in the area I found the Neilson Hays Library which was a cool reprieve from the madness outside and I had a long conversation with the two Australian volunteers who run it.

I meandered around the streets and had a look at Laai Sap Market. Considering this was a Cosmopolitan City I was the only white face in there, it was mainly locals buying clothes and housewares. There were lots of stalls selling the smallest bra's you have ever seen, the size of espresso cups, I don't know anyone with boobs that small.

There is an unfinished skyscraper here called Sathorn Unique Tower. It was started 20 years ago and was never finished due to the financial crisis that hit Thailand in the nineties. It is an ugly skeleton amongst the backdrop of the modern chrome and steel buildings. The locals avoid it completely as they believe it is full of ghosts. It is actually illegal to enter inside but there are lots of street people and wild dogs living within. It is nicknamed the Ghost Tower on account of the dead bodies (druggies) that tend to turn up in the empty rooms.

I got back on the skytrain and followed a sign to Saphin Taksin where there was a free boat ferrying tourists to the brand new Icon Siam shopping centre on the other side of the river. I don't really like indoor shopping centres but this place was fantastic, I wandered around open mouthed at the money that had been spent on this establishment. There was an entire Thai village complete with a river, bridges, lake and boats serving Thai food. All the shop keepers were wearing traditional dress and one man was even wading around in the river pretending to catch fish. The view from the top floor was amazing, you could see all of Bangkok laid out before you including the mournful Sathorn Tower. It certainly gives the shopping malls in Dubai and Abu Dhabi a run for their money with its opulence.

On the way back my ticket would not work on the sky train and I got into a heated discussion with the station master, eventually he let me through. I later discovered that I had used the wrong ticket, but I had paid the proper fare, so I didn't cheat them. Instead of going through the MBK to the hotel I think that I am being clever by walking along the outside of the building to avoid the shops, but even here there are a load of stalls and carts lined up along the wall and I end up spending even more money. Bah I thought I had it sussed.
I had another pizza for tea and roamed around the Thai Cultural centre looking at a superb photo exhibition of animals and scenery before I retired to my room for a long bath and bed.
I must say Bangkok is an exciting and amazing city but the heat, noise and crowds of people zap the strength from you and I was totally exhausted.

Day 21

Despite my tiredness I still did not sleep very well and opted to sit by the pool for a few hours in the morning. It was really hot and I fell asleep in the sun and woke up feeling very weird. There was a beautiful girl wearing a white bikini on the sun bed next to me, with her equally gorgeous boyfriend on the other side. They were simply stunning to look at, they made a beautiful couple and listening to their voices I think they were Israeli. Strangely enough I used to look a bit like her when I was younger, (a lot younger). They made me feel fat, old, frumpy and passed it, Oh dear I did get out of bed the wrong side this morning.

In the afternoon I took a gentle walk up the road to Jim Thompsons House. He was an American businessman who came to Bangkok in 1945 and restarted the silk weaving industry. His house is made up of five different teak buildings on stilts and is now a museum. It is also a lovely quiet haven in the centre of the city away from the noise and traffic and has a pretty little garden. I handed over my money to go on a tour of the house with a very bossy Thai guide. We had to put our mobile phones and cameras into a locker before we were even allowed inside, we also had to remove our shoes and are warned very sternly not to touch anything - as if we would dare.

The house was stunningly beautiful and full of Thai art and sculptures. The guide loosened up a bit now that we have shed our gadgets and shoes and tells funny little stories along the way. Following behind us is a very loud Korean group, they touched everything much to the consternation of their guide, who rolls her eyes every time she guides them on to the next room. Apparently Thompson disappeared whilst out walking in the Malaysian Cameron highlands in 1967. There are lots of theories but his body was never found, he may have been bumped off by the CIA or eaten by a hungry animal, no-one actually knows. There is a lovely shop selling silk clothes and bags at the entrance but they are way out of my budget but I noticed is was full of Americans and Japanese making expensive purchases. The museum was a very nice way to pass some time.

When I left the house I walked up to the Asia Hotel. I stayed here with my last husband about 27 years ago and at the time it was the most amazing hotel I had ever stayed in. Alas it has changed now and I hardly recognised it through the garish decorations and plastic flowers that adorned the lobby. On my way back to the hotel I noticed that the road had cleared and there seemed to be a lot of policemen around. As I attempted to cross the road I was shouted at by a uniformed officer with a gun and told to stay where I was, I decided best not to argue and I froze on the spot. A few seconds later a cavalcade of cars came roaring down the road with flashing blue lights followed by a stretch limousine. Apparently it was the Crown Princess on her way to a meeting. Drama over, I headed off for something to eat at the Siam centre where I was spoilt for choice with the amazing array of eateries.

On my way back I spent more money in the shopping centre before stopping for an ice cream in Svensens. I was just perusing the price list in the window when a Thai woman in front of me, who was yakking on her phone and not concentrating, suddenly changed direction, ran straight into me and stamped on my foot. I had had a loose toenail for several months and when I looked down it was hanging off and was only connected by a thin bit of skin. My beautiful gel manicure now looked really weird. I reached down and quickly pulled the whole thing off squealing with pain, at least the woman apologised.

I tried to speak to my friend Julie but we kept getting cut off so I gave up and rang Peter. He was keeping himself busy and was in the middle of a job so he could not speak for long. Feeling a bit dejected I entered a beauty parlour and paid for a foot massage. I love having my feet played with and find it really relaxes me: In fact I can hardly keep my eyes open.
I laid back in the reclining chair and reflected on my time in Bangkok. I had really enjoyed the city and apart from the dodgy taxi driver had felt quite safe on my own. The Thai people in general are very friendly. I had done lots of sight seeing but I still felt like I had only just scratched the surface, there was so much more to see here. Oh well I can always come back though it will have to be on my own again, Peter absolutely hates the place!

As I made my way back to my room I could smell that someone was smoking on my floor and the corridor stank strongly of cigarettes, this was supposed to be a non smoking hotel. I went back down in the lift to report it to reception. They took it all very seriously and sent up several security staff to investigate and put fans all along the corridor to kill the smell.
In my room I had a final sort out, finished all of my packing and had a relatively early night, I was off to LAOS in the morning.

5 LAOS

Day 22

After the lush foot massage I had a brilliant nights sleep and I woke up really refreshed and ready for whatever the day might throw at me. This was probably a good job as I had to get on another plane today flying into the complete unknown. I was not panicking quite as much as usual about the flight as my mind was on other things: I did not know a solitary person who had been to Laos and I just had no idea what to expect.

I had carefully repacked all the baggage and my hand luggage was now really heavy, the Burmese Celadon vase was wrapped up in there. The driver clearly strained something when he lifted my bags into the boot of the car. For the flight to the capital, Vientiane, I was allowed 25 kilos with my frequent flyer card but my case weighed in at 26.5 kilos, the check in girl did not bat an eyelid. Bugger, I now had to lug my really heavy hand luggage around Suvarnabhumi airport and I could easily have put the damned vase in the case and got away with it. It was only 7am but the airport was very busy and I luckily found a small trolley to put my bag on, carrying that weight I am sure my arms were longer than they were earlier.

I must admit I do not remember much of that flight. I had got up very early and I probably dozed. I know it was very smooth and took only an hour but I have no recollection of any food or drink being served. What I do remember was that the pretty Asian girl sitting next to me spent the whole flight looking through millions of photos of herself on her phone. For a whole hour non stop she scrolled on and on. I got bored nosing over her shoulder after five minutes and read the safety notice from the seat pocket in front of me, it was far more interesting: she was still looking at them after we landed. Nothing else of note happened apart from me nearly decapitating another passenger when I got my heavy bag down from the overhead locker.

Laos is supposed to be the poorest country in South East Asia so I was expecting an old jalopy to pick me up but my driver escorted me to a whacking big 4 x 4 that I needed a ladder to get up into. Everywhere I looked there were massive pickup trucks and jeeps. I also noticed that it felt even hotter than Bangkok and it was only 11.00 in the morning. There was a complete lack of traffic leaving Vientiane airport and we were at the hotel in 15 minutes flat. My guide informed me that he would pick me up tomorrow morning with the other two ladies who are on the tour, they were arriving later that evening. Good, I would have some company for a few days after being on my own in Bangkok for the last six days.

The hotel had been booked by the tour company who were guiding me through Laos and it looked OK from the outside. My room in this hotel was supposedly a Double Deluxe and was on the third floor at the back. It had a small window overlooking a scruffy piece of land which was inhabited by a load of chickens. I could not help but wonder what a normal room looked like (I found out later that the standard rooms have no windows). This Deluxe was very small and there was nowhere to put my suitcase so it sat open in the middle of the floor like a huge pair of orange jaws and I tripped over it every time I moved. By the time I left that hotel I was covered in scratches and bruises.
 There was a wet room which was strangely the same size as the bedroom, decorated with hideous burgundy tiles and had very bad lighting. But the room did have working aircon, wifi and looked clean enough. After all I was only here for two nights and it would do. I rang Planet Peter to let him know I was still alive and had safely arrived in Laos. He put the phone on camera mode so I ended up talking to the dog.

After a bit of a sort out I set off for a walk around the town. It didn't take long, what a funny little place. For a capital city it was tiny, there were no tall buildings or chain hotels, no Starbucks or McDonalds. As I walked up and down the shabby little streets, there was rubble piled everywhere. I am not sure if the buildings were being demolished or new ones being built, it was kind of hard to tell. Outside a temple there were six monks dressed in their saffron robes sitting on red metal scaffolding painting a wall, I can't imagine our local vicar doing that. There was a complete absence of shops, bars, restaurants and people. It could just be that it was very hot, 36C, and everyone was indoors unlike this ditzy female tourist who was walking around in the simmering heat.

I came across a money changer and transferred all of my leftover Thai Baht into Lao Kip. I was just wondering where to eat when I came across, wait for it, a pizzeria. Not exactly what I was expecting here, I went in and ordered some dinner and a beer. It was really cheap, it came to about £4 and was actually ok. I always think if in doubt have a pizza, as long as it is cooked in a really hot oven that will kill a lot of germs. I chose to sit out on the veranda which was a huge mistake, they could probably have cooked the pizza in front of me on the tiled floor it was so hot.

As I left the restaurant there appeared to be a few more people around and I came across the lively night market down by the river. It seemed to be for locals and there were lots of really cheap clothes and shoes mixed in with plastic children toys. It was very busy and I enjoyed the vibe, I appeared to be the only Westerner yet again and everyone totally ignored me. I purchased a lovely woven handbag for £2 and then following my map made my way back to the hotel. I felt perfectly safe walking around in the dark on my own, I certainly wouldn't do that in Bedford town centre.

I was a little nervous that there were probably millions of rats lurking in the builders rubble, but I made it back without seeing one. I don't mind snakes, spiders or cockroaches but I absolutely hate mice and rats. One evening last year I put the rubbish out after dark for the bin men. I was standing in the kitchen talking to Peter when I felt something run up my left arm inside my dress. I grabbed my sleeve and yanked the dress over my head. Looking down at my hand there was a small brown mouse looking back at me. I tossed the dress and the mouse on the kitchen floor, climbed on a chair and started screaming like a banshee. I could tell by the worried look on Peters face (and he never worries about anything) that he thought I had now finally lost the plot as I was in complete meltdown. He picked the dress up and shook it onto the drive, sure enough a little mouse fell out and ran off. He now found the whole thing riotously funny and replayed the whole thing on the security camera. Fortunately I was wearing by best underwear at the time. Mind you the dress went straight in the bin, I couldn't wear that again. Ever.

Back in my room I read through my guide book deciding what to do in the morning, updated my Blog and read all of my messages and emails. Donald Trump was in full flow on CNN and I dozed off watching him.

Day 23

I actually slept very well but had a very strange dream that I was in a James Bond film with Roger Moore who then morphed into Pierce Brosnan. I tried very hard to doze off again to be with Pierce (I think he is the most gorgeous man on the planet) but the moment was broken and I decided to get up. I had a shower in the wet room which was decidedly dodgy. There were exposed electric wires around the shower heater and I had to lay towels on the floor to stop me slipping around as I entered the bedroom onto the tiled floor with wet feet.

After a mediocre breakfast at the hotel where I was completely ignored by the waiting staff, I walked across town to the COPE centre. This is a rehabilitation centre for people who have been injured by UXO (unexploded ordnance). The Ho Chi Minh trail from Vietnam through Laos and back into Vietnam was at the time the most bombed place on the planet. Around 30% of the cluster bombs dropped failed to detonate and they estimate that there are still 80,000,000 unexploded bomblets still buried in the ground. 20,000 people have been maimed and injured since the end of the war by these UXO, mainly children and farmers. My guide book warns never to go off the beaten track when out in the countryside. It is a sobering place but full of hope. They are trying very hard to help the injured by supplying prosthetic limbs and giving physiotherapy to help them adapt. I leave them a small donation and buy a few trinkets in their little shop.

On the way back to the hotel I come across another local market and have a wander around. Everything seems very cheap but it is all a bit plasticky and tacky, there is nothing much of any quality. I try to buy a fake watch as I was fed up with the green fob watch. For some reason the stall holder expected me to part with $50 for it, on your bike mate! Back at the hotel I changed my clothes and went down to the lobby to meet my guide and fellow travellers.

It turned out they were two elderly sisters from California on a whistle stop tour of Asia, two days here, 1 day there, etc. They were called Julie-Ann & Sheila and they muttered between themselves. A lot. I had to strain my ears to make out what they are saying half the time. The older one had picked up a chest infection and moaned constantly about it. For Americans they were not that friendly and tended to keep to themselves as we started the tour. It was a boiling hot afternoon and the car thermometer read 37C.

We visited three important temples which compared to Thailand were virtually empty apart from several wedding couples having their photos taken. They were all wearing the traditional Lao dress and they looked beautiful against the temple backdrop. The last temple was called That Luang which my guide book tells me is the most important religious building in the whole country and was completely covered in gold leaf.

After the temples we went to Patouxai which is supposed to be Vientianes equivalent of the Champs Elysees. Laos was ruled by the French several times and they have allegedly left their mark. It was nothing like Paris not by a long shot - not even close. The only similarity was that the monument looked a bit similar to the Arc de Triomphe, there any resemblance to the Parisian Capital ended.

By now I was feeling the heat, sweat was running down my back and I had a sheen on my upper lip. The guide did not produce any cold towels or bottles of water like they did in Burma and by the time we got back to the hotel I was like a wet dishcloth. The old girls whittled away on the way to their room, they didn't suggest I join them for dinner, so after a shower and a bit of a cool down I headed out on my own again.

According to my guide book there was another night market around the back of the town so I set off to look for it. I followed the map but it was nowhere to be seen. It was starting to get dark and I didn't want to get set on by the rats so I changed direction and ended up in the area where I was the previous evening. Funnily enough I came across yet another Italian restaurant. It had aircon so I sensibly decided to sit indoors tonight. It was entirely void of any other diners and I was shown to a table in the centre. I ordered my dinner and then rang Peter.
He was doing the laundry and I could tell he had a bit of the hump about it. I do everything in our house, shopping, washing, cleaning, ironing, cooking, decorating, gardening: he does nothing. Before you jump to conclusions and I hear howls of protest, I work 9-5pm four days a week. Some days he gets up at 1am (I have never in my entire life got up at that time to go to work) and he normally does not get home until 6.30pm so it is an arrangement we have fallen into. He has another 10 weeks of this and he is clearly not enjoying himself.

Whilst I am waiting for my meal two gentlemen come in and are seated next to me. I would guess that one was around 70 and the other about my age. They were both American and the first thing they do is send in a thrusting lunge about the Brexit mess, I parry with a caustic comment about Donald Trump. Game over and the ice was broken. We sat chatting and laughing about the state of world politics for ages. They both had Laotian partners and owned houses here. I imagine there was a big age difference between them and their companions, if you get my drift. Their partners had gone out together for the evening to a nightclub so the Americans were having a boys night out. Who would know there was any nightlife here, it must be well hidden and only known to the locals. They were going to Luang Prabang tomorrow, what a coincidence so was I, it turned out that we are going on the same flight.

We sat and amusedly watched two German tourists arguing with the waiter about the extra charges which will be applied to their bill if they pay by Mastercard. This information about credit card transactions in Laos is available everywhere, so I do not understand what they were getting so upset about. In the end they flounce rudely out without ordering anything. We console the waiter who apologises to us for their rude behaviour, it was not the restaurants rules, this is the law here!

After dinner I walked around the night market again and ended up buying a classy Rado watch for £2.50 which was more in my price range. What a bargain! It even came with a battery and actually worked.
On the way back to my hotel I saw the most enormous cream coloured Bentley parked by the side of the road. I didn't see anything as opulent as that in Bangkok, someone certainly had some money around here.

Day 24

I slept very well and in the morning decided to wash my hair. That was an accident waiting to happen, as I blinded myself with shampoo, couldn't find the towel and skidded all over the wet room floor.

The two old girls and myself are picked up in another enormous 4X4 and driven to the airport. They mumbled all the way there, something about jelly beans. Again no-one even looks or cares at how much my bag weighed, I was not even using my frequent flyer anymore as we were with a different airline and I should only be allowed 20kilos. There were numerous flights to Luang Prabang each day, I just think the plane goes back and forth, but for my flight there was allegedly a 45 minute delay. Talking to some regulars this is quite normal for Laos and the plane will go when it goes, they told me to completely ignore the flight timings on my ticket.
I looked around the tiny departure lounge and spotted the Americans from last nights Italian restaurant. I went over, they were delighted to see me, and I asked them how their girlfriends got on at the disco last night. They pointed to their partners. Sitting next to them were two beautiful young Asian males with silky black hair wearing funky clothes, trendy trainers and lots of silver jewellery. Oh Dear what a mistake to make! Please let the earth open up and swallow me! I had got so used to seeing ugly old men with pretty Thai girls in Bangkok that I naturally presumed it was the same here. After I hastily apologised they introduced me to the boys who were charming and lovely. I made a mental note to myself not to presume anything from now on. What was strange was that the two boys were entwined around each other and were virtually ignoring their American partners who just sat watching them. All a bit of an odd set up if you ask me.

The flight took just 30 minutes and only flew at 17,000 feet. I actually enjoyed the amazing view as we came into land, everything looked green and lush as we flew in over the mountains. It was over so quick I didn't really have time to get myself into too much of a state. I had been expecting the airport to be a small shed in the middle of a field but it had a proper modern luggage carousel and everything, quite bona fide.

Transport was waiting for us three women and we were whisked off to our hotels. I was staying in a different one from the old girls which wasn't a problem as I hadn't warmed to them.

My residence was a collection of wooden low rise buildings in small clusters on a side street off the main drag. My room was basic but enormous. It was also very dark due to having six windows with all the shutters closed. When I opened one of the shutters I realised that there was no actual glass in the window frame, so I closed it again as I did not want insects getting in my room. I gave everything a really good spray with a can of Raid that I had bought with me for exactly that purpose.

The Wifi worked really well as it had done in Thailand and Vientiane. It's funny how sometimes I can't even get a get a signal in my kitchen but here it was very strong. I checked in with Peter, he had just woken up and was having a Saturday morning lay in with the dog.

We were due to meet the guide in half an hour, so I headed for a local coffee shop and grabbed a quick coffee and doughnut for lunch. It was all very normal in there, just like any cafe or bakery at home. The hotel was only about 100 yards from the 'centre' so I sussed out where to go in the evening.

We first went to the Royal Palace which is now a museum. What a place, I felt like I was on the set of The King and I, except that is set in Thailand not Laos. I expected Yul Brynner to waltz pass with Deborah Kerr at any minute. Unfortunately they do not allow anything to be photographed and you have to leave your camera in a locker, which was a shame. The throne Hall was decorated with red silk and covered in paintings of court life, it was quite magnificent and very atmospheric. The two old girls mumbled their way around. I came across a photo of Ho Chi Minh dancing with the last king of Laos and there is a tatty flag on display that was taken on one of the Apollo space missions. This is sadly all there is left of the 600 year dynasty of the Kingdom of Laos.

Afterwards we made our way along the main road to Wat Xiang Thong with the two old girls constantly wittering amongst themselves. Luang Prabang is obviously not very big and everything here was walkable. This Wat is the

most historic monastery in the whole country and very important to the Lao people. It was not enormous or even particularly elaborate but it is the only temple in Laos not to have been destroyed by any of the invaders and is currently undergoing extensive renovations with US money.
I liked it here, it had a nice feel and nowhere was crawling with tourists.

Back at the hotel I unpacked and had a big sort out of my stuff. An old skirt and a bra ended up in the bin as they were just too uncomfortable. I attempted to speak to my husband but he was busy at a Luton football game and passed me over to speak to my all time favourite Paramedic. I received a weird message from my friend Jane who was simultaneously travelling in Cambodia - something about having to share a room in Vietnam with me, not exactly what I had planned.

I went out for some dinner and noticed that it had cooled down considerably and was a pleasant temperature. I roamed around the excellent night market, it had some beautiful textiles produced by the different ethnic groups and there were some lovely clothes for sale, much nicer than all the tat in Vientiane.
I bumped into the two Americans and their charming boyfriends and ended up going for a beer with them at the Villa Santi where they were staying. It is a beautiful hotel and I would have loved to have stayed there but the tour company wouldn't let me as they only had contracts with the smaller hotels in town. The two boyfriends were wrapped around each other again and the Americans were just letting them get on with it, it was all very weird.

I walked back to the hotel, it was pitch dark once I got out of the night market and for the first time since that night in Bangkok I felt slightly vulnerable as I ducked down the narrow alley to my hotel.
When I arrived in reception there were 4 Asian men (I think they were Chinese) sitting around a table playing cards and drinking a bottle of whisky. Draped around each of them was a young lady from the hotel 'Spa' supposedly giving them a shoulder massage. I wondered where that was all leading to as I wearily climbed the wooden stairs to my room.

Day 25

I slept in fits and starts, every time I moved the bed creaked really loudly, I pitied the people in the room underneath me, they probably thought there was a honeymoon couple in my room with all the noise the bed made.
It was lovely and cool in the morning and I made my way down to the breakfast area. It was a truly awful affair, all the dishes were cold and congealed, there was sticky rice with everything, the only good thing on

offer was the coffee, it was delicious. Breakfast was included in the price of my room but I didn't bother with it again as it was so horrible.

Today the guide was taking us down the Mekong river to the Ou Pak caves. When he picked me up, only Julie-Ann was with him. Her sister had decided to stay at the hotel and have a rest, the chest infection was getting her down. Without Sheila, Julie-Ann warmed up and was quite chatty. We walked down to the riverside to find our long tailed house boat. Getting onboard was interesting. There were empty plastic petrol canisters all strung together which formed a sort of floating pontoon. There were no handles and there was nothing to hold onto. You had to really pull in your upper core to be able to balance, my core has been hidden for ages and I found it very tricky. The guide and pilot had to assist both of us aboard.
The pilot, his wife and their new baby live on the boat, there was a complete living section at the back complete with a laundry room and kitchen. Julie-Ann and I were the only passengers and we had the whole thing to ourselves.
The scenery was stunning, huge limestone crags covered in lush greenery and surrounded by forests. The tiny baby was asleep in a bouncy chair by her fathers feet in the cockpit oblivious to the noisy engines. The wife appeared every now and then from the back of the boat, where she was doing her washing, to feed her husband and the baby. It was all very relaxing and tranquil watching the world go by. We passed some huge water buffalo with massive horns frolicking in the water with their offspring. There was a monastery on the river bank where all the monks were unloading a boat full of bricks and tossing them to each other in a chain gang up the hill. There were two day beds and I stretched out feeling like the Queen of Egypt floating down the Nile. Everything in the world seemed right at that point.
We saw lots of tiny villages and fishermen out in their boats with their hand made nets trying to catch their evening meal. We then floated underneath an ugly eyesore. There was a huge engineering project going on down stream where they are building an enormous concrete bridge. It will cut down the time of the villagers journeys whenever they need to go into town. It completely ruins the landscape but I suppose that is progress for you.

We reached the caves and there were a couple of very dodgy moments trying to get off the boat onto another floating platform. This one was made of metal oil drums lashed together with a bit of rope. Julie-Ann it turns out is 77 and was quite sprightly, I am not and I needed a bit of help from the guide. Eventually off, we climbed the steep steps up to the caves. Inside there were 4000 statues of Buddha of every varying quality, placed in every nook and cranny and some were up on really steep limestone slopes. They were made of stone, china, rotting wood and some of the newer ones were neon green resin or made of yellow plastic. Apparently during Lao New Year all the villagers arrive and clean every single statue, it gives them merit with Buddha. It had obviously been a while as they were all dusty, covered in cobwebs and bird/bat droppings. It must have been a death defying moment trying to put the statues up in some of their locations. There was an amazing view from the top and I spotted elephants on the other side of the river. That was where we were going for lunch.

Julie-Ann and I were seated at a table in a wooden restaurant on stilts overlooking the river. It was a delightful spot and the view was stunning. The restaurant was full of tourists, they had all come to ride the elephants which were lumbering back and forth along the river through the undergrowth. I am glad we were not doing that, I am not sure I would feel very comfortable about riding such an animal as a gimmick. I wouldn't even go on a camel in Eygpt. Laos used to be called the Kingdom of a Million Elephants, but sadly they estimate there are only around 800 left in the country and 400 of them are in captivity, and these were some of them. The poor things laden down with fat, sweaty tourists waving their cameras around in all directions.

The guide proceeds to tell us that when we get back to Luang Prabang that afternoon we would need do the rest of the tour which was planned for tomorrow. Both of us are not happy with this and feel we are being rushed. Also we had paid for a three day leisurely tour not a crammed two day tour. I also expect Sheila would like to see some more of the town if she is feeling better. I can tell from the look on his face that he is not happy with us but we stick to our guns, and I smell something fishy going on.

After a surprisingly good curry lunch we explored the local village. There were numerous shacks selling locally made colourful fabric and textiles. Julie-Ann bought two hand made scarves for £1.50 each. Back onboard we cruised slowly back towards town. It was very hot but having been on the water there was a good breeze and I did not feel quite as exhausted today. Julie-Ann had been chatty like any normal American today and I now knew everything about her life and family. The pilot's baby had not made a sound all day and you can tell that the wife was happy with her lot. I had a mooch around the boat and took a look at their living area, they did not seem to have many possessions. It was a very simple life but they seemed content with it.

When we arrived back at the dodgy jetty I walked off in the direction of the Villa Santi where I ended up having an early dinner at a traditional Lao restaurant as the sun set over the Mekong. OMG the food was really fiery and spicy and I could feel it burning my insides on the way down. I think I actually lost my voice at one point and led me to believe I may have permanently damaged my vocal chords. The young waiter was delightful and we ended up discussing English Premiership football of which I know absolutely nothing. But I chatted away about the merits of Liverpool, Chelsea and Manchester United as if I was on the terraces supporting them every Saturday.

On the way back to the hotel I ended up buying some fabric made by one of the hill tribes. I haggled quite fiercely and ended up getting it for about £12.00. My idea was to get it made into a pencil skirt for work (it is still in the spare bedroom). I also bought a solid silver necklace and matching earrings for £11.00 which I was delighted with. That market was really fabulous, not a piece of tat in sight. I could have bought a lot more but I was conscious of the weight of my bags. I don't know why as so far no-one had even questioned it. I ended up having a beer and a iced doughnut in the local cafe, a very strange combination before bedtime.

Back in my room I spoke to my friend Jane, she was travelling with a bloke she had met on a previous trip to Africa . For some reason she thought it might be fun to travel to Cambodia and Vietnam with him. It turns out that he was a bit boring and she had had to spend a lot of time on her own as he doesn't want to spend any money eating out. They are not a couple, just companions and she was looking forward to getting to Vietnam to spend time with me for a few days. They had decided to extend their time in Vietnam but the hotel only has one room for the first night and she was asking if she could share with me. As it is only for one night I don't have a problem and we ring off.

I took some laundry down to reception. They were a right bunch of miseries in there and don't speak unless they are spoken to and never crack a smile, not like the Burmese or Thai people who are always smiling. I am made to pay up front for my washing, do they really think I am going to abscond without paying? I certainly wouldn't get very far with all my luggage.
I laid in bed watching 'Paul" which is one of Peters favourite films. I have never watched it all the way through and it is very funny.

Day 26

I woke up in a daze at 5.30 am to the sound of drums banging, outside it was still dark. What was all that noise? I later learned it was the monks walking the streets collecting food and alms from the locals or Tak Bat as the ceremony is called here. They do this every day and it is a bit of a tourist attraction. I really wanted to see it but I could never manage to get out of bed early enough.

After breakfast in the little cafe at the end of the road, I met up with Julie-Ann, Sheila and our new guide. Sheila was feeling better and looking forward to this mornings outing. It turned out that the first guide had gone to a party for his brother and this one had had to step in to cover for him as we declined to do the rest of the tour yesterday. My sixth sense had kicked in and I had known something wasn't right.

We headed off for the local market which was in a back street near my hotel. You would never had known it was there. There were lots of unrecognisable but colourful fruit and vegetables for sale and you could smell that some of it was starting to rot.
I am not a vegetarian in the UK but whenever I travel abroad I instantly become one. The meat here is not chilled and sterile or wrapped in cling film like at Tesco. It is covered in flies and bugs and I am sure some of it was still moving. When I went to China a few years ago I refused to eat anything that I did not recognise. Our guide there told me ' in China we eat everything with four legs except the table and chair' I came home a stone lighter.
There was an interesting stall selling insect larvae and locusts, sold in bags as snacks. (You won't find them in your nearest Asda). The locusts look like they have been fried in batter and actually did not look that horrible, a bit like long crisps with wings. Our guide wolfed a few down but we all politely decline, we had just had breakfast. We then came across a lady selling snake wine by the glass. This is quite common in Asia and I had seen it before. A huge glass demijohn full of an unknown clear liquid, laying in the bottom are a selection of dead snakes, centipedes and scorpions. Quite how old this wine was you could not tell but it was festering in the hot sun and would probably have poisoned you. It looked quite disgusting.

We reached Phousi Hill which is the spiritual centre of Luang Prabang: we were going to attempt to climb to the top. Sheila got about 25metres in and wimped out, so Julie-Ann and I set off with the guide. We followed a zigzag path at the beginning which then turned into steep steps. You could not set a proper pace because the steps were uneven and of different heights and it was murder on the hip joints. We were surrounded by jungle, it was very hot and humid and there were flying insects everywhere. We reached the top where there was a 360 degree view of the whole area, covered in a heat haze. That Chomsi temple is at the top and there were a few people around taking photos, it was again very peaceful. The guide informed us that at sunset the whole place is crawling with tourists so I am glad we had come up early.

Coming down was a bit treacherous in places, it was very narrow with no hand rails and scores of tourists were pushing their way up towards you. I am not very good with heights, I go up easily but descending when you can see everything laid out in front of me makes my head spin. I remember years ago I froze on a platform at Sigiriya in Sri Lanka and the guide had to physically come and get me. I literally could not move and he had to talk me down step by step. I felt such a twit! Once at the bottom I just carried on as if nothing weird had come over me

On the way down we passed a house that was built into the hillside. There was a lot of noise coming from inside so being nosey I poked my head through a window. Inside an industrial size washing machine was chugging away, the owners must have a laundry business.

It was not what you would expect to see on a holy mountain.

We found Sheila sitting in someone's house, they had offered her a chair and cup of tea. We walked slowly up to Wat Sene which is one of the monasteries that lines the main road. It was a very peaceful place and I just sat under a tree absorbing the serene atmosphere whilst the girls poked around inside the buildings. I watched one of the monks hanging out his washing. I wonder if it gets boring wearing the same outfit every day? Does he ever have to iron it for special occasions? How often does he have to replace his flip flops?

I left the Americans wittering amongst themselves now they were back together and took myself off to Ock Pop Tok. This is a crafts centre set up by local women which employs female weavers from the local villages for a decent wage. I had a look around the shops, the fabric and wall hangings were spectacular if a little pricey. I had a spot of lunch in the little cafe there and then walked back to the hotel.

It was really hot by now and the streets were almost deserted. I found a little shop that sold Haribo gummy bears and stocked up on my favourite treat. I decided to sit on the veranda and read but even in the shade the heat was intense and I retreated to my air-conditioned room where I promptly fell asleep for the rest of the afternoon. Total bliss.

After a very solitary dinner, I spent most of the evening on the phone. Peter, my sister, Julie and Maureen, they all wanted to know what I had been doing and I ended up telling my stories four times over. I updated my blog with my latest adventures and picked up of all my emails. There was also an email from Ivan raving about my trip and wishing me well.

I did not sleep very well, I woke up freezing and then got very hot. I had a feeling it was not helped by the three hour snooze I had taken the previous afternoon and also I don't think drinking beer before bed helps with the hot flushes. At this point I could not really tell during the day whether I was having one or not as it was so hot outside but I was still plagued with them during the night even with the freezing aircon blowing. Please God it has been 5 years when am I going to get a break from this?

Next day I had booked a tour through the hotel to the Kuang Si Waterfalls which were about 30km outside town.
It was an interesting journey. The driver collected me first then drove around six other hotels doing pickups. He then decided that he had forgotten someone so we then went round the town again. By now I had been in the bus for about 45 minutes and we had still not even left town. At last fully loaded the driver now realised he was running late and had to make up some time. He obviously fancied himself as the Lao version of Lewis Hamilton. He swung our mini van around every bend and corner completely oblivious to any other traffic, overtaking anything that got in his way. This was a narrow twisty mountainous road and he thought he was in a Formula One racing car not a Toyota minibus full of passengers. I had grave doubts as to whether we would get there in one piece. Nerves jangling and feeling really sick we eventually pulled up in the car park on a hand break turn, where the driver then informed us we had to pay him the entrance fee to get into the park. It was not very much but one grizzled old American became quite aggressive about it, and claimed that he had not been told the entry fee was not included in the price of the day trip. It all got a bit heated between him and the driver and I was glad to leave them to it.

As I entered the park, I feared the American may have had a point as I had not been given a ticket and no-one even asked to see one. Had we just been ripped off by our F1 driver? He roared out of the car park on three wheels, hurtling back to Luang to pick up his next load. I took a photo of his number plate as the whole car park was full of similar white mini buses and made my way up the hill.

I have to say the falls were spectacular. They cascaded down the hillside into a series of eight turquoise pools, the colours were amazing. You could actually swim in two of them and there were lots of tourists splashing around in the water. I decided not to go in as there was nowhere secure to leave your stuff and I had my big camera with me, if I lost that I would lose all of my photos taken so far. Watching the swimmers I noticed one girl with a perfect body and long blond hair wearing a blue thong wading around seductively in the shallow water. She had quite an audience and even I couldn't take my eyes off of her, she was exquisite : I hated her guts on sight.

There were several monks roaming around with their mobiles, taking photos of all the swimmers and secretly the gorgeous girl. I found out later that the previous day a Chinese tourist had had a heart attack and died in the water whilst everyone was splashing around him. It had taken an hour before any sort of medical assistance or defibrillator had arrived. Whilst they were waiting some of the tourists were taking photographs. How callous and awful for his wife who was with him. He was given CPR by a group of Australian backpackers but unfortunately they could not revive him. I thanked the lord that I had not been there as I know I would have ended up getting involved.

The Lewis Hamilton of the Lao minibus world arrived to take us back to the town. It was a curious selection of people - not one word had been spoken on the way there and it was very quiet on the way back. There was a young Spanish couple on the front seat who couldn't keep their hands off each other (get a room please), a selection of Japanese wearing interesting hats and gloves (they did not speak one word) and three very polite German lads. There had been two Koreans on the way there but they were not at the pick up point so we went back to Luang without them. I ended up on the back seat with the gnarly American who now zoned in on me and wanted to discuss politics of which I know or care very little about. He was the first Donald Trump supporter I had come across so far, I tried to be tactful but he got verbally aggressive whenever you did not agree with his point of view. I was trapped at the back of the bus and there was no getting away from him. I had to listen to his viewpoint on everything from the Military to Starbucks. He stunk of booze and fags and of course he told me his entire miserable life story. I was also a bit suspicious that he may have taken some sort of substance as his pupils were like huge black saucers. He told me that he had a Lao girlfriend who had just thrown him out and he was laying low for a while. I am not surprised she dumped him, he was foul. He then decides to come on to me and starts chatting me up: OH NO, NOT IF YOU WERE THE LAST MAN ON EARTH MATE!!

Did I imagine it or was the journey back slightly slower? I actually got to admire some of the scenery whenever my unpleasant companion stopped yakking for half a second or amused himself by trying to look down my vest top. The driver eventually came to a stop at the end of my road and ordered everyone out, no-one was getting driven back to their hotel much to their chagrin. I almost sprinted down the road to get away from 'My new friend' I tried to sit outside on my terrace and read but the heat drove me inside for the rest of the afternoon.

That evening I found a restaurant overlooking the night market and got talking to a group of English people who were on an organised adventure tour. It was definitely not my sort of holiday. They were going kayaking and caving along the Mekong the following day. They were all around my age and were obviously having a mid life crisis and felt that they needed to behave like teenagers. We had a good laugh and swapped numbers to meet up in Vietnam should our paths cross.

I decided to have a bath this evening which was lovely. Unfortunately when I pulled the plug out all of the water from the bath came up through the shower plughole and soaked the bathroom. It was full of black slime and goodness knows what else and ended up all over the floor. It took at least an hour before the water subsided back into the shower drain and I got down on my hands and knees to clean it all up. Just what you needed before bedtime.

I sent an email to the travel company checking that I would get checked straight through to Danang the day after tomorrow and they replied saying yes that should happen. The last thing I wanted to do was to collect my luggage in Hanoi and have to check in all over again to get to Danang. This had been worrying me a bit and my mind was put at rest.

Day 28

I took another precious sleeping tablet that night and had a long lie in the next morning. After a quick doughnut at the coffee shop I went for a really long walk along the river looking at the lovely Asian shop houses and old French mansions, somehow managing to keep mainly in the shade. There are no 5 star hotels in Luang Prabang, and apart from the Villa Santi all the accommodations are small and bijou. There are absolutely no swimming pools anywhere but there is a large Pullman resort about 5 miles outside town which has all the creature comforts you could desire. There were some very upmarket craft and clothing shops along the far end of the main road selling some beautiful but very expensive apparel. The shops were full of Americans flashing their cash, no budget conscious English tourists in there. This part of town also had some gorgeous guesthouses and restaurants and I stopped to have a coffee and an iced bun.

I came across a small bamboo bridge that crossed the Nam Khan, a smaller river fed by the mighty Mekong. During the rainy season the bridge is completely engulfed by water and is rebuilt every year. There is a small charge of 20p to cross. It doesn't look that bad at first but part way in I realised the bridge was a potential death trap. It wobbled and creaked and was held together with plastic cable ties, it was also definitely leaning to one side. There was a sort of hand rail but as the bridge twisted and undulated it was quite low and you either needed to be three feet tall or go along on your knees to get any benefit or security from it. I heaved a sigh of relief when I reached the other side.

I clambered up the bank and was just examining a small shrine when I was summoned over to a little shack by a tiny wrinkled bare chested man. From his hand movements he indicated that he lived in this wooden abode on the river bank. So we sat on a log together and communicated in that special way where I speak English and he speaks Lao. Neither of us has any idea what each other is saying but it was a lovely moment. At one point I am sure he mentioned Manchester United.

The temperature was starting to ramp up so I headed back cautiously across the bridge and made my way back to the hotel. I laid on the bed in the cool contemplating my time here. Lao is a beautiful country but the people are probably the least friendly I have met in any of my travels throughout the whole of South East Asia and I hadn't quite taken to them - the staff in the hotel were positively surly. But it had been a never to be repeated experience and I had really enjoyed my time here.

To finish off the evening I went to a nice restaurant that I had visited three times so far. As I made my way there the heavens opened with vivid lightening and thunder and I ended up soaked to the skin. Tonight the service was awful, I got given the wrong dinner and I had to ask three times for my beer. The American from the waterfall trip was in there too, shouting at the waiters and causing general chaos.

I think it was about time to leave, I was off to VIETNAM in the morning.

6 VIETNAM

Day 29

I woke up at 6am with a bit of a start - I then proceeded to have three bouts of rampant diarrhoea. This was the last thing I needed today as I had two flights to get through (it turned out to be the most stressful day of the whole trip). I shovelled some Imodium inside me and fought a savage battle with my luggage trying to get it down the stairs to reception. I am sure I woke all the guests with the amount of noise I made as I banged my case down the wooden steps. The surly reception staff didn't offer to help and just sat watching me. Lazy gits. I had purchased another shoulder bag at the market so I was now carrying three pieces of hand luggage along with my enormous suitcase.

My driver at least helped me with my luggage and we left Luang Prabang behind and drove to the tiny airport. At check in I was given the alarming news that I could not be checked in all the way through to Danang. I would have to clear immigration, collect my luggage at Hanoi and catch a bus to the Domestic terminal to check in all over again for the flight to Danang. I was not prepared for this and my insides turn to liquid again and I needed to head for the nearest toilet. The only upside of this saga was that I did not get charged for overweight baggage which at this point of the trip I had fully expected to being shelling out for, my luggage weighed in at 28 Kilos.

I exited the toilet and headed directly for the departure gate, there was no lounge, no shops and just a small cafe. At the gate is the smallest plane I had ever seen, complete with old fashioned propellers. Oh My God, I retreated back to the toilet again and I swallowed some more Imodium. By now I had worked myself up into such a state I was convinced I was about to die on the flight.

To get on the plane you entered through a back door, it was with a heavy heart that I mounted those steps. The plane was full of mosquitos, buzzing around everywhere, there were hundreds of them. I pulled my trusty scarf out of my bag and wrapped it around my bare shoulders for some protection. There was a German girl next to me and she was terrified too. She said that we would feel the turbulence more as we were on such small plane. I hadn't even thought of that particular horror amongst my own fears and my insides turn to liquid again. Eyes firmly shut, bum cheeks squeezed tight, hands gripping the arm rest, and praying to any God that could hear me - we steeply took off up over the mountains.

As was usual the flight passed perfectly okay and only took 1 hour, just flying at 20,000 feet. I was sat next to the propellors and kept a close eye on them to make sure they kept spinning. We were served a very strange mid morning snack which consisted of a stale roll containing tuna and lemon curd mixed together. A least that was what it tasted like.

We landed in Hanoi and that's when the fun really began. There were only six desks open in Immigration and the queues were enormous. Resigned to a long wait I got in line. Shuffling along at a snails pace I reached the desk exactly one hour and ten minutes after we had landed. You can't complain or make any sort of fuss - they will shoot you. At the desk I whipped out my special £156.00 visa but the official was not impressed and demanded to know if I was there to work. I thought that was the whole point of having a tourist visa? Welcome to Vietnam: passport stamped, I entered my second Communist Country of the trip.

I collected my extremely heavy luggage and made my way to the bus stop via customs. At some Vietnamese airports they have a very strange system of x-raying your luggage as you leave the airport. I just think they are being nosey and want to see your smalls. I heaved my bags up onto the conveyor belt and collected them at the other end.

When I arrived at the bus stop for Terminal 1 there must have been at least 50 people waiting in the queue ahead of me. When the bus pulled up there was a foot high gap between the pavement and the first step of the bus. I must have been looking a bit bewildered as to how I was going to get on with my suitcase and all my bags, when a young man swooped down on me, grabbed my case and hoisted it up the steps. I was now standing on the top step right next to the driver, sandwiched between the gearstick and this helpful chap. As with all airport bus drivers he drove like Sterling Moss and it took considerable strength on my part to hang onto my bags, stay upright and not end up sprawled across the drivers lap. We pulled up and I practically fell out of the bus as everyone was now pushing me from behind to get off in a hurry. Fortunately the young man helped me off again with my bags.

I had arrived although in a slightly dishevelled and undignified manner at the Domestic terminal.

I scanned the departures board and could see that my flight to Danang was not on there yet: it looked like they only show on there two hours before. My flight was at 14.30, after all the faffing around it was now 11.45, so I sat surrounded by my luggage waiting for the flight to come up on the board which I estimated would be around 12.30. I was so agitated by now that I could not stomach the thought of any food, I was so close to the finish line but Hanoi airport still hadn't quite finished with me.

By 13.00 my flight was still not showing on the departures board and I was starting to panic, so I decided to go in search of some customer service advice. I found the airline desk and spoke to a charmless unhelpful woman behind the desk, the conversation went as follows:

Did I not know that the flight time had been changed? - No I bloody well didn't.

Well it has, you should have received an email from us - Well I didn't.

Why haven't you received our message that we sent you - I don't know, did you actually send me one?

Of course we did, we told everyone on the flight - Not me you didn't.

Your flight is now rescheduled for 15:15 you stupid English woman - Thanks a lot for your help and consideration.

I go back to my seat to find it had now been taken over by a very noisy family and there was nowhere else to sit down, so I had to stand and wait. Fortunately a few minutes later my flight showed up on the board and I was able to check in and get rid of the heavy suitcase. I headed off for the departure lounge where I got chatting to some Americans who were on my flight: they had all received emails to tell them of the flight time change. Huh lucky them.

There was then a tannoy announcement that the flight was now delayed until 16.00 - I had now been at Hanoi airport for 6 hours and badly wanted to leave. I had been there so long I was starting to think about buying a house. Three other flights to Danang had already left, I so wished I could have been on one of them.

Eventually we were called to the gate and the passengers were loaded. It was an enormous shiny new plane and there were only around 50 people on it. I moved seats to sit by the emergency doors, where there was a charming man sitting on the aisle. He was another American and looked like a young

Howard Keel (from the TV programme Dallas). I think he would do very nicely for my friend Tracey. He had the most perfect teeth, silver fox hair and twinkly blue eyes and was very fit. He had just flown in from India where he had been trying to set up a charity now that he had retired. I asked him what his job used to be: an airline pilot. The flight was a little bit bouncy and he was not impressed with the chap flying our plane. I can't ask about his reasons whilst we are up in the air, he might frighten me to death, and I changed the subject very quickly.

We came in to land over the paddy fields and I peeked out of the window, I felt like I was coming home. The city of Danang has expanded hugely since last year and there were building sites everywhere. The American gentleman who I learn is called Ray had lovely manners and he gallantly offered to carry my hand luggage for me through to the luggage carousel where I was once again reunited with my suitcase. We swapped numbers and arranged to meet up for a drink in Hoi An whilst he was there. I felt a bit of matchmaking going on here as I think he and Tracey will get on like a house on fire.

As I attempt to leave the terminal I was stopped by a very officious young lady who demanded to see my boarding pass. She verified it against the tag on my case to check I had the correct luggage. Satisfied she lets me go and I exit the building. Hurrah at last I am out, no more aeroplanes for 9 weeks! As I was nearly 2 hours late I was worried that my driver may have given up and gone home but he was waiting outside with a sign that reads Ms Janic Coulso. I am sure that's me, so I get in the car and we head for Hoi An.

I was astounded by the amount of building work going on all the way along the coast as we followed the beach road. Plot after plot of new hotels and luxury apartments, it was all very different from six years ago when I first came here, it was all deserted beach and palm trees back then. There was a lot more traffic and there seemed to be more cars around than before. I noticed an enormous VinPearl resort that was still a building site last year, now it was completely finished. It was now an enormous resort with shops and restaurants. It sits glistening in the sun amidst it's manicured gardens and is apparently full of Asian visitors.

45 minutes later, I am deposited at my hotel. It was on the Cua Dai Road with the river opposite. A tiny little girl with shiny black hair, big framed glasses (she looked a bit like Thelma from 'Scooby Doo') wearing red Vietnamese traditional dress greets me with a welcome drink and offers me a seat whilst she checked me in. Her name was Anna and it was love at first sight. (I have never wanted children of my own but I ended up completely falling for her and we became very close. Even now we speak every week)

She cannot quite get her tongue around my name so she ends up calling me Jen for the whole time I am there.

She showed me to my room which was fantastic. I had only paid for a bog standard room but I later found out that I had been given the best room in the hotel. They rarely have guests staying more than a few days (they tend to have large groups on organised tours), I was staying there for 9 weeks so they had wanted to make me very comfortable. My bedroom was in the new wing, on the top floor with a stunning view of the paddy fields out the back. The bed was enormous, I could not touch either side when I lay across it. There was a balcony with soundproofed doors, which was a good thing as there was a lively back packers hostel next door. There was a huge flat screen TV (which I used a lot) The bathroom fittings looked new and I had a bath, separate shower cubicle and two sinks. It was spotlessly clean and so was the bed linen which I noted was also ironed. All in all I was thrilled to bits with it.

My luggage was brought up by one of the bellboys who also act as concierge and security guards. He introduced himself as Toby Hot Boy - he looked about 25 but was actually 42. He was tiny but must be very strong as he had lugged my case up 4 flights of steps (there was no lift) and he had not broken a sweat. He kindly helped me to sort out the safe. I had tried to do it without my glasses on and had now jammed it shut and could not get it open again. He goes off to fetch the master key so we can reset it. For some reason the safe is screwed to the wardrobe floor in the furthest corner and we had to lay flat on our bellies to get to it.
For the first time in four weeks I completely empty all of my luggage and put everything away. When I was growing up I never had my own bedroom, I had to share with my sister, and as I have been married to someone practically all of my adult life I have always had to share a room. This was to be my bedroom for 9 weeks and I arranged it exactly how I wanted it. It felt great knowing I did not need to live out of a suitcase anymore.

Once organised I went out in hunt of some dinner as I was starving, not having eaten all day. Anna was on the front desk and introduced me to Sunny who was her colleague on that shift, another pretty girl who I loved to bits. She was as tall as me, thin as a rake and never stopped smiling, her name certainly suited her. I asked if I could have a chair and table for my balcony as there was nothing to sit on out there and they promised they would arrange it for me.

Financially I appeared to have hardly spent any money so far. All the Thai and Lao cash had gone but I still had around $400 left, along with £500 in cash that I hadn't touched. (Tracey and Peter were bringing me some more cash out with them) so I decided to use up all the dollars first before I started on the Sterling. I changed $50 up at reception, I would change the rest in town as I would get a better rate there.

The girls recommended a good place up the road to eat. By now it was dark but I wandered off outside trying to avoid being hit by the kamikaze motorbikes - there are no pavements here. I clambered over bits of broken palm tree and piles of rubble all in the dark with an odd light flickering here and there. The restaurant was a very rustic type of place, the lighting was very bad, I could hardly read the menu. They had a lovely little dog with three legs who had been hit by a motorbike who was very friendly and liked to sit on the diners laps. The owners let their young children do some of the serving, they are obviously training them up for the future. It had to be done and I ordered seafood spring rolls with seafood rice. The food was good and I encountered my first La Rue beer of the trip. I never drink beer at home but I love this stuff and it only costs 50p per bottle. Fed and watered, I now felt that I was officially in Vietnam.

I felt very proud of myself at that moment, I had made it through four countries, four cities and endured 8 different flights on my own, all without mishap. A lot of people had frowned when I told them I was going to do this trip, they thought it wasn't a good idea to attempt it on my own. My mother positively hyperventilated when she realised what I was going to do. Some people had actually said' What do you want to go there for'? 'What are you going to do all day on your own?'

But some had also said I was an inspiration to them (mainly women of a certain age), they would never undertake such an adventure travelling solo and thought I was being very brave. Well, I had done it, I had survived so far and had loved every minute of the journey, now I could finally switch off my worry meter and relax. I staggered back to the hotel in the pitch dark, did not encounter any rats (there a millions here), did not get run over by a motor bike and fell straight into my fantastic bed.

It had been a really long and trying day but I had made it. - I WAS IN VIETNAM.

Day 30

I ended up sleeping for 11 hours, which was a small miracle, and woke up to beautiful sunshine streaming though a crack in the curtains. When I pulled the drapes back, two wooden chairs and a table had appeared on the balcony, the girls came through for me whilst I was at dinner last night. The view of the paddle fields had changed this morning with the sunlight on it and it was even more gorgeous.

I located the breakfast room and ate an enormous meal, consisting of omelette, delicious french bread & real butter, Vietnamese pancakes, fruit and yoghurt which I hoped was going to get me through until evening dinner. There was also an Asian assortment of noodle and rice dishes but I don't really fancy them this early in the day, just the smell put me off at this early hour.

The restaurant staff were delightful but apart from Enly, the manager, they spoke very little English but still bent over backwards to assist, nothing was too much trouble. You just needed to point at your omelette ingredients, which they cooked and delivered to your table. This was only a 3 star hotel but I could already see that the service is better than some of the 5 stars I had stayed in previously in this town. Particularly the expensive one we stayed in last year up on the beach, which shall remain nameless, where the staff positively ignored us most of the time.

There was a helpful and friendly young chap on reception this morning called Eric. He had a very strange haircut, it looked like his mum had put a pudding bowl on his head and cut around it with blunt scissors. Dodgy haircut aside he was soon added to my list of wonderful staff.

Examining myself in the full length mirror, I could see that I had lost quite a lot of weight, the Eric Morecambe shorts were positively hanging off of me and looked even more ridiculous than before. It wasn't that I hadn't been eating, I just hadn't consumed any processed food except for the jelly teddy bears. Pretty much everything I had eaten had been cooked fresh from the start, even the pizzas. I had also been drinking gallons of water, so my skin looked clearer and with a bit of a tan I was looking extremely healthy. Even my nails which are always chipped and broken looked half decent. My hair was looking a bit long and I remembered that I must try and look up the hairdresser when I went in to town.

I decided to get a taxi to An Bang beach which is about 5km from the hotel. The beach at Cua Dai has been decimated over the years by the Winter Typhoons and last year it was all a bit of a mess up there. I had never been to An Bang, Peter could never be bothered to go that far, so now was my opportunity - I could do exactly what I liked.

An Bang is where all the young back packers and cool people hang out. The beach was lovely and clean with golden sand but it was very crowded. You were pounced on the minute you set foot on the sand by the sales women trying to get you to use their sun beds. I have noticed over the years that the women seem to run all of the businesses here. It turned out that the bed rental here was rather expensive (by Viet prices) as I had to shell out £3.50 for a bed and umbrella. That's a lot of money over a two month period.

Ensconced on my little bit of the beach I settled back to catch some rays. It was a lovely temperature and there was a good breeze - perfect.

The entertainment was provided by the myriads of Chinese and Korean tourists who descended onto the beach just to have their photos taken. They do not sunbathe, go in the sea or spend any money in the bars or restaurants. They just pose in different positions and take zillions of pictures and videos of each other prancing around. They also have absolutely no concept of personal space and were practically sitting on my sun bed with me whilst someone videoed them. I hope that video never ends up on Youtube - 'Chinese tourist on beach with angry Englishwoman in the background'.

I stayed there all day until the heat started to go out of the sun and the sky took on a totally different quality of colour. It is usually completely dark here by 6.30pm so I left before the mosquitos came out for their evening dinner. It was just my luck, I got in a taxi with a driver who didn't have a clue where my hotel was. He could not speak any English so I had to type it into his satnav which then took us on a 10 km roundabout route back which I then had to pay for. Nothing unusual there then, satnavs in Vietnam work the same as at home.

I had a lovely long bath and went out for some dinner. Jane rang me to say she would be arriving on Monday at 7pm, it would be good to have some company. Peter rang me to say he had found the mouse run under our kitchen cupboards and had been devising a cunning plan to stop them getting in. Hallelujah!!

I slept in fits and starts. I had not quite got the aircon at the correct temperature yet and I had to keep getting up during the night to turn it up or down, I completely forgot that it had a remote control! Fortunately I could roll back and forth into the cold spots in the big bed every time I had a hot flush. I also forgot to turn the sound off on my phone, so it kept buzzing all night with messages from friends who had forgotten that I was 7 hours ahead of the UK and would be in bed.

Day 31

I went for breakfast around 9.30 where I appeared to be the only resident left in the whole hotel. All the other guests had been up and were checked out onto their tours hours ago. There were two more adorable girls on reception today called Helen and Misa. I could tell that Helen was a bit of a sexy girl and seemed very popular with all of the male staff, Misa was just dead cute. I was also introduced to Greenie who was the assistant guest manager and was a complete delight. We hit it off instantly and she was another one I fell in love with. She speaks very good English so we could have a proper conversation (I still speak to her every week as well).

I decided to walk up to Cua Dai beach today as I could not face the crowds at An Bang again. It was about a mile away and I set off with my rucksack on my back. I was wearing my baggy Eric Morecambe shorts and my very inelegant walking sandals with a Viet Cong jungle hat pulled firmly down over my hair. It is really important to wear a hat here if you are walking around in the heat. I know I looked a complete state but who cares? At home I usually wear full makeup and vertiginous heels but when I am on holiday all of that goes straight out of the window.

The beach at Cua Dai was a still complete mess and covered in huge sandbags that looked like big slimey slugs. You could not walk properly along the seashore, you had to hop from one sand bag to the next. The sea has eaten away at the land in parts and some of the restaurants were looking very precarious, as if they were going to collapse in to the sea at any moment. In a few years time they will be entirely washed away unless something drastic is done. I could see a crane and bulldozer further up the beach where they were putting in some sea defences made up of huge rocks and boulders, so at least they are trying to do something about it. There was a tiny bit of beach left with a few beds and umbrella's and I plonked myself down on one of them. A very small man appeared to collect payment, this was much cheaper here and cost about £1.75. If you faced towards the sea you could pretend that the mess behind you was not there. It was obviously less crowded here and there were a lot of locals swimming in the sea and having picnics underneath the palm trees with their families. I know it was ugly but I preferred it to An Bang, it had a more village feel about it. I stayed until I started to cook in the hot sun and then walked back to my hotel, feeling very sticky, sweaty and covered in sand.

My toenails still looked really weird, As they were painted dark red they look odd and the missing nail was very noticeable, so I decided it was time to get a new set done in a salon on the Cua Dai Road. The girl did a really good job and even managed to disguise my missing toenail by painting the bare skin and sealing it with her UV machine. They were now a lovely pale pink colour and looked great. It only cost me £7 and I promised to return for further treatments.

I had a quick shower and got on the 5 pm free shuttle bus to town. Ethan was the driver and he was another person added to my fabulous staff list. He made me sit up front with him, right by the aircon vents, and squashed everyone else in the back. They were all French and we could not understand a word they were saying anyway. I was just going in to town to get my bearings so I would remember my way around when Jane arrived and also to change some money.

Oh Dear, it was early Sunday evening and the place was heaving with Chinese/Japanese/Korean and Vietnamese tour groups. They ambled around in enormous groups and it was difficult to avoid being whacked in the face by their selfie sticks which they waved around with no thought for anyone else. I remembered this from last year and made a mental note not to go into town again until after 7pm when most of the big groups leave town. The Old Town bans traffic and is a walking zone only but it doesn't stop cyclists or cyclos. People who have not been on bicycles for years were causing chaos in the back streets and alleyways. The cyclos carry the tourists around and you have to step out of the way sharpish before they take the skin of the back of your legs with their wheels.

I think it would be much better if they banned all traffic from the centre. On my first visit here there were much fewer visitors, but with each passing year there has been more and more. I read some statistics that in 2017 there were 3.2 million visitors to Hoi An which was an increase on the previous year of 21.6%. We are now in 2019 and the figures must have doubled yet again, it certainly felt like it, the crowds were enormous especially around the bridges. Just outside the town are huge coach parks which are full every evening, they are from the monolithic hotel complexes along the beach and Danang sea front.

The local government needs to be very careful here, the Old Town is small and quaint and can only take so many visitors at a time, you just need to look at what is happening to Venice with the cruise ship business.

Mind you I still love it here, it is my favourite place on earth.

I found a money changer but then realised I haven't actually brought any money with me. My marshmallow brain had obviously melted in the heat and was now just a pile of goo. I had a few quid left in my purse and managed to just afford a pizza for tea (what else?). I sussed out where the bus stop was in relation to the rest of the town and got the early bus back to the hotel where I laid in bed watching Avengers: Age of Ultron. Not normally my sort of film but I enjoyed it anyway.

I emailed Derek and Ivan to let them know what I had been doing. I updated my Blog and rang my friend Elaine. She was in the park with her grandchildren who were running her ragged and I promised to call back later in the week.

Day 32

I slept much better and got up slightly earlier than yesterday. The French group were noisily having breakfast together before being whisked away on their coach tour. Enly told me that there was another huge French group arriving later that evening and the staff were very busy. I checked with reception that Jane's friend had a room for tonight, I really did not want to share with him as well. Anna tells me that two rooms were now available and they will get a room each so Jane doesn't have to bunk in with me. Phew that was a relief.

I walked up to the beach again sporting another strange outfit, it was very hot and windy today which is always a bit dangerous for sunbathing. The boys sorted out my bed for me and I promptly fell asleep in the sun resulting in some very strange red lines later on.

Around 3pm I took a 2 mile walk along the coast road to find an old friend of mine. Linh runs a beauty salon across the road from the Sunrise hotel and I met her a few years ago. She looks about 16 but is actually 36 years old and has two teenage children. She was thrilled to see me and we had a long chat. She speaks very good English and we understand each other very well. She tells me all about her family, her father died last year and she has set up a shrine in the salon in his honour which I have to say is a bit distracting with it's flashing disco lights and wafts of strong incense. She moans about her teenage daughter, seems they are the same the world over. She then moans about her husband, definitely the same the world over! Business hasn't been very good lately and she is thinking of relocating the salon to the front of her house to save on rent. She lowers her voice when talking about the Asian tourists (as if they can hear her) she can't stand the Chinese, they are very rude to her.

It has been lovely to catch up and I book a massage for Jane and I later in the week. Linh then insists on giving me a lift back to the hotel on her moped.
So with every bone in my body telling me not to, I climb aboard her tiny moped without a crash helmet and she drives me back to the hotel. When we arrived the reception staff found this all hysterically funny and even Toby Hot Boy came over for a look. 'Have you made a new friend Jen?' they all shout ; 'No guys, just an old friend'. I suppose it was comedic. Linh is so tiny and was covered from head to toe, wearing a full crash helmet, gloves and Ninja face mask with this huge Westerner on the back wearing baggy shorts and flip flops. Yes, I probably looked ridiculous.

There was a small bar next door that takes in laundry (they also sell beer for 40p per bottle). They always had numerous articles of clothing hanging on the washing line below my balcony. I spied a proper washing machine in the middle of their lounge so I think it will be OK, my clothes were not going to be washed in the river or battered on a rock. I gave them a huge bag of dirty washing which cost me £3 to be laundered and would be ready tomorrow evening.

I received a short message from Jane saying they had been delayed and would not be there until 8pm. I walked off in a different direction tonight and ended up having dinner in a pretty little restaurant which had very friendly staff and tasty food. There was a nice ambience to the place and it was very pretty. They also had atomisers attached to the trees sending out wafts of mosquitos repellant, just my sort of place. A group of very well behaved European male backpackers were at the table next to me and I photobombed their selfies which they found very funny. I expect they did, they will tell their friends about the strange old woman in their pictures. Jane rang me mid-meal, they were still at Ho Chi Minh airport, their plane had been delayed yet again.

On the way back to the hotel I spotted a large supermarket and went in. I did not actually want to buy anything, just have a look for any future purchases I might need. A very persuasive sales lady won't let me leave without buying something and ends up selling me a bottle of Dalat Red wine which set me back £3.

Back at the hotel I take a photo of my strange sun burn lines and sent it to Peter. He replied with a very short message: 'nice tits!'
I ended up laying on the bed with a glass of wine watching Deadpool which I thoroughly enjoyed. The wine was a bit rough around the edges to say the least but it was an improvement from a few years ago. Back then it was undrinkable and you could have run a jet engine with it, I later heard NASA were interested in using it for their rockets! I was on a tour at the time with some hardened drinkers and even they couldn't manage to drink it. I stayed awake until 10.30 but Jane still hadn't arrived so I turned in for the night.

Day 33

I awake early to someone banging loudly on my door, I staggered out of bed and wrenched it open with my eyes still shut. Jane bounded in to the room full of the joys of Spring questioning why I was not up yet. Err I am on holiday and don't normally get up until after 9am.
We ended up having breakfast very early, far too early for me. She was full of it and was chatting away ten to the dozen - give it a rest love, I am not

even properly awake yet. It turns out they eventually arrived at 11pm last night after a 4 hour delay at Ho Chi Minh airport. She's had a bit of a nightmare along the way with her companion. He appears to have a problem paying for food, so she has had to eat out every night on her own which wasn't quite the plan when they decided to travel together. It was her first time in Asia and she had wanted company in the big cities. He also abandoned her, allegedly, to go off on a sexual encounter in Ho Chi Minh City. He sounded like a right weirdo to me. He put in an dishevelled appearance at breakfast, refused to sit with us and doesn't look me in the eye when he speaks. Yes, he was definitely odd.

We decided between us to get a taxi to An Bang beach, Jane wants to sunbathe as she hadn't had a chance so far on this trip. We were instantly pounced upon and ended up sitting on the worst two beds on the whole beach in that they were situated next to the picturesque fisherman's coracles. All day long we had people literally standing between us to have their photos taken, it was really irritating and very rude. Jane and I were mid conversation when one of them actually perched on the end of my bed, mind you she did not stay there for long as I edged her off with my toe! Jane told me all about her trip so far through Northern Vietnam and Cambodia. I went to Cambodia the first time I came here so I can picture it all in my mind. We ended up chatting all day and totally forgot about the hot sun so that when we get back to the hotel I was a bit red in parts and she looked like a boiled lobster.

We got the shuttle bus into the Old Town, it was Tuesday evening and much calmer tonight. I gave her the city full tour. The ancient town of Hoi An used to be a flourishing port 200 years ago. It still has the original family chapels and Chinese merchant houses which are mostly painted yellow with back tiled roofs. Colourful lanterns light the streets, all the tiny boats are covered in fairy lights and the river is full of floating candles. There are brightly lit shops selling all sorts of goodies, over 400 tailors and there are restaurants to suit all budgets and tastes. It is very pretty and atmospheric. I have never been anywhere else like it and fortunately Jane could see why I like it so much.

I took her to one of my favourite restaurants. We sat out on the rickety balcony overlooking the river drinking banana daiquiris. Afterwards I took her along to the Japanese Bridge. This is not a late night town and the shop keepers were all packed up by 9.30pm even though this is peak season, only a handful of bars and restaurants stay open and they are all closed by midnight. This is not an ideal destination for anyone looking for a lively nightlife. It is a different town once the lights go off and it was very dark and eerie on the way to the taxi rank.

Back at the hotel we finished off the bottle of Dalat red in my room which somehow Jane managed to spill all over my white bed linen, I then spent the rest of the evening trying to wash it out with soap and a flannel.

Day 34

Next morning we go back into town on the bus, Jane's friend was still completely absent - she said he was laying on his bed watching football on the TV wearing only his very short hotel dressing gown!
 I would always stress to visitors that they must see the old town in the daylight as well as the dark as it looks very different . We got persuaded onto a rickety wooden boat by one of the constant hawkers which took us up the Thu Bon river. There were life jackets on the backs of our seats, not sure if that was worrying or comforting. There is an island opposite the Anantara hotel where there is a 'Universal' type theme park being built along with a huge hotel complex. It is a bit of an eyesore, the town really doesn't need it, it will just mean even more tourists. It is all for the Asian visitors: they do not appear to be very interested in the actual history of the town and prefer to watch a show about it. It's a bit like Animal Kingdom in Florida, some people think they do not need to go to Africa if they have been on the safari ride there. I don't know of anywhere on the planet that has African lions and Indian tigers living together.

Jane wanted to do some shopping, so I honed up on my haggling skills. Having been here before I had a pretty good idea of what most things should cost. The shopkeepers really tried it on, some of them were asking 500% more than we actually ended up paying. I understand they need to make money and the rent here is very high, it is a prime tourist spot after all, but even so some of them would sell their own grandma to make a few quid. I purchased some more insect repellant, I was on my sixth bottle and had not been bitten for ten days so it must be working. I also purchased a 'I love Hoi An' mug. I was fed up with the piddly little cups and saucers at breakfast and I wanted a proper builders cup of tea.
We ended up sitting in a traditional building drinking Vietnamese cold coffee, it is not to everyone's taste but I love it. When we got back to the hotel we sat out by the pool and had a swim. Jane went off to find her funny little friend and invited him out to dinner with us but he firmly declined : something about three's a crowd. Dickhead!

We started the evening with Happy Hour next door where I retrieved my laundry, it was a bit creased but definitely smelt clean. The beer worked out at 20p per bottle for the next two hours. It is like lemonade and you have to drink pints of it for it to have any sort of alcoholic effect. By then you need to go to the toilet and I was back and forth to the hotel loo - A lot.

We ate at a local restaurant and Jane hit the vodka. She was still shocked at how early everything winds up here and we are back at the hotel by 9.30. In reception we had had a bit of fun with the girls and took a load of selfies with them. They all had to rush to their handbags to check their hair and makeup and put on their lipstick: Jane and I both looked like we had been hauled through a haystack backwards. The Vietnamese do this very strange thing with their hands and fingers when they have their photos taken. I tried to copy it but it just ends up looking like the 'V' sign.

I Face timed the girls at work, they were still in the office, my friend Tracey cannot contain her excitement she will be here in two days time.

Day 35

When I go in for breakfast the next morning there was great hilarity amongst the staff over my gaily painted mug, for some reason they all want to know exactly how much I paid for it. This I found is a recurring theme here, they always want to know what we have paid for anything. I had brought my own tea bags as well, they only use one teabag to a huge pot and it was like drinking dishwater.

This morning Jane has somehow talked me in to going out on a bicycle. I was not keen but it's a way to see the countryside. There are a series of cycle paths out the back of the hotel so we were going to stick to them and not venture onto the main road where I imagine we would be instantly mowed down and killed. Toby Hot Boy sorted us out two knackered bikes and put some air in the tyres as an added bonus. They were very upright cycles with baskets strapped on the front, I felt like Miss Gulch from the Wizard of Oz. They were also death traps in that the brakes did not work properly, I had to put my feet down to stop mine. It had been a long time since I was last on a bike and I was all over the place trying to balance. Jane was having trouble with her handlebars, they seemed a bit loose.

In the course of time we got going and the scenery was amazing. We discovered lots of little Homestays, hotels and cafes that you just would not see from the main road and would never know were there. Huge water buffalo with massive curled horns and cows wandered around freely and we did a good obstacle course through the manure, squashed rats and snakes. I really enjoyed it and we planned to go out again the following morning. The downside of riding a bike was that my bum cheeks were very saddle sore that evening!

We walked up to Cua Dai beach and sunbathed for the rest of the day. Jane had to keep her stomach covered as it was still very sore from the sun burn two days ago. I actually ventured into the sea. It is really rough along this coastline and the current is very strong -you can get knocked over when you are only in knee deep. I am not a strong swimmer and it unnerved me so I got out.

There were three young bucks messing around on the beach, I would guess they were around 30 years old. They were dead fit with amazing bodies and one of them was covered in tattoos and wearing very small microscopic swimming trunks. Jane and I spent a thoroughly nice afternoon ogling them through our sunglasses.

At some point later in the afternoon we walked along to Linhs salon for our massages. We both had to strip down to our knickers, climb on the table and lay flat on our fronts, Linh had called in a colleague to do Jane. Linh instantly whipped my knickers down, I might as well have just gone naked. They both then proceeded to climb on top of us and start trying to flatten us out with their knees and elbows. They say that Westerners joints are all wonky and they have tension knots everywhere. This is a bit of an understatement and some of the massage was quite painful as Linhs strong little hands start to break up the lumps and bumps. Every time I moaned in agony she asked me if it was painful. When I replied in the affirmative she just carried on and I gritted my teeth. I don't know what was going on with Jane as it was very quiet from her side of the room, had she fainted with the pain? No she was so relaxed she had fallen asleep.

After the massage and the business side is concluded, Linh produced a plate of mango which we sat and ate together. She chatted away about her business. The hotel across the road used to be her main source of income, indeed a few years ago she was always booked up, now she says the hotel is full of Koreans and they don't really do massages or beauty treatments and her livelihood is suffering. Because Jane is with me today she doesn't offer a lift on her moped and greatly relieved we got a taxi back.

After a shower and change of clothes we got the bus into town and went in search of the hairdressers. Well that turned into a Anneka's sort of treasure hunt. We went around in circles looking for this place and even ended up in someones front yard. I actually had a map to follow but we could not even find the road. We asked several people who all pointed us in different directions. More by accident than design we stumbled across it - it was now closed for the next four days. I did manage to book a hair appointment through their website for the following week. There were some enormous scaly brown cockroaches sitting on the door sign bathing in the glow from the electric light, they don't bother me but Jane made a hasty exit.

Afterwards we went in search of dinner. Jane pointed out a place called Cuisine Dannan which I had never been to before so we decided to give it a try. The food was amazing and the staff were simply delightful, I will definitely come here again.

Day 36

The following morning we went for a really long bike ride. I was starting to get the hang of it again, they say you never forget how to ride a bike. Out the back of our residence is the Hoi An Chic resort which is small low slung Eco hotel surrounded by trees and bushes. I am no Eco warrior but I discovered it does have one overwhelming feature - around the side is a garage full of original Willys jeeps left over from the war. I absolutely adore these little vehicles and would dearly love to own one. The hotel uses them to transport their guests around, it would be worth staying here just to ride around in one all day. The drivers and staff get used to me hanging around over the next 9 weeks as I am constantly in their garage gazing longingly at their jeeps.

We walked up to the beach again and sat there all afternoon on a couple of beds which the boys scurried around organising for us. We had been sitting there for a while when a group of 6 well dressed middle aged Korean women appeared on the beach. They were horsing around and jumping up in the air whilst having millions of photos taken and were generally being very silly. They edged towards the shoreline for a paddle to have even more pictures taken. Oh Dear a huge wave hit them from behind and knocked them all off of their feet. They were flapping around in the surf like stranded whales, trying to fight with the strong current just to get upright. Their straw hats had gone all limp, their sunglasses had been swept away and they were dripping wet. Jane & I found this very amusing and laughed our heads off. Fortunately the Koreans saw the funny side too as they squelched off to their bus with their ruined soggy crocheted hats in hand.

Back at the hotel, I spoke to Tracey who was due to catch a 5pm flight to Hong Kong this afternoon, I can't wait to see her.
Jane and I headed into town early, we were going to the theatre to see the Bamboo Cultural Show. The name doesn't inspire but it was an interesting evening. The theatre was contained in a huge bamboo dome and the show consisted of a load of acrobats dressed in black throwing poles and wicker baskets around. It was very clever and fast moving, I had never seen anything quite like it. It was a shame that the theatre was only 25% full, they were all Europeans, not an Asian soul amongst them, probably the word 'Cultural' put them off. It also cost a whopping £24 per person, which may be another reason why it was so empty.
Jane made the decision that we were going to eat on the other side of the river tonight on An Hoi Island. I never eat there as for some reason it is considerably more expensive, sure enough we end up paying for a mediocre dinner with over priced beer which she then moans about. I did try and warn her!

Day 37

In the morning we headed in to town again as Jane wanted to finish her shopping as she was going home later that day. I like visiting the Old Town early in the morning, it is never crowded and the light takes on a entirely different quality. We mooched around the shops for a while, I took her to a very cheap clothing shop I know. You can get flowery shorts for £2, elephant trousers for £3 and a dress for £4 - 5. Jane bought some trousers and I ended up buying a pretty pink dress which they let me have for £4 - I did not bother to haggle, it was cheap enough already.

We spent the rest of the afternoon on the beach where we ended up having very strange club sandwiches and beer for lunch before Jane got ready in my room to leave for the airport with her funny little friend.
So far all he had done was run up to Cua Dai beach, eat 3 portions of breakfast daily and then lie on his bed watching football on TV all afternoon and evening. He had not even ventured into the Old Town - even if he is tight with money, there is a free bus, it doesn't cost anything. He has made no attempt to look around the town and declares in a loud voice in reception when he checks out that the whole place is a bit of a dump. I take extreme exception to this, I know Vietnam is not to everyone's taste but he has made no effort at all and is now slagging the whole place off. I can't bear to even look at him, but now that he is leaving he wants to have a conversation with me. I am having none of it and I barely grunt in his direction when he offers to sell me his leftover currency. I refuse, he can keep it as a souvenir, he has not put any other money into the Vietnamese economy.
Their car drives off, I wave goodbye and they disappear from my view. I have really enjoyed having Jane here for company, we have got on well, and I shed a little tear as she left but blimey she has bent my ear every night about my volunteering job. I had made it clear to everyone at home that I was having some time out, I have been a volunteer for 27 years and maybe it was time for a change. I had not come up with any answers yet but she hasn't let it drop and I am fed up with talking about it. I ring Lisa and let her know that I still have not made any decisions about anything to do with the Unit. She is mightily relieved as she is not enjoying running it in my absence and realises now that it is a lot of work for a voluntary role.

I pick up a call from Peter to tell me that a sick friend of ours, had been diagnosed with terminal cancer and they don't think he will be coming out of hospital. This is really sad news, I was just dancing with him at the last Christmas party and now it looks as if he is going to die three months later.

You never know what life is going to throw at you, these days you need to achieve your dreams early if possible. My old dad got Parkinson's disease at age 55 and my parents spent their early retirement years just trying to get through each day, let alone chasing their dreams. I remember vividly the last time I saw my father, the only part of his body that he could move were his eyes and they followed me around the room. He couldn't talk, smile or move. He died a horrible slow demise in a nursing home where he eventually choked to death all on his own aged 70.

Maureen and her husband have done loads during their marriage, and she has no regrets now that he is ill and frail and I think that was why she positively encouraged me to do this trip now whilst I can.

When you have a health scare it does make you think very hard about the future and the past. I was very ill when I first contracted Graves Disease. This is where your immune system turns inwards on itself and attacks your thyroid which then knocks everything else out of kilter. I could barely walk, my heart raced so hard and fast that I could actually hear it and I kept losing weight despite devouring every piece of food in sight. I lost nearly two and a half stone in six weeks and I know I looked awful and it was a very worrying time. After some initial blood tests at the local Doctors, Peter ended up paying for me to go private to see an endocrinologist, as there was a 13 week wait on the NHS. She took one look at me and diagnosed Graves disease: she said that if I had waited much longer for treatment it could have been fatal. She also said that 50% of women who get it only ever have one bad attack which is usually set off by a traumatic event. I asked her if the menopause could be responsible for this and she said undoubtably yes. My sister also has Graves but she is always ill, fortunately (so far) I have only had the one bad episode and that is one of the reasons why I was here in Asia now.

The hotel car picked me up at 6pm and we drove to the airport to pick Tracey up. I was prepared to be waiting for ages but she came through really quickly and I swooped her up into a big hug. For some reason all of my friends are a lot shorter than me; Julie, Elaine, Lisa and today I notice that Tracey looks really small as well. We talked incessantly on the journey back to the hotel. I wanted to know all the news and gossip from the office and we rabbited on and on. She related the story about a temp that they were going to employ who has turned out to be a complete psychopath and has been stalking the management on the internet. I privately think she should actually fit in quite well then. The way she tells the story is hilarious and I was in stitches, the driver viewed us warily in his mirror, were we going to wet ourselves all over his car seats?

We dumped all of her stuff in her room which was in the main building above reception. She handed me over an envelope with my £500, it was still warm, she had carried it in a money belt all the way from UK. She also handed me a bag of goodies that I had given her to bring out for me. Hurrah, I now had some more stylish clothes and was restocked up on toiletries. Even more important though: she had bought me an enormous bag of Haribo.

We went for a few beers next door so she could wind down and we could properly catch up. Tracey knows our sick friend well and says that everyone was in shock at work about it.

Like Jane, Tracey had never been to Asia before and was not scared of it, she just wanted to embrace the whole thing and put herself firmly in my hands. I had worked out some day trips with Greenie and we agreed to book them in the morning. I left Tracey to unpack and catch up on some sleep whilst I retired to my room where I watch 'Jurassic Park' on the TV for about the sixth time.

Day 38

Next day I took her up to Cua Dai beach and we stayed there all day. Tracey was quite happy to sit under an umbrella, whilst I roasted myself in the sun. My tan was coming along nicely and I was past the point of going red, even so I still slapped on the Factor 30 all over. I know it is bad for me but having a tan makes you look half a stone lighter and much healthier - I am sure there are worse things I could be doing to my body. I tried to enter the sea again but the current was just too strong for my liking.

Later in the afternoon we walked along to Linhs for a massage. Tracey and I giggled like a pair of kids, especially when the masseur climbed on top of her and started walking up and down on her back, she wasn't expecting that! Linh soon put a stop to all the hilarity when she started digging her fingers into the soles of my feet, she takes her job very seriously. Afterwards a very large pineapple appeared which Linh then forced us to eat. This resulted in poor Tracey being up half the night with acid indigestion. I had also been bitten on my right hand which was swollen and painful so I was back on the antihistamine, I am pretty sure it happened in Linhs salon, in fact I am certain it did.

Day 39

The following day it was very overcast so we decided to go into town to do some shopping and Tracey could have a look around in the daylight. She was taken aback by the traffic around the back streets. Jane and myself had got accustomed to it but this was Tracey's first experience of Vietnams motorbike traffic and I guided her across the roads like a little old lady. You basically have to wait for a gap and then walk slowly straight into the road in front of all the bikes. Do not stop, hesitate or run and never, ever, step backwards. All the bikes then just go around you - Easy Peasy!

She loved the town and I dragged her all over in the muggy heat. Looking at all the lovely clothes for sale she decided that she would like to buy a dress. Well that was an interesting experience. Most of the shop keepers took one look at us and claimed they had nothing big enough. Sure enough unless you were a perfect size 6, nothing would fit our well covered frames. We eventually came across a shop with a business savvy owner that does stock proper European sizes. Unfortunately they also wanted to charge us an inflated amount of 1,000,000 Dong for it (£35).
I was so cross as I know this was an outrageous price that I did not even bother to haggle, I grabbed a bewildered Tracey and we headed for the door. Before we had even reached the bottom step the shop keeper chased after us and suddenly offered us the dress for 250,000 dong (£8) which was a bit more like it. Without saying a word we got it for a much more realistic price. If they had said that price to begin with Tracey might have bought two dresses which would have been better business for them. We also bought some elephant trousers from my cheap little clothing shop, all the tourists wear them, even the blokes, they are so comfortable and only cost £3 a pair.
We ended up on the roof terrace of the Royal Hotel having drinks. This is the highest hotel in the old town and you can see the whole of Hoi An laid out in front of you right up to the beach. There is a fabulous roof top swimming pool where the sun beds are actually in the water. It is a spectacular hotel and I usually come here with Peter for Happy hour cocktails. Because it is a high end hotel it is usually full of Japanese visitors and sure enough they are everywhere, sunbathing fully clothed.

In the late afternoon we ventured out into the paddy fields on bicycles. Tracey had not been on a bike for years and was very wobbly, but she was game for anything. It was still cloudy but very humid and we were both dripping with sweat when we got back. After a shower we decided to go back in to town for dinner on the shuttle bus. We were the first passengers waiting when from inside the hotel came a rugby scrum of French tourists who literally pushed us out of the way and totally filled the bus up. Toby Hot Boy grabbed us and pulled us out of the way. Two minutes later Ethan turned up in another bus from the sister hotel and we had it all to ourselves.

I took Tracey to the Banana Leaf restaurant. This is probably my favourite place to eat in the whole town. We sat out on the balcony admiring the view across the river. Tracey didn't eat very much, I don't think she is a fan of anything too foreign.

We were just eating our meal when a woman from the table behind us rushed into the loo. She then proceeded to barf like a dog which echoed throughout the whole restaurant. Tracey went a bit green around the gills, she doesn't do other peoples sick. It didn't bother me, I just carried on eating. The womans husband suddenly realised that the strange barking noise was coming from his wife so went over to find her. The poor woman came out of the loo looking as white as a sheet having publicly puked her guts up and they quickly departed. Poor lady, she looked awful!

As we were leaving town we came across a Vietnamese couple who were having a set of wedding photos taken. Couples here have several sets of photos taken before the big day and the brides get to wear two or three different outfits. This groom looked very uncomfortable as he was wearing tight trousers with old fashioned blue braces and pushing a bicycle which the photographer obviously thought was a good idea. The bride looked ethereal in a lacy meringue of a dress.

We purchased another bottle of Dalat red tonight and sat out on my balcony listening to a noisy drunken party at the backpackers place next door. I looked this place up on the Internet and weirdly it costs twice as much to have a private room there than it does to stay in my lovely hotel.

Day 40

Next day we were booked on a mini bus trip to Bana Hills (or Brigadoon as we nicknamed it). There is an old French hill station up there but that is not where we were headed. Oh no, we were off to Sun World at Bana Hills. This is an entirely fictional invention of the Vietnamese who have built a complete French village at 1467 metres above sea level. There is a bridge up there which is held up by huge concrete hands and the view is supposed to be spectacular. We will have to get on a very steep cable car to get up there, this I am dreading as I do not like heights.

The mini bus arrived, it was full of backpackers who were on various stages of their gap year. Tracey and I climbed aboard and you could see them glaze over and lose interest instantly as these two old birds got on with them.

This morning it was still very overcast and I cannot imagine we would be able to see very much. The journey to Bana Hills took 1.5 hours. We drove through some beautiful lush scenery before we pulled up in an enormous coach park, they are obviously expecting a lot of future visitors. The entrance is very Disneyesque, we ascended several sets of escalators accompanied by jolly Music before we arrived at the cable car station.

Tracey & I climbed aboard one of the pods along with a couple of Korean women. I sat next to them so I could only see forwards or upwards, Tracey sat opposite and could see the whole vista below us.

Off we go, it was completely terrifying and very steep, I had to keep my eyes tightly shut. After a couple of minutes everything disappeared into the thick clouds and you could not see a thing anyway. One of the Korean ladies then proceeded to be silently sick into a paper bag which somehow didn't even smudge her spectacular scarlet lipstick. Tracey was now looking a bit green, someone else's puke two days in a row, it was as much as she could take.

At last we arrived at the Golden Hand Bridge and all piled out of the pod. I was actually very grateful that it was cloudy because you could not see a thing beneath us. It always makes me feel dizzy when there is a gap between me and the ground. The huge Chinese and Vietnamese tour groups were jostling to take selfies on the bridge and we fought our way through the middle of them. In the end we photobombed anyone who got in our way. We were behaving like two naughty school girls on a day trip.

We were led to Le Jardin D'Amour by our guide. It was a good job we had a guide as we would have got lost in the fog. I love gardens and I am sure these were very pretty but by now it was so foggy you could not see your hand in front of your face. It was also much cooler up here but still felt muggy and damp. Apparently there was an enormous seated Buddha in front of us but we could barely make out the concrete base. The clouds cleared for 2 seconds and we see his face and spot a few tulips but it all then disappeared again in to a swirl of white mist. We found all of this hugely comical and can't stop laughing, we had paid £40 each for this trip and cannot see a thing.

We then got on the second cable car to take us up to the fantasy village at the top. No kidding, there is a proper French village on top of the mountain complete with shops, hotels and restaurants and it was heaving with visitors. After an interesting buffet lunch where we fought hard with the other visitors for the spring rolls, we were given some free time to wander around on our own.

A huge group of brightly dressed European dancers appeared out in the main square. I was beginning to feel like I was having an out of body experience, it was like Disney on acid. The Asian tourists were lapping it up and joined in enthusiastically with the dancing to the loud if slightly distorted music blaring from the loud speakers. It was all completely weird and bizarre and I could have done with a large glass of something alcoholic to take the edge off.

There was even an entire railway station but with no trains. I was stopped by a young man who wanted me to take his photo with some friends on the station steps and he handed me over his iPhone. That was a big mistake mate. I took a few photos of them, turned it onto selfie mode and took numerous pics of Tracey and myself. Chortling with glee, we climbed the hill up to the temple and pagoda. Strangely we were now at the highest point but it was not quite so cloudy and at least you could see the buildings properly.

On the way down we bumped into the wedding couple we saw the other night in Hoi An, they were having yet another set of photos taken. He looked a bit happier this time wearing a full velvet tuxedo and she was wearing another fantastic feathery cream dress.

I was actually very glad when it was time to leave, it had been a surreal experience, not my type of thing at all. The whole place is just a rip off of Disney and Universal, even the cuddly toys for sale bear close resemblance to well known cartoon figures, and believe me Tracey knows her Disney characters.

The cable car down is one straight line and we climbed into a pod with all the backpackers. I ended up clutching onto the arm of the man sitting next to me every time there was a rumble from the cables above, fortunately his girlfriend didn't seem to mind (too much).Tracey and I made them all laugh and they realised we were not that bad for two old girls. I told them about my trip so far, they were impressed that I had done so much on my own. None of them were brave enough to tackle Burma and I earned some serious street cred.

I am not dead yet I tell them!!!

It was a mini bus full of jolly people on the way back, I think we were all glad to escape the craziness of the place. Everyone agreed that the day out had been a never to be repeated experience but we had had such a laugh. Immediately we arrived back at the hotel Tracey and I dived into the bar next door and had a cocktail or two to get over the weird adventure and to numb our senses.

I took Tracey for a pizza tonight, it was much more in her comfort zone. Whilst she devoured her margarita pizza, I tucked into fried squid cooked with lemongrass and wrapped in a banana leaf - It was absolutely delicious. We roamed around the streets looking in all the shops and met up in a bar with Ray, the American I met on the plane from Hanoi last week. I can instantly see Tracey and he are quite taken with each other - I just knew it. I made myself absent by getting into a lively conversation about Brexit with two hilarious gay Germans at the bar, where I proceeded to drink far too much beer.

At some point on the way to the taxi rank I needed to go for a wee. There is a large modern public toilet in the centre of town which costs 10000 dong (30p) to use. I paid my fee and entered the cubicle. Along one side of the toilet was a panel with lots of buttons, levers and varying instructions. Of course I did not have my glasses on so I could not read any of it. I finished my wee and pressed the first button. A jet of water goes straight up my jacksie, I then pressed another and a waft of warm air blow dries my nether regions. It was the most erotic experience I had had in six weeks and was well worth the fee! I thoroughly recommended it to two other ladies who were on our shuttle bus and they promised to give it a go.

Day 41

The next day was D day - I was having my hair cut. Leaving Tracey lounging by the pool I made my way nervously to the hairdressers. The stylist came out armed with a proper pair of hair dressing scissors and not chop sticks which was a good start. We had a bit of a chat and she summoned a young girl to wash my hair which cost me £3 extra. I was thinking that was a bit steep but the hair wash involved a full head massage and actually took 20 minutes to do, it was worth every penny and was very relaxing. I watched very carefully as the stylist cut my hair, she then blow dried it whilst making comments about me having a messy look?? When she had finished it actually looked ok, not quite as good at home but it was passable and felt much better. The whole thing cost me £10 which is £34 cheaper than my usual fee. When I got back to the hotel all the girls cooed over my haircut telling me I looked beautiful, (they are obviously back on the drugs this morning).

We ventured out on the bikes again in the late afternoon, I was starting to get good at this. Through the paddy fields and up to the duck farm today. I rang Peter and asked him to bring me a cycle helmet when he comes out, I will feel able to take my life in my hands and go out onto the main roads then.

I took Tracey to a local place down the road for dinner where she proceeded to pick every bit of greenery out of her dinner. She is a very fussy eater, I just eat everything that is put on the table unless it is meat when I have to then pretend I am a strict vegetarian.
We FaceTimed the girls in the office so they could speak to Tracey and I caught up with my sister. I asked after my mother (she doesn't understand technology at all and I have no way of contacting her which doesn't cost serious money), my sister hasn't seen her but knows she is following me on my blog.

The week was passing so quickly, Tracey goes home in two days so today we are off on another mini bus trip with another load of youngsters on their gap year, hopefully it will be better weather and we might be able to see something.

First stop was marble mountain which overlooks the city of Danang and the airfield. The caves here were of religious importance to the Cham people and were also used by the Vietcong during the war as they could watch what the Americans were up to from here. It is a nice place to visit but it was a hot and a very steep climb up the uneven steps which is probably why it is was not overcrowded with visitors. There is a very small lift but you can queue for ages and it has a habit of breaking down. The view was amazing and as it was a clear day you could see all the way along the coast from Danang to Hoi An.
There were lots of brightly coloured temples and pagodas dotted around, covered in orchids and tropical plants and it had a very calming atmosphere. We entered one of the caves that has a small temple which is dedicated to single people who wish to pray for a partner, Tracey entered inside and had a few words.
When we got to the bottom of the steps we wanted to have a look in the shops but we were whisked away by the guide and taken to a very posh marble showroom out on the coast road. There were some beautiful huge carved statues that had eye watering prices attached. We asked the price of a couple of small marble elephants, they wanted $40 and for a stone Buddha I was interested in they wanted $65. We left sharply without making any purchases.

We were taken to a private house in the middle of nowhere for lunch. It was a private house (probably the bus drivers) and there were two plastic tables set out in the scrubby courtyard. The food was horrible, I pushed it around my plate and just ate a bit of rice and the dessert of bananas, I noticed that most of the backpackers at least attempted to eat most of it.

After lunch we were separated out onto different buses heading in different directions, we were driven back to marble mountain to go into the Am Phu Cave which is entered at ground level. It was enormous and had some interesting religious images and statues, including a purple neon light up Buddha, obviously not an original icon! The cave itself is quite magnificent and has holes in the ceiling that lets in shafts of daylight which reflect on the stalactites and stalagmites. It was much busier in there than the caves at the top and there was a lot of pushing and shoving going on as you descended the steep steps.

Back on the bus we were off to the Son Tra Peninsula or Monkey Mountain as it is sometimes called. Its nickname comes from the hundreds of monkeys that roam all over the landscape. We spotted a few who were combing though a load of rubbish and plastic bottles left in the car park. I am not very keen on monkeys, when I was in Bali one jumped on my head and wrapped it's fingers around my hair so I couldn't shake it off. This was all a diversion, whilst I was screaming and carrying on, another monkey quickly reached over Peter's shoulder, rummaged though his shirt pocket and fled off with a wad of his cash. They are much cleverer than they look and I steered well clear whilst Tracey went over for a closer look.

We came across the Ling Ung pagoda which is set in a park full of immaculately crafted bonsai trees. The statue of the Goddess of Mercy is reputedly the largest lady Buddha figure in the whole of South East Asia at 67 meters high. It is only five years old and is in a very picturesque spot where you can see the whole of Danang laid out before us with all the blue fishing boats moored up in the harbour. The sun had come out and it was very hot as the bus party split yet again. Tracey and I ended up on a bus with just a young Spanish couple and we set off to go up the Hai Van Pass.

The Hai Van Pass is a spectacular twisty mountainous road that really got put on the map by Top Gear. Since that television programme thousands of tourists have ridden over it on rickety old motorbikes, myself included. I didn't actually drive it, Peter did on an old Russian Minsk and I sat on the back. The scenery is staggeringly beautiful and you look down over a pristine piece of beach which I am surprised no-one has built anything on yet as it would make a beautiful resort. I imagine the logistics of getting building materials down to the beach is probably why it is not yet developed.

At the top of the pass we got out of the bus and climbed up to the derelict observation base. Strangely enough there was another wedding couple up here having their photos taken on top of an old concrete look out post. The bride was having great difficulty climbing the ladder with her enormous dress blowing around in the breeze. She had a big entourage of people trying to hold it down and stop it getting caught by a big gust of wind which could sweep her off of the concrete block. I espy that she was wearing white flip flops underneath her petticoats, perhaps not the best footwear to climb a ladder in.

There were several stalls up here selling jewellery (mainly pearls) and ornaments like the ones in the posh marble shop. I got my stone Buddha here for £7, a set of dragons for £6 and Tracey bought some elephants for £5, they were exactly the same as the ones in the expensive shop.

As we made our way back to the bus the clouds swooped in and everything suddenly started to disappear in a white swirl of mist - It was time to go. We drove down the Pass just staying slightly ahead of the clouds, keeping the amazing scenery in sight. It was a spectacular vista to watch the clouds following the bus down the mountainside. It was such a vision that I got a bit carried away, accidentally managed to switch the camera setting onto Sports mode and ended up taking 175 pictures of the same view.

After a well earned shower and another change of clothes we headed into town to have dinner with another colleague from work (different office though) who was also currently travelling in Asia. Neither of us had ever met her before, we had only ever spoken on the phone. We met up with her and made for a nearby restaurant. It was apparent almost from the start that she could not wait to get away from us and join her much younger friends. I did not understand this - she had messaged me to meet up with her not the other way round. If she didn't want to meet up with us she could have pretended she had lost my number in a technical glitch on her phone, I know that is a favourite line when you want to get out of something. After a very quick and awkward dinner where I felt like I was conducting an interview trying to pull teeth to get a conversation going, she sprinted out of the restaurant so fast she beat Usain Bolts world record for 100 metres and left scorch marks on the floor in her wake.

Tracey and I met up with Ray again in a small intimate darkly lit bar. Actually every bar is dimly lit around here. I had chocolate cake and a beer, not quite sure what Tracey has as I did not see her again until breakfast, when she turned up with a big smile on her face !!

Day 43

It was really humid in the morning and I was struggling with the heat today. I could not get my temperature to regulate and nothing seemed to cool me down, not even the swimming pool where we stayed all morning. Tracey passed out on her sun bed and slept until noon.

After lunch we made for Linhs salon for another massage. I thought I was being clever and had opted for a foot scrub instead of a massage, unfortunately this turned out to be another extremely painful ordeal. I think Linh actually used a bit of Dremel on my feet as she removed several layers of skin, but I did end up with the smoothest feet and it lasted for the rest of the trip. Tracey had a decidedly dodgy moment when her masseur removed her own flip flops and offered them to her to wear. What with all the vomit in the last few days, now she had to contend with wearing other peoples warm footwear.

I emailed Peter with a huge list of presents I wanted him to bring out for the staff consisting mainly of boxes of chocolates and sweets that they will go mad for: they love chocolate here. He tells me that there is an offer on in Tesco and he will go shopping for me. I also asked him to bring me some more toiletries and a further selection of clothes. He switched his phone onto camera mode and goes through my wardrobe and drawers with me shouting out each item I want. A pair of shorts, two vest tops and a bra have gone in the bin this week as they have had the guts washed out of them.

For Tracey's last evening I take her to the Cuisine Dannan restaurant that I went to with Jane. The staff greeted me like a long lost member of their family and we had a delicious meal with a few drinks. It was really muggy again tonight and I just could not cool down, the alcohol was not helping either as I had hot flush after flush. The lovely staff brought me out an electric fan and I sat dead in front of it, relief at last! After dinner we ended in up in a little cafe I know, called for some reason Pineapple. We had huge lumps of chocolate cake and more beers before making our way back to the hotel.

Day 44

Tracey's last day dawned, she has really enjoyed herself and we have had a great time. It is always dodgy going away with someone else but it had been brilliant fun and we hadn't stopped laughing the whole time. She checked out at reception and Toby Hot Boy brought all her luggage up to my room.

We went into town so she could finish off her shopping. Considering the weather forecast was for rain, it had turned into a lovely day. She decided she wanted to buy her granddaughter a Vietnamese conical hat and we got one hand painted with pink flowers on it for about £1. We then decided to buy our boss Steve a 'Good morning Vietnam' T-shirt as a bit of a joke. We had a bit of a heated debate in the shop as to what size would fit him, of course we completely underestimate it and he can't even get it over his head when he tries it on!

Back at the hotel we had a few beers before Tracey's car arrived to take her to the airport. At this point I got a bit choked up and ended up crying when she left, I was now alone again until Peter arrives here in two weeks time. I had been perfectly OK being on my own but it had been nice to have someone to go out with at night. Eating on my own is the one thing I hate the most about travelling solo, everything else I can deal with. The reception staff all fussed around me, they had been wonderful and I hear there were big plans for a big night out when Peter arrives. I managed to pull myself together and went off in search of some dinner and a stiff drink.

I ended up in the Dingo Deli which is a bit of a walk towards town. They have a very strange system in here of asking you to write down everything you want to eat which you then give to the waitress, this is supposedly to avoid any confusion in translation. Somehow I am served with a plate of corn chips, bowl of salsa, tub of sour cream and a side plate of four slices of cheese, it was supposed to be a Caesar wrap. Hey ho, I woofed everything down and wandered back to the hotel along the busy main road in the dark.

I ended up having a particularly busy evening in my room. I did some smalls laundry and painted my nails. I spoke to Lisa about the voluntary unit, everything was going OK and everyone was helping out. I caught up with my nephew Joel who tells me everything he had been up to, some of it I am not really sure if I want to know. He is always very honest with me and doesn't hold back. I am fairly open minded and not easily shockable and he regales tales about his latest forays into the LGBT world, GULP! REALLY!! I then managed to get hold of my friend Elaine again, minus the grandchildren, who went off into an angry tirade about an event that had gone a bit wrong. Eventually she calmed down and asked me about my trip and we had a long chat.

Day 45

I had a really bad nights sleep, I just could not settle down and I ended up switching the TV on at 2am and watch Ironman. This didn't really help much, so I played Angry Birds on my IPad until I eventually dozed off around 5am.

I had a bit of the hump the next morning (missing my mates), and think I am hallucinating on the way to the beach. Sitting on a chair outside a hotel bar is a sour faced Vietnamese woman dressed as a leprechaun wearing an oversized green top hat. (I think I would be cross as well if I was made to dress like that in this heat) She looks bizarrely out of place until I realise it is an Irish bar, so obviously it must be St Patricks Day. Sure enough the bar is rammed full and everyone is drinking Guinness - it was 9.30am.

Up at the beach the boys see me coming along the beach and hurriedly get my usual bed ready for me. There was a really nice looking bloke on the bed next to me wearing bright luminous pink shorts. He was about 50, from Wales and did not stop talking, he turned out to be extremely boring. His wife was sitting in the shade and doesn't even look up from her book, maybe he bored her too? He told me that he has been changing his money at an actual bank and this morning they would not take his £20 notes. I told him to go to the money changers in town but he insists he gets a better rate in the bank but complains that it takes an hour every time he goes in there as he has to go through a rigmarole with his passport and fill out several forms each time. When he told me the rate he was getting, the difference was literally peanuts. If he changed £1000 at the bank he would only get around £10 more for all that hassle, I couldn't be bothered with it. He spent all day talking crap and drinking beer until he eventually nodded off, good some peace at last.

I was in such a dopey daze this morning with the lack of sleep that I totally forgot to put any sun cream on and my back had gone another funny shade of red.

I took another huge bag of laundry next door and asked if it could possibly be ironed as well. For £4.50 she agrees to do it - Bargain.

After dinner I spent the evening playing word games with Anna and Sunny to help them with their English. They had both been to University and are very bright, they speak a bit of French, English and German. They are so smart that do I wonder what they are doing working in a three star hotel, they should be out seeing the world and having grand adventures - I know, I am starting to sound like Donna from Mama Mia but without Pierce Brosnan hanging around (unfortunately). They both had boyfriends, Anna's relationship is very serious, Sunny currently has half a dozen suitors all fighting for her attention - Go Girl. Neither of them have ever been out of Vietnam and the chances of that ever happening are very slim. They cannot get their heads around the different time changes and cannot imagine flying the long distance from Vietnam to Europe. They earn the equivalent of £50 per month, which is nearly the same amount I pay for a haircut, no it is never going to happen.

Day 46

I had another terrible nights sleep. I just don't understand it, I should be worn out every night. I was walking around 14,000 steps every day, normally I only manage 1000 and I should be knackered. I was knackered but I just could not sleep.

I had a long and complicated discussion with Greenie about going on a trip to the Imperial City of Hue which is further up the coast. She wants to come with me and is trying to arrange it with work and her husband, she says her family will look after her children. This is a great idea as it will be great to have someone with me who speaks Vietnamese. I offered to pay for the hotel and meals for two nights and she says she will pay for the sleeper bus which is around £9 return each. That sounded perfectly fair to me.

It was a beautiful day today in the Nam, just perfect. The humidity had died down a bit and there was a nice breeze. I complained to Enly in the restaurant that there was never any bananas or pineapple left for me at breakfast, it all gets gobbled up by the early tour groups. She goes off to speak to the chef, returning with a plate of bananas. Every other day after that I received a little plate full of fruity tit bits just for me from the kitchen.
There is one waitress in the dining room that I just cannot take to, she always appears to be sneering at me and making comments to the others. I may be mistaken and she is just talking about her boyfriend but I could not warm to her at all. She also doesn't actually appear to do much work either, apart from her everyone else is lovely.

Opposite the hotel is a tributary of the Thu Bon river and this morning there were hoards of tourists bobbing around in fishermen's coracles all wearing conical hats. I crossed the road with Toby Hot Boy to take a look. It was very picturesque and I took a few photos including some in black and white which were very effective.

Up at the beach the sky had cleared and you could see all the way to Danang, I could even make out the Goddess of Mercy perched up on the hillside. There was also a very good view of the Cham Islands. When it is very hot these are barely visible in the heat haze, Jane did not even realise they were there as she never saw them, but today you can clearly make out all seven islands. I fell asleep for most of the day, I think that's the probable reason as to why I can't sleep at night. I finished my last book and was wondering where to get another. I sneaked across the road to one of the big hotels I have stayed in where I know they have a free library full of used books. I quickly swapped mine for two of theirs and scurried off before anyone could stop me.

After a shower at the hotel Linh arrived to pick me up on her bike. I was on my own now so there was no excuse to get a taxi and she firmly insisted on picking me up. I have said I would only go on the bike on the condition that she brings me a crash helmet to wear. She passes over a small helmet that would just about fit an orange and perched precariously on the back we pull onto the main road, through the rush hour traffic and up over the bridge towards the beach. No-one drives very fast here, I don't think most of the bikes can actually go any faster than 25 miles an hour but it doesn't stop them zipping perilously in and out of the other vehicles. Though the bridge only has room for one car or bus at a time it doesn't stop the bikes, there is a complete free for all and I shut my eyes whilst I hanged on tightly to Linh's microscopic waist as we weaved in and out of the traffic. Once out onto the coast road the traffic cleared a bit and I am not quite so in fear of my life.

I was so blasé and comfortable with Linh by now that I let her do what she wants with me rather than telling her what I would like. Today she decided that she was going to have a go at breaking down my cellulite, it certainly needed it. OMG the pain was excruciating. Her tiny strong fingers seemed to get right inside my legs and she tried very hard to break up all the lumps and bumps. I screamed all the way through,
"Is it hurting Jan?" "Yes Linh, very much" and she just kept on going. After the massage she decided to paint my finger nails bright blue whilst I ate a whole plate of bananas lounging in a chair with my feet up. I tossed her my purse and told her to help herself to whatever I owed her. When she dropped me off she warns me not to walk very far tomorrow or maybe she meant I won't be able to walk very far tomorrow.

I ate my evening dinner in the bar next door, it was completely empty and I was the solitary customer. I was also the only guest in the hotel tonight, as three groups left this morning and another two are due in tomorrow. I had a delicious mango and seafood salad washed down with a couple of beers. I collected my laundry which was all freshly ironed and still warm. Back in my room I washed out my trusty scarves, the water went brown, I could not believe how dirty they were.
I had a long conversation with Peter, in my absence he has ordered another Indian motorbike which Maureen positively encouraged him to do. Where the hell are we going to put it? He was so excited, like a small child at Christmas and I knew it was a mistake to leave them two alone together for long. I opened another bottle of Dalat Red in despair, I now know I am starting to get the taste for it, I can't say it is delicious but it definitely takes the edge off.

Day 47

As I haven't been sleeping very well I decided that I would get up very early tomorrow and go for a long bike ride. Of course I slept very heavily and missed breakfast completely, so in the end I got on the shuttle bus with Ethan and went into town. I set off walking across the bridge onto Cam Nan Island. I had never been here before and I combed the whole island traversing all the little streets and paths, before crossing back to the Old Town. I wandered off along unexplored roads and alleyways and came across a garage with three massive Harley Davidsons. These were the first 'proper' motorbikes I had seen here and I showed the owner some photos of Peters (other) Indian on my phone. We then had a long conversation where we did not understand each other at all but do grasp the mutual love of motorbikes. By now it was very, very hot and I was feeling a bit jaded so I made my way back to the bus stop.

When I returned to the hotel I was greeted by an agitated Greenie: the hotel were refusing to let her have the time off to go to Hue with me. They were just too busy and needed her go and help out at their sister hotel as they had a few staff shortages. I was a bit disappointed but I had been to Hue before so I know I would be OK. She had pre-booked me a hotel (her choice) and also sorted out my ticket for the sleeper bus which I paid her for.

I stretched out by the pool and tried to relax but I had a niggling stomach ache and felt a bit out of sorts. The thought of food made me feel slightly nauseous and I can't quite put my finger on it but I did feel decidedly weird, then the realisation hit me - it was yesterday's massage. This happened to me before after a vigorous massage, in fact that time I had a violent upset stomach all night. Linh had warned me not to walk very far and looking down at my phone I could see that I had just done 26,500 steps in the hot midday sun. Fortunately for me the diarrhoea did not arrive this time but I felt exhausted and decided to have an early night, it was going to be a long day tomorrow.

Day 48

A new day and another adventure beckons. I set my alarm for at 6.30am but when I tried to get out of bed, I had a major problem - I could hardly move. The pain in my bum and legs was pure agony, but on a positive note the area around the tops of my legs and buttocks did look a bit smoother if a bit bruised. I also had four nasty mosquito bites on my right bicep in a cluster which have swollen up and I looked a bit like Popeye when he has been on the spinach. I must have got them at Cam Nan yesterday so I now have to go back on the anti histamine tablets.

Greenie had somehow arranged for the sleeper bus to pick me up at 7.30 directly outside the hotel rather than me going to the bus station. How did she manage that? I can't imagine that happening in Bedford.
By 7:45 it had still not arrived so she rang the bus company, it was on its way. It eventually turned up at 8.00am, I could have had an extra half hour in bed. I go to mount the steps when the driver started shouting 'shoes' at me. "Oh I understand, you want me to take my shoes off before I get on?" he nodded firmly. It was a very painful process climbing up those steps, I

can tell you. With my overnight bag, shoulder bag and shoes clutched in my hand I edged down the bus, the driver wasn't hanging about and drove off before I had found somewhere to sit and I went flying. I somehow launched myself into a sleeping compartment that was level with the floor, next to the window and got myself organised. For my £9 (return) ticket, I got a fully reclining seat which was a bit like Business class on a plane but without any luxury whatsoever. There was a cubby hole for your feet and I had use my bag as a pillow.

There were three lines of seats running through the length of the bus and you had to climb a metal ladder in bare feet to get into one at the top, not an easy feat on a moving bus. There were a few European backpackers lounging at the rear, the rest of the passengers were Vietnamese, they were all wearing anoraks with their hoods up and face masks, not sure why, and you couldn't tell if they were men or women. It was not too uncomfortable and I settled down for a bit of a nap.

Why it is called a sleeper bus I will never know. The driver was obviously on a mission to win a medal for the quickest drive to Hue and drove like a complete lunatic, overtaking every vehicle in sight, weaving in and out of the traffic on the motorways and constantly beeping his very loud horn. Mobile phones were ringing all the time, including the drivers, and the woman next to me coughed all the way to Hue (Now I know why they were all wearing face masks). The only time it went quiet was when we drove through the Hai Van Pass tunnel. The drivers cannot overtake in there and needed to maintain a constant speed, also everyone lost their mobile signal. It was a total of 18 minutes of peace apart from the hacking cough next to me.

Every now and again we stopped in very odd place (definitely not on the itinerary) to load or unload stuff from the underneath containers. I can't call it luggage as some of it was decorating materials, reels of wire, heavy duty cables, cans of paint, bags of cement and some huge boxes full of beer.

Four gruelling hours later we pulled into Hue bus station. I had no idea where we were in relation to the city centre and there were taxi drivers everywhere touting for business. I was rescued by a Vietnamese chap who said he was part of the tour company in Hoi An who the bus trip was booked through, he would take me to my hotel for the cost of £1.

I now had a bit of a dilemma, do I go with him or get in a taxi, both of them could rob or kill me! I was saved by a young German couple who decided to take up his offer and the three of us got in his van. The van was a total write off and had obviously seen better days, it had four bald tyres, a huge dent in the bonnet, no glass in one of the windows and no aircon. It was noon now and felt even hotter than Hoi An as we set off in the mobile sweatbox for the city centre.

We pulled up at the hotel which Greenie has booked for me. From the outside it didn't look promising as it was completely covered in scaffolding and blue plastic sheeting. I will give the driver his due, he said he would go inside and investigate for me. Fortunately it was just being painted on the outside. I entered the hotel to check in, the huge lobby looked OK except there was a complete absence of any furniture or decoration. There was a very beautiful new marble floor that had obviously just been laid and was covered in brick dust.

I was given a room on the top floor which was a bit odd to say the least, I am presuming Greenie's idea of luxury is slightly different to mine. I had a big room with a double and single bed with black lacquered carved headboards, the white linen was spotless. Oh Goody, there was a big flat screen TV on the wall. The floor was on two different levels and on a large slightly raised platform there was a typically Vietnamese solid wood three piece suite and coffee table sitting beneath an enormous, ugly and very dirty chandelier. I pulled back the curtains and looked out at a lovely view of next doors side wall.

The bathroom had a completely enclosed bath with strange sliding floor to ceiling doors but it was clean and the room looked fairly comfortable, I was not planning on spending a lot of time in here anyway.

I sorted myself out and set off to the Imperial City. I had a map and could see that my hotel was slightly out of the centre, I really don't know why Greenie chose this place for me. I started out on foot, the Palace was about a mile away, but is was so hot that when I got around the corner I decided it would be best to hail a taxi to take me the rest of the way there. I got ripped off by the driver, he did not switch his meter on but told me it would cost me 40,000 dong (about £1.40). On the way back from the centre later I got in a metered taxi and it cost me 17,000 dong. It is not the money I object to just the principle that they think it is fine to scam the tourists. This city depends on tourists and it isn't a good idea to give it a bad reputation.

The Imperial City of Hue is impressive, it is built in a similar lay out to the Forbidden City in Beijing. It is nowhere near as well preserved as Beijing though due to all the damage caused by incessant wars and conflict and it has been seriously flooded several times over the years. Many claim the Tet Offensive in 1968 caused the most destruction in 200 years and there are still bullet holes in some of the monuments and buildings.

Unesco started a renovation project here in 1983 and the city achieved World Heritage status in 1993. It is an amazing place and is so large that all the visitors are spread out and it never seems overcrowded. This was my fourth visit and I had a good idea in which direction to go as I wandered in and out of the courtyards and pavilions. I can see a lot of restoration work had been going on and some of the buildings look like they had just been painted, the colours were so fresh. Some of the older buildings are faded and covered in mildew but somehow they seem more interesting than the newly painted ones. It was boiling hot and there was little shade, after a couple of hours I was melting and had had enough so I left through one of the side entrances.

Across the road is the War Museum. There are tanks, helicopters, cannons and aircraft left over from the war with America. I read a fact in my guide book that says 60% of Vietnams current population were born after the Americans left. Whilst the West still vividly remembers the war, the majority of the Vietnamese have either moved on or were not around to remember it, they are only interested in the future. Which is why the vehicles are all slowly decaying in the heat and humidity and are covered in mould, mildew and vegetation. It shows how popular the museum is as I am the only visitor.

When I first came here in 2013 there were no cafes or restaurants around this area but now there is a row of eateries outside and I slide into the air conditioned iciness of a coffee shop to cool down. The menu is all in Vietnamese and I pointed at a slice of cake and indicate an iced coffee which were brought over to my table. The cake was nice but the coffee had huge square lumps of a brown jelly like substance floating around in it, I have no idea what it was but it did not look very appetising and after a couple of sips I ended up leaving it.

I headed towards the antiquities museum, this is another place I have never made it to as I have always run out of time before. It is set in an old wooden pavilion on stilts and has huge electric fans wafting cold air around. I stand in front of each fan as I make my way round the glass cases displaying the Emperors sumptuous clothes, furniture and possessions. Again I was the only paying visitor in there.

As I left the Imperial City through the imposing arches and walked across the moat, I came across a few stalls selling tourist tat. They had a nice T-shirt that I fancied and I asked the price - it was £1.80, I did not bother to haggle, everything here was at least half the price as in Hoi An. I then attempted to cross the road at a busy junction, it was just impossible, nobody would slow down enough to let me cross. In the end I stood next to a local man and walked out with him into the middle of the road where all the vehicles just weaved around us. I crossed the Trang Tien Bridge and walked along the Perfume River waterfront to what I would call the city 'centre'.

It is really two roads with a few shops, some hotels and a lot of restaurants. It was a bit early and the restaurants only had a few customers. I chose the 'Army' restaurant. It is uniquely decorated with ex army clothing and equipment, bomb shells and old motor bikes. The tables are made up of wooden crates full of bullets with a glass top. I had a very nice meal with a couple of gin and tonics. The entertainment was provided by the waiting staff who were obviously having some sort of very boisterous staff meeting and there was a lot of hilarity going on, they were very amusing to watch.

By now the bites on my bicep are even bigger and the itching was driving me mad, the antihistamines did not seem to be working and I needed something stronger. I ventured into a local pharmacy where I was sold a tube of cream (a whopping £3.50) which the pharmacist said would help, I rubbed a big blob in. Almost instant relief!

By now it was dark and I flagged down a taxi to take me back to the hotel where I had a lovely cooling bath, noticing that I now had another two bites on my right leg. I wondered how I would fare if I did not wear any insect repellant, I think I would get eaten alive. I spoke to Peter, he was off on business to Germany in the morning and was just dropping the dog off at my sisters. I spent the rest of the evening in aircon icy splendour, laying on the bed stuffing my face with Haribo teddy bears watching The Mummy - Tomb of the Dragon Emperor on the TV.

<u>Day 49</u>

I took a sleeping tablet last night out of necessity and only woke up once during the night. I had been wrapped up underneath the big duvet with the aircon on freezing and I was very comfortable.

I wrapped my arm in a big bandage today to try and prevent me from scratching it, so I looked like I had been in the wars. Wearing another stylish (NOT) pair of Eric Morecambe shorts and my new T-shirt I looked a complete state, but as there was absolutely no chance of bumping into anyone I know I was not at all bothered - comfort was the keyword today. (Some of my friends would be horrified if they saw the state of me, I don't even go into the garden to mow the grass looking this bad).

I went in search of breakfast which was on the 12th floor. I found this a trifle odd as I was on the third floor and there was nothing else above me. I followed a sign along the corridor which lead me to the back of the hotel, hidden around a corner were a set of funky new lifts with mood lighting and soft Muzak playing. At the rear was a much more modern 12 storey wing, who would have known it was there! I thought there appeared to be a lot of people checking in last night and had wondered if the hotel was big enough.

The restaurant at the top had amazing 360 degree views of all of Hue, the staff did not speak any English and everything was done by hand signals and smiles. There was everything you could possibly want to eat for breakfast as well as some strange Asian dishes that you possibly wouldn't! There was an enormous car park below which was crammed full of motorbikes, not a car in sight. Vietnam has a huge import sales tax on cars which is why everyone has a motorbike, they simply cannot afford a car. Mind you the way they drive their motorbikes I cannot even begin to imagine the carnage on the road if they were all driving cars!

I got the concierge to call me a taxi to take me to Dong Ba Market which is across the river. He deposits me there for a fee of 17,000 Dong, which is correct. I have been here before and it is a maze of tiny market stalls and shops underneath varying pieces or corrugated iron and tarpaulin roofs. The good thing about this place is you can walk through, come out the other side and then re-enter a different way and not see anything you have already looked at. They sell everything here - fruit, veg, meat, jewellery, clothes, shoes, souvenirs, washing machines, huge fans and aircon units, fake watches & sunglasses, makeup, fabric, you name it they sell it.

I headed first for the fruit and veg section, it is very colourful if a bit smelly. All the vendors are women and they look very picturesque in their conical hats, they are all completely covered up, with only their eyes showing, wearing full Ninja face masks, I don't know how they do it as it was boiling hot at 38C
Most of this veg would never make it into British supermarkets as it is of varying sizes and a bit knobbly but I bet it tastes of something unlike our watery cucumbers and tomatoes we eat at home. I don't really eat salad in the UK as it just tastes wet, but here it looks very appetising.
Everything was vibrant, smelly and noisy, the Vietnamese stall holders were all yelling at each other and numerous motorbikes laden with goods were weaving in and out of the pedestrians: it was complete chaos and I loved it. I tried to avoid the butchery section entirely as I was nearly sick last time I went in there, a lot of it was alive. It wasn't when I left, if you get my drift. It was also very slippery underfoot with blood and visceral substances all over the place and the smell was disgusting. I can see lots of baskets of live chickens & ducks being unloaded and I veered in the opposite direction. I examined shoes and clothes, fortunately none of it looked large enough to fit me, there was certainly nothing bigger than a size 10. I was trying very

hard not to buy anything when I came across a stall selling a certain brand of trainer. Now I know these are actually made here so I am not sure if they were genuine or not, they certainly looked it and I ended up buying two pairs for £18. I also purchased a bottle of gold nail varnish from a lady who assured me that it was normal polish not gel.

Pleased with my purchases and dripping with sweat I sauntered back across the bridge. Halfway across I was stopped by a couple who had just arrived on the train and were looking for the market. We got into a long conversation and decided to get out of the sun and go for a drink together. They were a very 'cool' English couple, she was something in television and he was something in graphic design. They were not young , I would say around 40ish and lived in Majorca. We had a bit of a laugh together and I pointed out the places to visit on their map. They were off to Hoi An the following day and did I know anywhere good to stay? I gave them a list of places and we arranged to meet up for a drink when they got there.

Back at the hotel I had yet another shower and changed my clothes again. This afternoon I had booked a car and driver through the hotel to take me to the Emperors tombs which were around 10 miles down river. This had cost me £15 for the whole afternoon and I had been told by the receptionist that my driver would take me wherever I wanted to go. There is a small hitch to this promise, when I get in to the car he cannot speak a word of English! I had to whip out my guide book and pointed out my desired route on the map.

Once out of the city the jungle scenery is jaw dropping and there are some beautiful hotels and houses hidden in amongst the trees. I have absolutely no idea which direction we were heading in, we could be going anywhere, my driver is obviously not very talkative and the journey passes by in almost complete silence.

I had chosen three places to visit - The tombs of Minh Mang, Khai Dinh and Tu Duc. The tickets vary in prices according to popularity but they are roughly between £3-£4 each.

I visited Minh Mang's tomb first. It was in a beautiful setting with lakes on each side of the pavilion and temples, surrounded by trees and lush greenery and I thoroughly enjoy the tranquility of the place as I wandered around. The buildings and gateways have been well preserved by Unesco and the colours are bold and vibrant - I took lots of pictures as it was very photogenic. It was very quiet, peaceful, serene and uncrowded.

Unlike the second place that I went, the tomb of Khai Dinh. The road outside of this place was heaving with coaches and taxi's and was complete traffic carnage. It was not much better when you got through the entrance. First of all there were 127 steps to climb which had no shade and were in the glare of the full afternoon sun. There were no hand rails and people were pushing and shoving to get up and down, it was very difficult to go around them as each step was so steep with nothing to hold onto. There were literally thousands of tourists here waving their selfie sticks around and by the time I got to the top I actually felt physically sick. I found a small bush and sat under it to try and cool down and get some water inside me before I even attempted to enter the tomb. All the outside decor here is grey and black, it's not very pretty but the statues and buildings are very striking against the blue sky and mountainous backdrop. It is quite high up here and there are glorious views of the pine covered mountains in the distance.

Once inside the tomb there is a complete change of style, everything is covered in brightly coloured murals made up of pieces of porcelain and glass and there is a huge bronze statue of the emperor sitting on top of his tomb. It is very pretty and also totally unexpected after the starkness of the exterior.

What is interesting is that this was the last but one Vietnamese emperor's tomb, he died in 1925 and there are actual black & white photographs of him hanging on the walls dressed in all his regalia. He was succeeded by his son, Bao Dai who was born of one of Khai Dinh's ten concubines and was the last true emperor of Vietnam.

By now the heat was unbearable in the tomb and it was not much better outside. I gingerly made my way back down the steps, narrowly avoiding breaking my neck when I get pushed sideways by a gang of noisy Koreans who were not looking where they are going.

I somehow managed to find my driver amid the chaotic melee out on the road and relished five minutes of aircon in the car before arriving at the last tomb of Tu Duc. It was also very beautiful here and once again the buildings have all been renovated with Unesco money and are in good repair with vivid colours.

Tu Duc had 104 wives altogether, I wonder how he coped when they all went menopausal? Mind you, Asian women do not seem to go through the same miserable time as us Westerners, they think it is something to do with their diet.

It was very tranquil, there was hardly anyone there and I sat on a wall under a tree trying to absorb the atmosphere and reflect on the meaning of life. I suddenly realised that there was actually no-one around and looked down at my classy Rado watch. Oh no, the place had closed, I was now panicking that I had been locked in, there was just me and the dead Emperor. I remembered the film I watched last night and broke out in beads of sweat as I practically ran towards the nearest side gate, which wasn't the one I came in through. Fortunately it was still open and I let myself out. Now I had no idea where I was in relation to my driver, so I sprinted off in a very unladylike fashion in what I suspected was the general direction of the main entrance. Thank God, my driver and the security guards had been looking for me - I was rescued!

At my request my driver dropped me off in the city centre and I went into a restaurant for dinner. I was absolutely minging and really should have gone back to the hotel for a shower but I was starving hungry and thirsty after walking around all afternoon. There was only one other table occupied and I sat in a pretty little corner next to a wall covered in flower pots. I had just started on my first G&T when a local family group entered the restaurant. There was a mum & dad, what looked like two sons and two daughter in laws or it could have been the other way round and three youngish children. They sat across from me, the way they behaved was pure slapstick.
First of all the children ran wild around the restaurant, playing musical chairs. One of the sons then whipped out his mobile phone and proceeded to take numerous pictures of the children in various poses. They were obviously used to this as they posed like professional models every time he pointed the camera in their direction. The daughters in law then decided to get in on the camera action (after applying their scarlet lipstick) and he then takes around a thousand pictures of them in every conceivable nook and cranny of the whole restaurant - with the exception of one - my table. They posed and pouted, gesticulated madly with their hands and fingers and generally got in the way of the waitress who was trying to serve the customers who were actually in there paying for dinner. Between the 9 of them they only ordered 2 coffees and two ice-creams. I was just about to tuck into my dinner when one of the women realised she had not had her photo taken in my dining space. So whilst I am trying to eat, one of the women squeezes between the wall and my table to pose next to the flower pots whilst her husband snaps away. They were completely oblivious to the fact that they were being beyond rude. By now I was so used to the way that some of the locals behaved I just ignored them, but the poor waitress was mortified and kept apologising. I told her it was OK, not to worry and left her a big tip to cover her embarrassment.

It was dark by now and I was just relishing the thought of a cold shower back at the hotel when I received a message from the 'cool' English couple I had met earlier on the bridge. Did I want to meet them for a drink? So instead of going back to the hotel I met them in a seedy little bar around the corner. (I later discover they preferred seedy - I will explain later) I am not sure how long they had been there but they already appeared to be well under the influence and it was only 8.00pm. She did all of the talking whilst puffing away on her fags and relates funny stories about TV personalities she knows, I think she is just name dropping until she uttered the magic words - Strictly Come Dancing. This is my absolute all time favourite programme and my very guilty pleasure. I hardly watch TV all year but as soon as Strictly hits the screen I am completely addicted. I tape every show, the results show, It takes 2 and I watch it all live as well. I know nothing about dancing but I hold long debates with other fans over the merits of Block Steps, Chaine turns and Botofogo's. I steadfastly refuse to answer the phone if it rings on a Saturday night and Peter knows it is useless to even try to speak to me when it is on. (Just for the record my all time favourite celebrity dancer is Mark Ramprakash followed by Danny Mac who should also have won).

Anyway this cool lass knew quite a few of the celebrities who had been on the show and had met a couple of the dancers at various parties. I was suddenly all ears and we talked about it non stop as her boyfriend glazed over more and more. After about two hours they were both legless and now wanted to take me to a karaoke bar. I was having none of it and got a taxi back to the hotel, I was totally mystified as to how they got so drunk, I only had three beers.

Back at the hotel I had a long cold bath, my clothes were limp with sweat and I was absolutely filthy. I got a message from Peter, he had arrived in Germany and had met up with all his mates, he will forget all about me now for a few days whilst they drink extensive bottles of beer, "Network" and examine shoes in every detail.

I laid in bed watching A Good Day to Die Hard, the Vietnamese obviously have a taste for violent films as this appeared to be the least bloodthirsty thing on the TV. I took another sleeping tablet as I knew it was going to be another long journey back on the bus tomorrow.

Day 50

I was awoken by drilling from above at 7:15 am. It was really loud and made my teeth rattle so there was no chance of going back to sleep. When I complained to the receptionist she claimed the noise was coming from the site next door where they were building a cinema. It was definitely coming from above my room and when I go up to breakfast I can see several workmen crawling around like ants down on the roof below. So she told me a pack of porkies, next door indeed!!

After breakfast I took a casual stroll along the Perfume River. It was still very overcast and the humidity was up through the roof. There were lines of colourful boats tied up that take tourists up and down the river. On a sunny day it is lovely but on a grey day like today it looked miserable, like a dull October day in Bedford. I sat and watched a gorgeous little boy, around three years old, munching on a huge piece of French bread, I had no idea where he had come from and I was a bit worried that he appeared to be on his own. One of the boats started to pull away to to head up river, I heard a shout and this child suddenly flung himself over the jetty wall and landed on the prow of the boat. My heart was in my mouth but he has obviously done this all before - I was so glad that I did not have to jump in the filthy water to save him.

I met some friendly Americans out for a stroll and pointed them in the general direction of the historical sites. They must be very rich, they were staying at The Governors Residence which is the best hotel in town.

Back at the hotel I had yet another shower and changed my clothes again - I now had a huge bag of sticky semi-damp dirty laundry. My insect bites had all gone down, the cream worked really well and I no longer looked like Popeye's older sister.

I was picked up by a tiny non air-conditioned mini bus which was crammed to the gills with other passengers also getting the Sleeper Bus to Hoi An. I am pushed in and the door slammed behind me, I was practically sitting on some young chaps lap. Well I didn't mind if he didn't. We were deposited at the bus station and I unfolded myself out of the bus. This time I had a few minutes to select my seat and get organised before the driver pulled out in a plume of diesel fumes at 1pm.

Everything was going great, I was thinking we should be back in Hoi An by 5pm, if the journey to get here was anything to go by. We pulled into Co Lang, which is a village at the bottom of the Hai Van Pass. There was a lot of business being conducted outside whilst the driver and his colleague begin to fill the compartments underneath the bus with shellfish - buckets and buckets of it. The bus started to take on a decidedly fishy aroma, but they had not finished yet. We drove further into the village and picked up even more containers, I watched the women wheeling out boxes of oysters in old pushchairs and wheel barrows. We had been in Lang Co for nearly 45 minutes now and my body decided it needed to pee. There was a tiny loo at the back of the bus which I fought my way into, the smell was disgusting, a putrid combination of strong urine mixed with fish. Of course the driver now started to pull away whilst I was mid stream, simultaneously trying to prevent my shorts and knickers falling onto the wet floor with one hand and holding the door open a crack as the light was broken with the other. I staggered back to my seat and hastily clean myself with my hand gel, I was now much more comfortable and settled back into my seat to relax. Ha! Fat chance of that happening, this driver used his horn even more than the last one and there were the interminable phone ringtones going off every nano second.

We eventually pulled into Hoi An at 6.15PM. The driver pulled up outside my hotel to make a delivery of oysters to the restaurant next door, we were supposed to be going directly to the bus station. I decided to make a run for it and tried to get off of the bus, the driver was having none of it, he said I had to go to the bus station first. I can see his companion was still unloading buckets of shellfish and I yell at them that this is my hotel and I was getting off now whether they liked it or not. I struggled down the steps with my bags and ended up barefoot in the middle of the road smelling like a piece of cod!!

I am welcomed back by Anna and Sunny with hugs and tears as if I have been gone for a year. Greenie then appeared, she was absolutely sobbing her heart out and looked like she had been crying for a week. I had only been gone three days and there had been a big staff reshuffle, she had been moved up to the beach to their sister hotel on a permanent basis along with Eric. She had worked at my hotel for a long time and was very upset. I wrapped her in my arms and gave her a big cuddle, she didn't faint from the smell of me and promised her that I would go up to see her during the week. (I secretly hoped none of this had anything to do with me and she hadn't been moved by the management because we were getting too friendly, you never know what undercurrents go on in places like this).

I am informed by Sunny that my friends had arrived and were in the room below me?? Who?? What friends?? I suddenly twig it was the 'cool' couple and I go off to find them. They arrived three hours ago by private car, the lucky buggers! I took my new friends into town on the shuttle bus and we ended up having a meal together at the Banana Leaf restaurant. They were very taken with the town as I pointed out some of the highlights. Dinner was delicious as always and my new chums drank A LOT. By the time I left them they had already drunk two bottles of wine and it was only 9pm. They headed off to find a late night bar (good luck with that) whilst I got the shuttle bus back.

Day 51

When I woke up next morning it was very sunny so I set off for the beach and sat up there for a couple of hours reading. The clouds gathered in the afternoon and it came over very dark, I could hear rumbles of thunder and see flashes of lightening in the distance, so I set off for a walk around the houses along the beach. I popped in to see Eric and Greenie but neither of them were there, apparently Eric had had a motorbike accident and Greenie had been given a few days off. I must admit I was a tad suspicious that they had let her have some time off now when they previously told her she was needed there??

I was about 100 yards from the safety of my hotel when the heavens opened. I got absolutely drenched, by the time I arrived in reception I was dripping water all over the marble floor and one of the cleaners followed behind me with a mop. It proceeded to rain for a few hours so I sat out on my balcony but was driven inside by the humidity, which now it was raining, has gone up by several degrees. I spent the afternoon attending to some personal grooming issues. I painted my nails with my new polish that I bought in Hue. Because I had done no housework or gardening for nearly two months my nails were long and looked fab. I plucked my eyebrows, trimmed my fringe and completely de-haired myself everywhere else.

I met the 'cool' couple for a drink next door during Happy Hour. They told me that last night they ended up in a small bar at An Bang beach where there is a bit of a drugs scene. The penny drops, now I understand what they were up to. They were certainly taking a big risk. In fact anyone who goes to Asia in search of special substances has to be mad. Most South East Asian countries carry harsh penalties or even the death sentence for drug use. If you want to indulge in recreational drugs on holiday you are better off going to an English city, as far as I know no-one has faced the death penalty for drug use in Birmingham or Manchester.
It carried on raining all evening and huge puddles accumulated by the roadside. The high humidity was unbearable and I was really struggling with it. I had five more weeks here, please don't let it be like this every day. The mosquitos were out in force as it was so damp so I expected to get bitten again. So far I had gone through 9 bottles of repellant and had been bitten 19 times. I made a medical decision to take an allergy tablet every day to see if that helped. This did indeed turn out to be very effective. I may have got bitten again but as I was already full of antihistamine none of the bites irritated or itched and I was not bothered by the mozzies again for the rest of the trip. (This is something I will proceed to do in the future whenever I go anywhere tropical)

Day 52

In the morning the sun was shining and there was no sign of the huge puddles which had evaporated, but it was still very sticky. I had to sit in the shade as I literally could not bear the heat today, I swam in the pool at least six times but it still didn't cool me down. I do wonder if I was having some sort of menstrual period. I haven't actually had a proper one for 9 years since I had a Myrena coil put in due to a medical problem, but that doesn't mean my body doesn't go through the process now and again, my skin always used to feel warmer around my time of the month. These days the only cycle I am usually aware of is the one in our garage. Who knows what is going on inside me, I just wish it would end and I could feel normal again.

Whilst I was lounging around, I was approached by the somewhat creepy assistant hotel manager. I had seen him hanging around but this was the first time he had spoken directly to me. He started off the conversation with a remark about keeping his staff happy and that they were the most important aspect of the hotel. I felt a slight undercurrent here, he knew that I knew what had been happening with Greenie and Eric, was he trying to tell me something? I launched into a big speech about how this hotel was only a 3 star but it was actually the staff that get it the 5 star rating on Trip Advisor (these ratings are very important here, they take them very seriously) without those staff the hotel remains exactly what it is - just a 3 star establishment. He nodded pensively at me as if he was taking it all in. He says if he can do anything at all for me just to ask. Hmm this all sounds a bit fishy and 4 weeks late.

There was a new girl on reception today called Kayla who had just returned from maternity leave and was replacing Greenie. She didn't look old enough to have had sex let alone produce a baby, but I find out she is 28 years old. She was so thin she made some of the famous Supermodels look like heffalumps. How could she possibly have had a baby? Her waist is the circumference of my thigh and she must weigh about 5 stone. But she proudly shows me photos of her baby boy so it must be true. He was a proper little bruiser with thick black sticky up hair and looked completely adorable.

Linh picked me up on her bike and I went for a massage, today it was actually relaxing: she must be in a good mood. Afterwards I am forced to eat a whole pineapple and a plate of bananas whilst we talked over her business plans to move the salon to her home. Where she lives there are at least 6 other salons in that vicinity, so she will have fierce competition but even I can see that she needs to do something drastic - I was the only customer she had had for two days in a row and therefore my money is all she had earned.

On the way back on the bike (I had given up with the tiny helmet) I asked her if we can get some beer. We pulled up at a supermarket and I bought a 24 can slab of beer for about £5. This then goes on the bike balanced between Linhs knees as she drove me back to the hotel. They carry everything on bikes here, food, furniture, panes of glass, building materials, potted trees & plants, animals - the funniest thing I ever saw was a chap with a chest freezer strapped on the back of his, he must of had incredible balance to stay upright.

When I got back there was a bit of a panic going on in reception, there had been a fire at an electricity sub station up the road and it had knocked out the Internet in the whole area. The senior hotel manager asked me if I could write a notice for the guests explaining the problem and apologising for the inconvenience. They know what they want to say but cannot work out the English grammar, I was only too happy to do this for them and they stick it up on a big white board for everyone to see.

I go in search of my cool chums who are both burnt to a crisp and don't feel very well. For two grown adults with amazing jobs they were a bit thick: they had walked 6 miles in the searing heat wearing no suncream and with no drinking water after a boozy night on the tiles! They were planning on going to An Bang again later tonight so I decided to leave them to it. I seriously think I was way too uncool for them anyway, they were verging on the ice side of ' Cool'. I like a drink but I don't smoke or take drugs and I think we may have run out of conversation.
After a solitary dinner I cannot speak to anyone as the Internet was still out and there was no Wifi, so I hit the Dalat red and watched two episodes of Scrubs on TV.

Day 53

After the dodgy wine I had the best nights sleep since the first night I arrived here. I slept in very late, got up in a bit of a rush and just made breakfast where the staff were starting to set out the tables for lunch.

At reception I asked Kayla if she knows how Eric was, she tells me there was some other trouble going on and nodded in the direction of Sunny who was sitting alone at the tour desk. Sunny smiles constantly but today she was frowning and looked very worried. Because the hotel was now short staffed as they have relocated experienced personnel, the previous evening she managed to lose a 500,000 Dong note (£17) that was given to her by a French guest to pay his bar bill. She was working the shift on her own trying to check out the huge tour group and maintains that the guest got fed up of waiting and must have walked off with the money. There is no way of proving this and she has been told by the management that they will take this out of her wages. She was frantically trying to ring the tour guide to get him to speak to the guest but he was not returning her calls. When you only earn £50 a month, £17 is a huge chunk. I instantly offered to give her the money, but she refused point blank. I had a bit of a think about this and mulled it over later on. To save face I then offered to lend it to her and she agreed to pay me back weekly. (We then conveniently forget all about it).

I passed the burnt out sub station this morning, what a mess. All the surrounding trees are black and charred and there were burnt out cables and bits of rubber laying all over the road. No-one will ever clear the mess up, it will stay there like a landmark. The beauty salon next door was very lucky that their palm roof had not caught fire. That would have brought a whole new meaning to hair removal!

When I returned to the hotel Anna tells me that 'my friends' had checked out and relocated to a hotel at An Bang beach. I wasn't sorry to see them go, they were starting to irritate me a bit with their 'coolness' and made me feel old with their celebrity stories and exciting jobs. I am a thrice married woman from Bedfordshire who works in an office and volunteers as a pastime. How can I compete with such dazzling lifestyles?
Actually it's been a good life so far, I have a beautiful house, a varied group of friends, I have travelled the world and seen plenty of life, why would I want to go and live in sunny Spain, take drugs and get drunk everyday?
Mind you on some days it sounds like the perfect life!

Peter had returned from Germany and been to Scotland on business these last few days, he was now on his way to visit our sick friend who had requested that he help organise his funeral. This was quite upsetting as he was still alive but he was obviously getting his affairs in order and had very strong opinions on what he wanted.
I did not envy Peter that meeting.

I embarked on a very long and arduous cycle ride out towards the beach along the new road in the morning. The road and a gargantuan new bridge have been built to enable the traffic to reach an enormous building site just outside of Hoi An where there is a huge new resort going up. I had a decidedly dodgy moment when I accidentally disturbed a pack of feral dogs which then decided to pursue the bike. I pedalled like mad, not easy on a bike with a loose chain and broken gears in 90C heat, fortunately they soon got bored of the chase and slouched back into the undergrowth, whilst I dissolved in a pool of sweat.

I took some more dirty laundry next door, this time the lady refused to charge me for ironing it. It was obviously a novelty for her to have a regular customer and she welcomed me into her home with open arms and genuine hospitality.

Later that afternoon I had an appointment to have my toenails gelled again and decided to treat myself to a French manicure as well. There was one small technical problem - we could not get the old nail varnish off, it was almost semi-permanent and my nails had a decidedly orange hue about them. At one point I thought we might have to use an industrial scourer on them and I got a bit alarmed when the technician produced a bottle of acid and did something with a paint brush to my nails. Whatever it was, after an hour long battle the end result looked fab and only cost me a fiver. The owners mother and grandmother arrived at the salon (they both look really old and wizened but are both younger than my own mother) and I am wrapped up in a big hug. We were like old friends now, they always waved at me every time I wobbled past on my bike, I could never wave back as I dared not let go of the handlebars.

As I walked back to the hotel I was about to pass a bar I had noticed before, I had read up about this place on Trip Advisor but I am a bit of an old fashioned girl about going into bars on my own. Oh well this time I decided to bite the bullet and go for it, nothing ventured nothing gained. There were a few people milling around inside so I pulled up a stool at the bar and ordered a beer. It was owned by a couple of friendly New Zealanders and we soon got talking. The clientele were mostly European and there was a large group of expats who were all working at the huge building site outside town, English, Australian, New Zealanders and French.

After some polite introductions I spent all evening in there sandwiched between Danny (English) and Mike (Australian) at the bar. They made me roar with laughter and told me juicy stories about the all the different countries they had worked in: Saudi Arabia, Bahrain, Dubai, Abu Dhabi, Oman, Iraq, Jordan, Kuwait and Afghanistan - all of the worlds top holiday hotspots.
All of these chaps were married and some of them had beautiful Vietnamese girlfriends but that did not stop them trying to chat up a 54 year old slightly bewildered English woman who had suddenly become the centre of attention!!!! They even offered to show me their erection process - a full tour of the building site, I thought I might take them up on it at a later date.
I put my new popularity down to the fact that I can generally hold a whole conversation, we talked about Brexit, football, eighties music, work in general and travel, whereas the girlfriends could hardly speak English. But then again their men are probably more interested in them for their slim young bodies and lustrous black hair, I doubt if they go out with them for their scintillating communication skills!!!

I love Vietnamese food but they serve real chips in here and I just could not resist, I scoffed a whole bowl full with a side helping of mayonnaise, they tasted fantastic!

I tottered off back to the hotel feeling slightly squiffy where the girls virtually pinned me to a chair in reception and held an inquisition as to where I had been all evening. I was usually back in my room by 9.30pm and I sloped off to bed like a naughty child.
Back in my room I had a good sort out and moved things around to make some space, Peter was arriving tomorrow morning.

Day 54

I was so excited that I woke up very early which surprised the hell out of the restaurant staff, they didn't know I could get up that early. I changed my clothes three times and finally ended up wearing what I had put on in the first place, I even put on a bit of makeup. I strangely felt a little nervous, we had not seen each other for 8 weeks, would everything feel normal or a bit awkward?

Eagle eyed Anna spied I was wearing makeup immediately, honestly nothing got past that girl, she should work for the CIA or MI5.
My car arrived to take me to the airport, the driver took an interesting route. Even I know to drive to the end of the road, turn left at the roundabout and keep going towards Danang along the coast road, but he headed off in the complete opposite direction towards the Old Town. I had no idea where we were or where on earth he was going? I wondered if he had an errand to attend to in town but he doesn't stop anywhere, I then realised he was just trying to kill time driving the long route instead of waiting around at the airport. Good plan, and I sat back to watch the passing scenery. He drove me through the outer suburbs of Hoi An, there were huge factories, garages and housing plots that I had never passed before and I recognised absolutely nothing. If he had stopped the car and ordered me out I would not have had a clue where we were.

At the airport I paced up and down outside the arrivals doors keeping a beady eye on the arrivals board, you are not allowed to wait inside the terminal building. It said the plane had landed but there was still no sign of him yet. Suddenly I spotted him, head and shoulders above everyone else. All of a sudden he was outside and walking towards me, he looked up and gave me a cheeky grin. I have to say that he looked a bit odd in that he was wearing jeans, trainers, a nylon fitted Indian motorcycle top, a bomber jacket and a flat woollen cap, perhaps not the best outfit for the suffocating heat. We had big hugs and kisses all round and made our way to the car where we found the driver sitting with his feet up on the dashboard eating his lunch.

I talked non stop all the way on the journey back to the hotel with Peter occasionally grunting in response. There was a welcoming committee in reception and Anna presented him with a huge bunch of red roses, Peter was bit taken aback and was not quite sure what to do with them, he's never been given flowers before.

Up in my room I unpacked all of his luggage which had weighed in at a whopping 29 Kilos. Apart from a few T-shirts, three pairs of shorts, two pairs of flip flops, his wash bag and some underpants, nearly everything else was for me. I noticed that he had packed all of his favourite T-shirts, the ones I hated and not his nicer ones, I was sure he had done it to wind me up as I normally do all of our holiday packing. He laid flat on the bed whilst I sorted it all out and put everything away.
He informed me that at last we have had some viewings of the house, but none of the prospective buyers could sell their own houses. The government had done a really good job scaremongering over Brexit and the UK housing market had completely slumped, nothing in our village was selling. He had also bought me out some important letters to sign about two of my pensions that I would be able to draw down when I got to 55, I chattered away non stop about what I was going to do with the all the money. I pointed out that he will shortly be living and sleeping with a pensioner which was secretly worrying that I am actually that old. I suddenly realised it had gone very quiet, when I turned around he was fast asleep and had not heard one single word that I had said.

When he eventually came to, I took him up to Cu Dai beach. He moaned all the way there: it was too hot, it was a long walk, his feet hurt, he was tired etc, etc, on and on he whinged. When we got there he goes straight into the sea for a swim with a warning from myself not to wear his new LTFC sunglasses. Completely ignoring my advice as usual, the vicious waves whipped his glasses off and they disappeared forever to Davy Jones locker. He then flopped down on a sun bed and fell asleep for the rest of the afternoon. As I sat reading my book, I was aware of a funny irritating noise, I can't quite put my finger on it at first, then it suddenly dawned on me what it was - snoring. I had not heard that noise for two whole months and I certainly hadn't missed it.

What a grand romantic reunion!! In the end I left him snoring his head off and walked along the beach to see if Greenie and Eric were around. Eric was on shift at the hotel and showed me his battle scars from the fight with his motorbike and a mad dog that had run out on front of him. He was very lucky not to have broken anything, he had some nasty cuts and lesions which his mum had covered in iodine and his foot was now bright orange and probably glowed in the dark. He told me that Greenie's son was sick and she had taken some time off to look after him.

 OK - I might believe you Eric, if not the hotel management.

Days 55-56

The next two days passed by in a similar sort of vein.
Peter slept all night long wrapped up in the duvet, snoring his head off - I did not sleep at all. We walked up to the beach where he slept all day long. We returned to the hotel to have a shower and get changed, went out to a local restaurant for something to eat and then retired back to bed again, where he slept all night whilst I had to keep the TV on to muffle out the noise of his snoring.
I might as well have been on my own again.

Day 57

On the third day there was a small miracle, he awakened and actually held a full length conversation with me, I was so shocked by this that I had to lay down again. To occupy his days and nights whilst I had been away he had worked non-stop and had filled his weekends and evenings with voluntary stuff : Even I can see that he was completely exhausted. This is a usual holiday for us, normally he always goes down with a cold as well once he switches off, fingers crossed this will not happen. Because he runs his own business he always tries to fit in two weeks extra work before we go anywhere so by the time we arrive he is so tired he sleeps for days. This particular morning he was more with it and wanted to go out on a bicycle. Hurrah movement at last!

Toby Hot Boy and his companion go through the selection of rickety old bikes to try and find one big enough for Peter (he is 6 foot 2). I had my usual Orange Peril bike number 9 with the dodgy gear chain and non existent brakes. I now had a proper cycle helmet and we could daringly venture out onto the main road, this opened up whole new areas to explore, we discovered some Koi Carp farms and several beautiful villas hidden amongst the greenery and vegetation. (I Googled the villas when I got back, they were for rent and were very reasonable).

We were cycling alongside a river when we spotted a woman in the water clinging on to a polystyrene box drifting downstream, she was still wearing her stylish conical hat. Her very dry husband was shouting instructions to her from the shore. After a few minutes of watching it became apparent that she was bringing in his fishing nets for him!

I think today was the hottest day by far of my whole trip and we were both soaked with sweat when we got back to the hotel. The humidity was up again and there was no breeze whatsoever. We both jumped in the pool and stayed there all afternoon. Incredibly today Peter had actually managed to stay awake for 8 hours in a row!!

I handed out all the chocolates and sweets over to Anna with strict instructions that they were to be shared by everyone: gardeners, laundry, maintenance, kitchen and cleaners as well as all the front office staff. I know she would sort this out for me fairly. I spotted some of the bar staff chomping away on the Haribo later that evening.
I also had some jewellery for all the receptionists and waitresses, it was only cheap costume stuff that I do not wear anymore, but they each excitedly chose a piece as if it was designed by Karl Faberge. Anna had had her eye on my fake 'RADO' watch since I arrived and I gave her that as well, she was delighted and doesn't give a hoot that it's not real. Peter had donated some old McLaren F1 baseball caps for Toby & Ethan and a ruck sack for Eric. I was a little bit embarrassed by their genuine pleasure in all of these items. It is just stuff that we had hanging around at home and would normally end up at the charity shop or in the car boot sale.
We all have so much stuff nowadays, I have a 4 bedroomed, extended three storey house and it is crammed full to capacity with things. There are wardrobes bursting with clothes, bags and shoes, kitchen cupboards containing every item and gadget you can imagine, a garage full of tools and man stuff, two motorbikes (now), two cars and two garden sheds full of goodness know what. Why do we need all of these possessions? Does any of it truly make us happy? As I get older I am starting to appreciate experiences more than having actually things. I always say that if I won the lottery I would get more joy out of giving most of it away than spending it on myself.

In the late afternoon, the heavens opened and a loud storm raged overhead so we are forced indoors. A saga now ensued as I attempted to pay my hotel bill with my credit card. My bill for two months came to a whopping 476,850,000 dong (around £1600). My credit card had one day left until it expired and Peter had brought the new one out with him. I tried to pay my bill with the new card but I was not wearing my glasses and messed up the pin number which totally disabled the new card. Fortunately the old card was still working and it all went through. Of course I was now left with no valid credit card. I had plenty of cash but I needed something in case of an emergency so Peter offered to leave me one of his. Thank god I paid it on that day, there would have been a real drama if I had tried to pay my bill on the day I left and my card wouldn't work.

Back in our room our toilet did not seem to be working properly since Peter had arrived, I wonder why that was? Definitely overuse. He spends more time in the bathroom than the bedroom. I reported it to reception and they promised to get it fixed immediately.

As Peter was now awake and fully conscious we decided to go into town on the bus to have dinner. I took him to see my new friends at Cuisine Dannan, they behaved like I had been gone for weeks, I got dragged in and welcomed like long lost family. Peter ordered the Hoi An pancakes. There was a very funny moment when the waitress asked him 'if he knows how to eat?' What she meant was did he know how to eat the pancakes which you have to roll yourself, so she then had to give him a lesson in pancake rolling. After yet another scrummy meal we then had to go on a shopping spree for some shoes and new sunglasses for Peter. Somehow all he had brought with him were a pair of trainers and two pairs of flip flops, of which one pair had already gone in the bin as they had broken. I was a bit sceptical that we would find anything big enough for him and several shops turned us away, the biggest they could offer was a size 8. After hunting around we eventually found a shop that sold size 10 canvas lace up pumps but they only had them in black not any of the vibrant or funky colours on display, they only went up to a size 7! Peter was very happy with his new purchases and decided to wear them, he later moaned on and on that he now had blisters from wearing new shoes with no socks. You just cannot tell them can you, some men are so daft!
We also ended up having to buy fake sunglasses which cost roughly £4 a pair, there was nothing decent for sale anywhere. Peter has quite a wide head and they snapped across the bridge two days after he bought them. We then bought another pair which do exactly the same thing: he literally ended up going through 4 fake pairs in 12 days. If he had listened to me on the first day he would still have had his nice new LTFC ones that fitted him properly!

At some point in the evening all the artificial lights went out in the Old Town for ' Earth Day'. It was very dark and atmospheric but everyone was walking about with their phone torches on which was defeating the object a bit. We ended up drinking beer in a pretty candlelit bar until the lights came back on, I was not going to risk walking around here in total darkness, the rats would be out in their millions.

It was quite late and we had missed the shuttle bus back so we got in a taxi. Oh Dear, tonight we got a frustrated racing driver. We were tossed around in the back seat as he drove like Sebastian Vettel, weaving in and out of all the cars, bikes and coaches. I actually put my seat belt on which was a first since arriving here. At one point I was sure we were about to have a high speed head on collision but he managed to pull back in the nick of time, gosh that was so close! We clambered gratefully out of the car at the hotel, the only tip we gave him was to tell him to drive slower next time.

Back in our room the toilet had already been fixed and we both hit the Dalat Red. By the stunned and painful expression on Peters face after one sip I could tell he was not a fan, so he started on the cans of beer. That wine is definitely an acquired taste.

We FaceTimed Maureen as it was Mothers Day and she proudly showed me the sickly and arse lickey cards that Peter had sent her - URGH!YUK!

Day 58

Next morning it was cloudy but bright and we ventured out on the bikes again. We were heading in the direction of the new bridge when a woman approached us in the middle of nowhere and asked us if we would like to go to the Coconut Village. We made noises about maybe later and she disappeared off into the palm trees. We reached the bridge where there is a huge traffic junction to cross. I took my life into my hands as I cycled across 6 lanes of traffic praying I wouldn't get killed, Peter just pedalled nonchalantly across, totally relaxed.

There were about twenty coaches parked up so this was obviously a tourist hot spot and we were not that keen. As if by magic the lady from the palms appeared again, she had obviously furtively followed us here, and offers to let us park our bikes at her house. Oh well we were here now it might be fun. We cycled through a row of cafes and shops and pulled in to her front yard and dismounted. An elderly gentleman came out of the house, he must be her father, and offered to take us around the Nipa Palms in his coracle for a small fee. In for a penny in for a pound, we agreed and Peter handed the dosh over.

We were led through the houses to the waters edge where a small round boat was tied up. We could only get in one at a time to steady the boat and the boatman handed us conical hats to wear. So looking like a complete pair of twats we floated off into the Nipa Palms. I have never seen palms like these before, they grow up out of the water (almost upside down) and some of them have huge brown papery flowers, very unusual. There were also a few water rats sitting in the tree trunks but fortunately they did not come near us, just watched us with their evil eyes. It was actually good fun bobbing around in the little boat and it felt much cooler out on the water. The boatman made me a ring and a headband out of the bark of the palm which he made me wear, I looked even more of a tit than I did before. From somewhere we could hear the sound of very loud music. As we rounded the corner we came out into the main tributary that runs out to the sea. There were numerous little boats bobbing around, full of conical hatted tourists, most of them Korean. On a floating buoy in the middle of them all was a young man with a full set of speakers and a massive amplifier. In one of the other vessels was chap who was dancing enthusiastically and spinning his boat around, all of this to the overwhelming sound of 'Gangnam Style' - boy he was really going for it. The Koreans were jumping around joining in with the dancing whilst all the coracles rocked perilously, it was absolutely hilarious and I have never seen such a sight. Peter and I agreed that we were glad we came as it was all so mad and surreal.

Returning to the ladies house she kindly gave us a glass of water each, I hope it was bottled and not out of the river. As we cycled back through the village I spotted some dresses for sale which I had seen in the Old Town, they never looked big enough but this lady had BIG sizes and I get a dress for £3.50, no haggling, which I am very please with.

The afternoon passed by lounging around the pool before getting a taxi to Linh's. Peter and her look so funny together, her head only comes up to his belly button. Peter promptly fell asleep the minute he laid down and snored his head off. Linh, her colleague and myself rolled our eyes at each other and sniggered quietly to ourselves.
He claimed later on that at one point his masseur touched his testicles - in his dreams!

We spent all evening in town trying to price up leather handbags. My sister was looking after our dog and I wanted to get her a nice bag as a present. This was quite a long and difficult procedure as the shops all charge different prices and you have to work out who is negotiable and who is overcharging. Anna had given me a figure that we should pay but it was very hard work reaching that point and we never did get that low with anyone. It takes ages to work the system but it is all part of the shopping experience here. If you do not haggle they will rob you blind and think you are stupid, but I do not want them to be out of pocket either. Eventually worn out with it all, we gave up for the evening and retired to the Pineapple cafe where we have huge lumps of chocolate cake and more beer.

Days 59-66

The next week with Peter passed pleasantly by. We just mooched about together. On one of the days the weather was deceptively hot and everyone got caught out by the sun, there were bright scarlet bodies everywhere you looked. Peter was so burnt that he glowed in the dark and his chest and shoulders came up in small blisters. His legs were so red he looked like he was wearing stockings when he took his swim shorts off. I made him squeeze himself into the bath to try and cool his body down properly to stop the burning and stop him moaning. It was his own fault, I had told him to be careful and sit under the umbrella, but men, they just never listen to us do they?

On one of the days we were on our way to the beach when we were approached by a chic looking French woman who was loitering about at the top of the beach road. She said she was working in PR and was trying to drum up some tourist interest in a new hotel. She showed us the glossy brochure and offered to take us for a look round, we had other plans that day but said we night pop in at a later date for look round. She then got a bit arsey and said we would have to come now if we wanted to win a prize? Peter by now was on the alert and was quite sure that it was Time share so we firmly declined her offer. Looking at the internet it was indeed Timeshare. What, here in Vietnam, is that allowed???

News comes in from my office at home that we are getting a new Manager as the other one has decided not to come back from maternity leave. I was very pleased as I get on really well with the new one, and we go out walking every lunch time. They informed me that it was starting to get busy with event bookings for the Summer and everything was getting a bit hectic and stressful. I felt a little bit guilty that I was not there helping them out, but it only lasted for a few seconds!

I needed to get my haircut again and I went off to the salon. This time the stylist seemed a bit distracted and definitely cut it with a knife and fork motion, it was all over the place. I had to trim it myself back at the hotel with my nail scissors, my own hairdresser in the UK would have a fit. Whilst I was in the salon the owner told me about an incident with an Englishwoman who had been in earlier and had 1,000,000 dong's (£33) worth of beauty treatments. When it came to settle the bill she had no cash on her but said she would go to the ATM around the corner and bring it

straight back. That was 5 hours ago. This was such embarrassing behaviour for us English, she had her finger nails and toes gelled, eyelashes tinted, and a cut and blow-dry. This would cost well over £100 in the UK and the beautician was very upset as it was a lot of money for her to lose.
(I found out later that the owners husband who is Scottish and deals with the bookings, emailed the English woman informing her that he would put her photo all over Facebook from the security cameras if she did not pay. They do not actually have such a system but it worked as strangely enough the money turned up anonymously in a taxi the next morning!!).

We went out on the bikes everyday and Peter was very impressed with my cycling skills. I certainly felt much more confident now that I was wearing a cycle helmet. He was particularly impressed by the way I avoided getting taken out by a woman on a bike that was heavily laden with vegetables. She had no brakes and had to stop with her feet, her front wheel missed my leg by 1cm and she got her trousers entangled in my chain! I was managing to cycle across huge junctions without any misadventure. Peter rides a powerful motorbike and he has no fear on two wheels so I felt I was doing well keeping up with him. There was another heart in my mouth moment when a chap on a motorbike, who for some reason was carrying an 8 foot long, wooden old fashioned hat and coat stand across his lap, nearly took me out on the main road but I managed to stay upright and narrowly avoided getting knocked off.

We had been told of a beautiful unspoilt piece of coastline a few kilometres away and we set out to find 'Hidden Beach'. It was so well hidden that 4 other people stopped and asked us if we knew where it was. We had to cycle through the Paddy fields, out onto the new four lane bypass and then down a steep narrow track, that was good fun on a bike with no brakes, I can tell you! I chickened out and walked my bike down the really steep bit. At the bottom of the hill was a piece of pristine beach with beds, umbrella's and a small selection of restaurants. The deal here is that the beds are free as long as you purchase a drink or meal in one of the huts. It was very peaceful, no noisy kids playing football or tossing a Frisbee around nor were there any photo mad tourists trying to sit on your sun bed with you. The sea was still very rough though, I went in once or twice with Peter holding my hand but the strong current unnerved me and I got out very quickly.

We rode out along the coast road to the lighthouse passing an enormous plush hotel that was not there last year, it was just a building site back then. It was now completely finished, plastered white with a garden full of beautiful tropical flowers and plants shimmering in the sunshine . Blimey, when they put their mind to it the Vietnamese are very hard workers to finish this in a year. My friend had to wait nine months just to get her kitchen finished properly in the UK. There was a really good view of the new building site from here, it looked like a row of jagged teeth in the distance, it was certainly going to ruin the skyline.

The land runs out at the lighthouse where there is a small port, with lots of fishing and pleasure boats moored up. What was horrifying to see was the amount of plastic bottles and rubbish floating in the sea, obviously washed up river from the Old Town. The Vietnamese have not really caught on to the plastic issue yet. Everyday I was given two plastic bottles of water in my room which also had plastic wrappings covering the lids. Over the 9 weeks I stayed, that equates to 126 bottles just for me and that doesn't count the other bottles that I had purchased myself. I know some of the bottles are recycled but not the plastic lid covers. This is a massive problem in Asia and they need to do something drastic about it now, some of this rubbish will be swept out to sea and will end up on the beaches as far away as Indonesia.

On this particular day I had been given cycle No.13, the dodgiest bicycle ever, it was really hard work - no brakes, a chain that kept slipping so you had to pedal backwards to get it to go forwards and was just generally unsteady. It was a complete deathtrap and I nearly came off of it when I got spooked by a cow that appeared out of the hedge in front of me and lumbered straight out onto the main road.

We visited Traque Vegetable Village which is basically just a glorified allotment - but what a fabulous allotment. It had rows and rows of neat lines of vegetables and flowers, all very orderly with not a weed in sight. Everything was dug and planted totally by hand and some of the workers looked very photogenic in their conical hats and wellington boots. I like gardening and I loved it here, it was right up my street. Peter got a little bit bored in the end, he doesn't mind eating veg but doesn't want to look at it growing, so I vowed to come back next week when he went home. On the way back we found a tiny little palm bar and ended up having a cold beer in the middle of nowhere.

I took Peter to see Greenie and Eric, they were thrilled to see us and meet Peter at last. I gave them their presents and picked Greenie up and swirled her around in the air, not sure why, just because I could. Her son had been very ill but was now on the mend and she had had a stressful few days. Eric was walking a bit better, his wounds were healing but it was going to cost him a lot of money to mend his motorcycle, there is no such thing as motor insurance here.

We went in to town most nights absorbing the special surroundings and general atmosphere, eating the fantastic food and just enjoying being together. We ate at all of our favourite haunts and tried some new places as well. One of the restaurants did cocktails during Happy Hour by the bucket and some nights we had a bucket each as well as some beer before we rolled back to the hotel usually by 9.30pm. We played cards in bed and Peter beat me every night, he is just too clever for his own good.

Since Peter had been there the weather had been getting hotter and hotter. We had been to the beach most days and I felt like I had sand in every orifice, I even had it between my teeth. My tan was coming on and I was starting to go much darker than my usual colour. I had put a little bit of weight back on but that was all due to the biscuits and sweets Tracey and Peter had brought out for me. My hot flushes were way out of control but as I was so hot most of the time anyway, I seemed to be coping better with them than I do in the UK. I did seem to be more carefree and not so anxious or worried about everything. I suppose not doing any washing, ironing, housework, cooking, shopping, gardening or work for nine weeks all helped. For the first time since I arrived in Vietnam my sleep pattern had calmed down and I was sleeping much better as well which all helps with the Wellbeing. I had the bedroom at a constant 16C at night time and Peter was going to bed with all his clothes on as it was freezing in there. And miracle of miracles I had not been bitten again since taking the anti histamine pills every morning.

Having my husband here had been lovely but God he is so untidy. Clothes, magazines, cables, laptop, phone all left laying around the room. Wet towels left laying on the bathroom floor, I was constantly tidying up after him. And why does he have to take his shoes off and leave them together in the middle of the floor? Not to one side or tucked under the bed. No, right in the centre of the floor - I nearly go arse over tit several times. Talking to my friends they all say their husbands are exactly the same, why is that? What makes an extremely intelligent man think that he has a little fairy who cleans up after him? Fortunately he had ruined some of his hideous T-shirts with the greasy suncream he uses, so I had been able to chuck a few of them in the bin with unfettered glee. I also had to throw away 2 more of my own vest tops and a pair of shorts which all came back from the laundry beautifully clean and ironed but covered in black stuff. Not sure how they could come back dirtier than they went in?

The days rolled blissfully on and suddenly it was Peters last day: it was also our 19th Wedding anniversary and we were in for a real treat.

Day 67

After a gorgeous day at Hidden Beach we were presented with another big bouquet of red roses and a bottle of Dalat Red (oh goody - my favourite) by the hotel management. We had been instructed by the reception staff to wait in reception at 5.30pm wearing a dress and looking beautiful - Peter could only manage shorts, I at least attempted to follow their instructions. We were loaded into a taxi with Kayla and driven to I do not know where, I could not find it again if I tried.

Waiting inside a big modern glass and chrome restaurant were Greenie, Eric, Misa, Helen, Sunny and Anna. They lead me by the hand out the back onto a terrace where there was an enormous ' Happy Anniversary' balloon and a lovely cake. I hardly recognised the girls without their uniforms, they were all glammed up wearing dresses and high heels. In their heels I did not feel quite so Amazonian around them as I was wearing flats (I did not bring any heels with me, they had gone back in the cupboard). This was the first time I had seen them without their hair tied up and they all looked so different.

They all wanted to have their photo taken with me, they were not at all interested in Peter. This was a new feeling, most people are all over him like a rash and I am the one who usually gets sidelined but here I was the complete centre of attention (and I have to admit it felt great). He ended up taking dozens of pictures of me with each girl in turn, obviously not until they had applied their lipstick properly. They draped themselves all over me and I wrapped them up in my arms. I felt strangely maternal to all of them, something very weird was happening to me, I had never felt this strange sensation before.

We sat at a long table on the veranda overlooking the paddy fields, it was a beautiful setting as the sun started to go down. I noticed that all the girls took several selfies of themselves at some point during dinner, so they were all at it too!! We whatsapped Tracey at work so that she could see everyone at the party and there was lots of laughter and kisses blown around whilst she was online.

Various dishes were brought out and we all tucked in, the La Rue beer was flowing freely. We had stir fried prawns, crackers, clams (called chip chips here), rice, soup and chicken (which was horrible and included all the bones and knuckle joints - Yuk) there was not a Spring roll or pancake in sight. Everyone ate with chopsticks except me, I just cannot get the hang of them, Peter is a dab hand. The Vietnamese are very untidy and throw all their empties and rubbish on the floor, some tables looked as if a tornado had hit them, there was so much debris everywhere.

Happy Anniversary toasts were made in unpronounceable Vietnamese which we tried to copy but could not get our tongues round. In the end we picked up on the word 'Yo' and turn it into 'YO YO' as a sort of 'Cheers' which they all found very amusing.

Greenie then made an announcement that my Anna was pregnant. WHAT! HOW! WHEN! It turns out that she is six weeks pregnant and it must have happened just before I arrived here. Does that technically mean I was going to be an adopted grandma of sorts? Will Peter be sleeping with a pensioner and a grandma in the future? Anna also told me that she was now getting married in May, we were both very disappointed (I was a bit devastated) that I would miss the wedding by two weeks. More toasts and YOYO's all round.

Greenie then informed us all that Kayla was having an affair with one of the kitchen staff which she vehemently denied. Please don't have a spat at the party girls! Phew, it was obviously a bit of a joke with everyone, it turns out she was just very friendly with one of the kitchen lads and they were all just gossiping, like any normal workplace. Helen then waded in with her news that she was now dating one of the chefs at our hotel. Oh God, please don't let it be the same fella! It turns out that her new beau was the one spreading the rumours about Kayla's chap.

I go back to my earlier point, girls are the same the world over.

After the meal the fun really begins when Greenie lit some enormous fireworks in the middle of the restaurant, which were decidedly dodgy to say the least. They were like huge sparklers and really dangerous (I bet there were no safety warnings on them). None of the other diners even flickered an eyelid, it was just normal behaviour here. I cannot imagine what would happen if you did that in the middle of Wetherspoons! The lighted fireworks were passed around between themselves and they took another load of photos which included Peter this time. Eventually the pyrotechnics fizzled out much to my relief. I really don't like fireworks as we saw a horrendous injury occur years ago at an organised display and it put me off them for good. If I ever go to a fireworks display you will always find me right at the back hiding underneath a tree.

They settled the bill between themselves and adamantly refused to let us pay for anything. Peter managed to catch sight of the bill, it worked out at £50 for the meal and drinks for the 9 of us. Where else in the world would you get that sort of value?

There was then another change of tempo and we all jumped aboard the motorbikes. I got on with Greenie, riding side saddle (not to be recommended) and carrying the Anniversary cake. Peter jumped on with Eric (I am surprised it did not tip backwards with him on the back) and we roared off in convoy into the dark night. Against all of my sensible middle aged instincts, we had agreed to go to a Karaoke bar.

Neither of us had ever been to a Karaoke bar before and I envisaged a shack with a few people sitting around and someone murdering a song on the microphone. Oh no not here, the Vietnamese take it very seriously and have whole buildings just for this purpose.

Once inside the foyer it was a bit like a palace : there was a waterfall and pond full of Koi Carp, a white and black marble floor, crystal chandeliers hanging from the ceiling, lots of Vietnamese glossy wooden furniture dotted around and huge murals of dragons were painted on all the walls. Are they sure this was a Karaoke joint or had we wandered into some rich persons house by mistake?

Sunny & Helen were in charge of proceedings, once booked in we were led up an ornate staircase where there was a long corridor lined with doors. I went somewhere like this in Amsterdam but that is another story! We were shown into our windowless booth and presented with a bowl of fruit and some cans of beer. It was about the same size as my hotel room with a light up dance floor, really loud music pumping out, and there were flashing lights beaming down from the ceiling and walls - not a good place for anyone suffering from seizures. There were some seats around the edge of the room and one wall was taken up by an enormous screen, fortunately for me there was also aircon blowing.

Eric called me over to the console to choose a couple of songs. Most of it was Vietnamese pop but we did find a Coldplay and a Bangles song which would be for me and Peter to perform. The girls were dancing so I threw myself onto the dance floor with my usual gawky enthusiasm. Peter unfortunately videos all of this. (Even when I look back at it now, I still laugh at myself. I looked totally ridiculous dancing with all these gorgeous young things, a bit like my grandma did at my wedding).

The singing began and Peter and I take to the microphones. Oh Dear! Nil points! We gave a terrible out of tune performance of 'Yellow' and 'Eternal Flame' and received a polite round of applause from our audience. After that it then got very serious. It turns out that all the girls have fabulous voices and even perform synchronised dance routines to each song, it was almost semi professional. Apparently they all practice their routines at home on a daily basis in front of the mirror. Oddly the song that they all loved the most and knew all the words to was My Heart Will Go On by Celine Dione!! Well, at least Peter and I could join in with that one as well, though I noticed that we were not given the microphones again.

I would never have thought our wedding Anniversary would turn out like that and it had been a brilliant if slightly odd evening.

Probably the best anniversary party ever.

Peter managed to wrestle the Karaoke bill off of a very flushed Eric and we insisted on paying for the entertainment, it cost £18.00 for one hour which seemed very expensive considering what the dinner had cost.

In the taxi on the way back to the hotel Peter reluctantly admitted that it was England 0 Vietnam 5 in the singing stakes. As with all Vietnamese nightlife we were back at the hotel and tucked up in bed by 9.30 eating our delicious cake.

Day 68

We were both up early next morning, Peter was going home. I had packed his cases for him, they were both full of my stuff anyway. Everything I had bought so far and a lot of things that I would not use again or did not need now that I was not moving around. When he got to check at Danang in they weighed 32.5 Kilos and no-one even commented on it. The girls all crowded around me as we waved him off to the airport, telling me 'don't cry Jen'. I managed to keep myself together this time but I did feel sad and a little bit lost. I had three more weeks to go and I was now on my own again.

I gave the staff on reception the rest of our cake to share between them and got the bus into town. I wanted to try and find a book exchange I had read about on the Internet. I had devoured all of the books that Peter had brought out with him and I desperately needed something else to read. All the books in the hotel 'library' were in German or French.

On Cam Nan Island was a book exchange run by an American expat from Hawaii. With my rucksack weighed down with eight books I set off across the bridge.

The shop was a funny little place. It was in a private house and was crammed floor to ceiling with books of all languages. I climbed up the tiny narrow staircase into the roof and selected my books. OMG it was so hot in there. I was dripping with perspiration as there was no ventilation whatsoever and my glasses kept slipping down my nose with the sweat which was also dripping into my eyes. By the time I got to the till I was soaked to the skin, I looked like someone had literally thrown a bucket of water at me. We did a deal at the till with my bag of used books and I left with my new reading material, as I emerged outside it felt positively chilly compared to the inside of the house.

I then went in search of a travel agent to book a boat trip to the Cham Islands. I have sat and looked at them every year, now I had plenty of time I wanted to visit them. I had been recommended a dive company who did boat trips by the New Zealanders in the expat bar.

Despite following a map somehow I missed the office, ended up on the wrong side of town and had to walk all the way back in the heat lugging my heavy rucksack. Once booked I handed over £30, this included the hotel pick up, the boat trip, lunch and the use of snorkelling equipment. I had now spent all of my cash and just had enough to pay for a taxi back.

When I got back to the hotel Kayla furtively corners me in reception to ask a big favour. I was agog with curiosity as to what it could be but it was not very exciting. In a few days time they had a big German tour group arriving which they had inadvertently overbooked by 4 rooms. Would I mind moving out to their sister hotel for a few days to help them out? I did not really want to uproot myself at this stage but they had given me the best room in the hotel which I had not paid for, so I agreed, it also meant that I would be able to spend a bit more time with Greenie and Eric. She told me that the boys would help me with all of my luggage and there would be no charge for anything. The sister hotel is a new 4 star up on the beach road and was much more expensive so I am sure it would be fine.

She then dropped a massive bomb shell into the conversation about poor Eric having gone down with Chicken Pox after last nights party.
I am instantly on the alert, this was very worrying for me. 20 years ago I caught Chicken Pox from my nephew, he had two spots, I had 200. He got better, I didn't. The Varicella virus turned into Encephalitis which affects you brain and spinal cord. I was off work for three months and ended up in Addenbrookes neurological ward for two weeks until they worked out, from a lumber puncture, what was wrong with me and sent me home to recover. At the time I was separated from my then husband and had to stay with my parents so they could look after me, as I could not walk or do anything for myself. I was very ill and was told to be careful around anyone with Chicken pox or Shingles in the future, apparently the virus stays in your system forever.
Oh bloody hell this I do not need, I sat next to Eric last night and also gave him a big hug at the end of the evening and Peter had been close up to him on the motorbike.

I spent the afternoon washing my smalls and rearranging my room, fretting all the time that I was now going to go down with Shingles. It would be sods law that I was ill as soon as Peter went home and would have to cope with it all on my own. I did not feel great that afternoon and I was beginning to imagine all sorts. My common sense eventually kicked in and I realised I was just coming down from the mad party last night and also I had just walked about a hundred miles around town in the noon day heat.

I must say my room looked very tidy without Peter in it. He messaged me that he had reached Singapore and now had an eight hour layover until his 11.30pm flight to Heathrow. I don't relish this thought as I would have to do it on the way back home as well. Luckily for him he has a business card and had been able to check himself into one of the private lounges for the rest of the day, I have no such luxury and will have to slum it.

Later that evening I went back into town to change some money and go for a pizza. As I was still feeling a bit delicate I decided to get a taxi straight back to the hotel instead of waiting for the bus, I really wanted an early night.
This was a big, huge, enormous mistake.
I was ushered into the front seat of the cab by the middle aged driver (all the other drivers had been young bucks, this was a first). Because I was so relaxed I was being a bit dopey and my common sense should have told me to get in the back. The driver flicked his phone cable into my lap and then slyly retrieved it, touching my thigh with his fingers as he did so. I let it go the first time, it could have been an innocent accident but then he did it again. Much to his surprise I yanked out the cable and chucked it in the footwell, I think he got the message. He talked non stop on the way back and asked me loads of personal questions which I don't really give an answer to and then he wanted to play a guessing game as to how old I thought he was. You stupid arsehole, I really don't care 20, 30, 100? Then to cap it all he started bloody singing, Oh God, please let me get out of this car. Of course he also drove the long route around town, down some very dark roads to get back, but I was getting slightly annoyed rather than alarmed at this point.
Safely back at the hotel I refused to give him a tip and he called me something obviously rude in Vietnamese, I retaliated and called him a tosser as I strode inside.

Whilst I was relating the story to the girls at reception and Toby Hot Boy, who had wandered in to see what the fuss was all about, an English man was being checked in by Anna. He introduced himself as Den and we shook hands, he painfully crushed my fingers together in a vice like grip. I had no idea how old he was, certainly no spring chicken, but I could see he had a real naughty twinkle in his eyes. He loped off with Anna to find his room, I hope she walked behind him not in front as I imagined that he was the type that would be ogling her from the rear!!

Day 69

I felt a bit fed up the next day and walked up to Cua Dai beach, I stayed there all day reading one of my new books. On the walk back I was stopped by Linh on her moped who offered me a lift. I had no idea who it was until she removed her face mask, anyway I hopped on and she delivered me back to the hotel without me wearing any helmet.

Helen and Misa were on reception duty and Helen was limping badly. When I enquired why, she showed me a nasty festering burn on the back of her calf. This had been caused by touching her bare skin against the hot exhaust pipe on her motor bike. It was about two inches long by an inch wide and had burnt through at least three layers of skin and was red, blistered and weeping. I know this needed covering up before it got infected, especially here in the Tropics, she had not cooled it down so it was still burning and she was in a lot of pain.
First Aid Jan to the rescue. We cooled it down in the bathroom and I put a dressing over the top and gave her a few spares, in the UK this type of burn would need looking at by a Health Care Professional but here that just wasn't going to happen. Misa rolled up her dress to show me her battle scars from her bike and then Kayla waded in to show me hers. They were all badly scarred on the backs of their legs, a simple bit of First Aid training then takes place as I tell them they must get it under a cold tap ASAP if it happens again.

After a lovely cooling bath I rang Peter who had just arrived back at our house. The flight was fine and on time, he had a lovely time in the executive lounge and we discussed all the films he watched on the flight. He said the weather in the UK was cold, wet and miserable, totally normal then.
As I was a bit fed up today I went back into town as I wanted to be surrounded by people tonight, I also felt that I fancied something different to eat for a change, some chips would be nice! Just along from the taxi rank I found a Mexican restaurant (what else) where the food was divine, a little bit pricey but worth it. They had the most enormous air cooling unit and I sat right in front of it, just perfect.

When I got back to the hotel I found Den sitting alone at the bar, he beckoned me over and insisted on buying me a drink or two. This turned into a very long evening!
I never did find out his age but he lives in Thailand and informed me that over the age of 75 he could not get travel insurance there, so I worked out that he had to be older than 75. He looked like he was in the middle of a permanent shrug but that was to do with an old rugby injury to his neck, in fact he looked a bit like a taller version of Uncle Fester from the Adams Family.

He hailed from London originally and told me that he used to run pubs, clubs and snooker halls in the East End for a living. I got the distinct impression that he had done 'time' at some point but I did not press him for the gory details. He retired in the eighties, divorced his wife and left his kids in England to go and live in Phuket, where he now lives in a luxury apartment with a 30 year old female, currently the fourth girl in a row! She can't speak English and he can't speak much Thai, apparently they communicate through food.

Well, please explain Den, how the hell does that work???

Do you lay a cucumber out on the table when you want sex???

Does she replace it with a French bean when she isn't interested?

Does she put out a radish or a turnip when you are being annoying???

I can't quite get my head around this weird courtship and I tease him mercilessly.

I can tell that he is as sharp as a whip, ruthless and also a little menacing, a bit like Reggie Kray in shorts. I imagine he was a handsome and striking man when he was younger. He drinks like a fish and I can see from his bar tab that he had consumed 8 G&T's already.

He was also very funny and made me laugh like a drain. I cackled so loudly that Sunny's head kept appearing over the top of the reception desk to check that I was not having some kind of seizure. He told me hair raising stories about the sex trade in Thailand and some of the revolting things (not for the faint hearted) that male tourists do to some of the girls out there. He had got into many an argument and fight defending girls in bars and I realised he actually did have some old school (if slightly warped) morals regarding women. He was here on his own for a few weeks as it was the festival of Songkran in Thailand, this is where everyone throws buckets of water at each other all week long. Last year he was arrested (again) for punching someone who threw water at him whilst he was on his way to a meeting, so this year he was laying low until the festival was completely over. He had left his young girlfriend behind to enjoy the festival with her friends.

He then suddenly turned the conversation completely on its head and started to question me as to why I was travelling alone and away from my husband for three months. I started to relate the whole story but he was having none of it and implied that there was something wrong with my marriage for my husband to let a woman like me go away on my own. Sorry what did you say, I don't understand ? What do you mean a woman like me? He said that if he had a woman as gorgeous as me he would not let me out of his sight for even one minute. I looked behind me to check that it was me he was talking about, OMG he was. I nearly fell off my chair in shock. Really? Honestly? I am a 54 year old mad menopausal woman with sticky out teeth, wonky feet and a fat arse, I am definitely not gorgeous, but OH

YES apparently I am. I look down at myself, I was wearing the Andy Pandy jumpsuit, there was obviously something about it that attracted the older man.

We continued to debate this for hours with me getting drunker and drunker and laughing louder and louder. Den just sat there with a deadpan face with his mesmerising blue eyes twinkling, you would never know he had drunk 15 G&T's. He then changed tack and decided that my husband must be having an affair at home to have let me leave the country for so long, either that or he was a complete blind idiot. Back and forth we argued the point, he was adamant that he was right and we ranted on long into the night.

At some point past midnight, I staggered off to my room, as I passed him he slapped me across the backside.
If anyone else had done that they would have swallowed their own teeth, I decided to let him get away with it - I did not want to find a horses head under my pillow.

Day 70

I awoke late with a bit of a hangover. No surprise there then! I set forth on my ancient bike to go to visit Traque Vegetable Village again. It was a lovely ride and I remembered the way there and did not get lost. This was a highly unusual event for me, at home I normally cannot remember how to get out of the garage.
There were lots of visitors there today all having the 'Traque experience". I cycled around the village examining the flowers and plants and somehow ended up in someones back garden, I soon got chased off by their guard dogs, another worrying moment as the bike would not get into gear and I could not get any speed up.
On the way back in the middle of a deserted track I was stopped by four English women who were looking for the village. We were having a friendly chat when from nowhere appeared hundreds of people on bicycles from all different directions, it was suddenly like the M1 of cycle paths and we were the ones causing the traffic jam. Anyway I had a lovely morning pottering around and I felt much more cheerful.

I sat by the pool for the rest of the day until I was forced out by a very loud group of French tourists who had just arrived. They took over the whole pool area, all got in together and completely disturbed the peace. They also left their foul smelling ash trays and cigarctte butts all over the sun beds.

I checked in with Peter, he said it was freezing a home, and I had a long chat with Julie before making my way up to the expat bar.

Most of the lads from the building site were in there, a few had gone home to the UK and were due back later that week. I ended up eating my tea in there, they didn't do big dinners, just little plates of delicacies and I ordered a few different plates which were all yummy.

I sat at the bar talking to Mike all evening about his Vietnamese girlfriends tailor business after I made an off the cuff comment about the problem of finding anything in town big enough to fit my European figure. He had suggested to her that she make some off the peg clothes in larger sizes for the tourists, rather than them having to spend time out of their visit being measured and fitted for clothes. This made really good business sense to me, but she was not willing to even contemplate doing it unless one of the other tailors in the street did it first. Every business suggestion he came up with she ignored and he held his hands up in that defeated way of "I tried to tell her so"

I ended up having far too much to drink (again) and reeled back to the hotel. I never gave a thought to my personal safety, wandering around in the dark late at night, I always felt very safe here. I probably would not even cross the allotments opposite our house alone in the dark at home.

Tonight Anna and Sunny were on reception and I was quizzed again as to where exactly I had been and who I had been with. I had been the perfect guest so far but I had got sozzled two nights in a row and they saw me off to bed with a disappointed look, just like my dad used to give me when I was a teenager and got in very late.

Day 71

It was the big day today and I was off to the Cham Islands on my boat trip. I was picked up on the dot at 8am and we drove down to the port, next to the lighthouse. They were a mixed bag of passengers, some backpackers, several mature singles and couples, some families with children and even a young couple with a tiny baby (what were they thinking of?) French, Danish, Swedish, South African, German, 1 English (me) and 1 American chap. By the time we got to the port, which took 10 minutes max, everyone on the bus knew every bit of the Americans business.

At the port we were directed onto the dive boat and we climbed aboard. It looked like an old wooden fishing boat that had been adapted with a flat dive platform and set of ladders running off the back. The cockpit was in the middle of the main deck and leading up to the bow there were bench seats on either side, up on the roof there were some loungers and deckchairs. I decided to sit downstairs as it was very hot and I wanted to be in the shade. The crew were made up of 3 burly Australians, a giant English chap and two Vietnamese, all of the crew were qualified PADI divers. First there was a full safety briefing and then the crew introduced themselves and explained how the day would run. We were going to visit two dive/snorkelling sites, then would have lunch on the main island before sailing back to Hoi An. Before we pulled out of the port everyone had to put their life jacket on, apparently it was Vietnamese regulations, but once out of the port we could all take them off and they were stowed away and we never saw them again.

We set off across the South China Sea towards the Cham Islands. It was a beautiful day, the sun was shining and the water was very calm. I got talking to some of the other passengers who could all speak good English, much to my shame. The giant English bloke introduced himself and his enormous hand engulfed mine as we shook hands. His name was Simon, he was about 45, and had been working on the boat for two years, he lived there with his Vietnamese wife and daughter. He reckoned he had the best job in the world and at that exact moment in time I could understand why.

We sailed to the first island which was totally uninhabited, where they dropped anchor. All the divers were pulling on their wet suits and arranging their Oxygen tanks, the rest of us were given snorkels and flippers. One by one everyone slid off the back into the water, and then some of us got back out very quickly. We had all been bitten by sea lice (no I have never heard of them either), it wasn't particularly painful but it did sting a bit. Simon squirted a shot of vinegar solution all over me and the stinging instantly stopped. Fortunately they had prepared a large barrel of it which was handy as there were a lot of people in discomfort.
This completely put me off of going in the water and I did not venture back in again at that site.

I chatted to two Danish lads who were into free fall diving, this is basically where they dive into the water with their bodies in strange funny positions, and who were showing off by jumping of the roof into the water. They were very pleasant, spoke brilliant English and had been travelling together for two years. Two Years! I was so jealous. How could they afford it? When were they ever going to get a job and enter the real world?

The guys on the boat were very relaxed but kept a careful eye on the people in the water, you could see where the divers were by the bubbles coming up. After an hour everyone came back up and we sailed off to the next dive site. When we got there 3 speed boats were already anchored up. In the water were about forty Vietnamese, all wearing life jackets, flapping about like a scene from Titanic. Simon told me that this happened every day, boat loads of them come out to the islands, none of them can swim so they just splash around.

I gingerly got back in the water and attempted to swim around the boat, I was really struggling as I was wearing a life jacket and flippers, I could not really make myself go flat to look down into the water as the life vest kept floating me upwards. Then one of my flippers slid off, I was trying to stay upright whilst fighting with the force of the water to hook my flipper back on and in the end I gave up. I took my flippers off and tossed them on the back of the boat and went for a gentle swim. There were lots of rocks around and plenty of fish around feeding off the plant life. There was a very dangerous moment when one of the speed boats started up and began to pull away over the water where our divers were. Our crew went mad and a loud shouting match ensued, I tell you I would not have argued with our crew, they were very masculine and masterful.

After an hour we headed off to the main island for lunch, by now the wind had picked up a bit and the water was a little bit choppy. We were too big to anchor at the beach so we dropped anchor about 100 metres offshore . Now this vessel had no life boats so I was wondering just how we were going to get to the restaurant, swim perhaps? From around the headland chugged a tiny wooden Vietnamese death trap of a boat which the crew tied up at the back. It was about one foot deep and was held together by different coloured odd planks of wood and would have been used as firewood at home. We were told to jump into the little boat from the dive platform which was a drop of around a foot with nothing to hold onto. The youngsters all leapt across fearlessly but some of us older ones found it a bit precarious and the youngsters had to catch us as we landed, once again I landed on some young mans lap - Lucky me, Unlucky him! Once the boat was full we set off to the beach, bouncing around on the waves, it then returned to get the others. The beach was a pristine ribbon of white sand, slightly spoilt by the gaudy rubber inflatable slides at the other end of the bay - all for the Vietnamese visitors. Dinner was served in a hut on the beach, it was ok but every dish was stone cold as we had been late arriving due to the faffing around on the tiny boat. I nibbled on a few things but noticed that the youngsters all wolfed down everything put in front of them. After lunch I ambled along the beach and sat under a tree to pass the time taking in the delightful scenery.

Getting back to the big boat was very exciting. Whilst we had been at dinner the wind had really whipped up and the sea had got quite rough and choppy. The Vietnamese boat man could not get up to the back of the boat and after three aborted attempts the crew told him to pull alongside instead. Now this little fishing boat was only a foot deep and there was at least a 3 foot height difference between us and the side deck of the bigger boat. They also did not bob together in the water, so at times there was a 5 foot height difference as one went up and the other one down. We were instructed to stand up one at a time, put your hands on the deck and push yourself backwards and upwards. My hips and knees are not what they were and I was grabbed by the scruff of my neck by two of the crew, lifted upwards and pulled onto the deck where I lay gasping like a stranded whale (fortunately this happened to three or four people).

The most perilous situation was trying to get the woman with the tiny baby aboard and it took about six people to get her back on deck safely.
The sea was really rough going back, the sun had gone in and the water and sky looked grey and menacing. It was quite chilly with the strong wind and I had to wrap my damp towel around me to keep warm. The boat was hitting the waves at such an angle that there was nowhere to sit to avoid getting sprayed with the sea water and by the time we entered the port we were all soaked to the skin, even the tiny baby. My hair had got wet and salty and then been blow dried by the wind and I looked a real fright. I had a magnificent silver bouffant that resembled Glenn Close's character in 101 Dalmatians.

Back at the hotel everything was covered in salt and I had to have a long hot shower to rinse it all off. I thought I might go into town for dinner. After my solitary meal I went for a drink at 'Pineapple', it really was the best place to get a fantastic piece of cake in town. The owners knew me by now, and I always got a friendly welcome.
Whilst I was stuffing my face, two English couples came in, Londoners who had the same accent as myself, and sat down at the table next to me. We got into conversation, they had arrived last night from Hanoi and were wondering where to go for dinner as they had had some lousy food at their hotel. They wanted a proper Vietnamese meal that would not give them an upset stomach or break the bank. I suggested 'Cuisine Dannan' and offered to show them where it was as it was on the way to my bus stop. As usual the lovely staff were all over me and dragged me and my new chums inside and gave us the best table. I forget their names but the two couples asked me to stay to have a drink with them, which then turned into several and for the third night in a row I arrived back at the hotel slightly tipsy and a bit dishevelled.
I got the full Spanish inquisition from Toby Hot Boy tonight, he was on the night security shift - I bet he was going to grass me up to Anna.

Day 72

I cycled to Hidden Beach in the morning except of course I knew where it was now, so it was no longer hidden. I arranged myself on my bed to soak up the rays and promptly dozed off, when I opened my eyes sometime later I spotted Danny from the expat bar lolling on a sun bed opposite me. I wasn't sure if he would remember me, as we were all a bit drunk last time I saw him a few weeks ago. But sure enough he knew exactly who I was, not sure if that was in a good way or not, and we spent all day chatting in between the frequent naps and cold beers. He had got back from the UK last night after visiting his family and was chilling out at the beach trying to get over the jet lag.

It must be an age thing, whenever I travelled when I was younger, I do not remember experiencing the crippling jet lag that I get nowadays, in fact I can't really remember feeling that bad at all. I remember flying from Melbourne to Sydney to Bangkok to London in one straight 26 hour hit, when I got home I unpacked and then went out all day. How on earth did I manage to do that? Jet lag makes me feel sick and woozy, I behave like a total zombie and it takes me days to settle back down. I have trouble sleeping at night at the best of times but after a massive time zone change I have literally no chance! Neither Peter nor my ex husband ever suffered from it and I put that down to them working shifts and getting up at all hours to go to work. Mind you Peter can fall asleep anywhere, I remember once he fell asleep on the sidelines at a football match whilst he was standing up!!

I left the beach, had a shower and got picked up by Linh for my weekly massage. I was having a bit of gip with my right leg, I think it was caused by all the cycling, and she set about trying to relieve the pain. What her scruffy little salon lacks in aesthetics she certainly makes up for in her knowledge and experience, afterwards the pain had completely disappeared. As usual after the business side was concluded I had to sit and eat large quantities of fruit whilst we chatted, tonight it was a whole pineapple just for me. I asked her if she would drop me off at the expat bar which she did.
Big Simon from the dive boat was in there tonight and he made a beeline for me, shaking my hand with bone crunching enthusiasm and talking about the boat trip, the other boys raised their eyebrows and made funny faces at me whilst we sat up at the bar talking. It was Saturday night and the boys had had a long hard week with their erections at the building site and were up for anything, they asked me if I would like to go to a late night music bar with them (there was one in town then). I was just thinking about it when my phone rang, it was Peter to say our sick friend had died. I was very upset, shocked and I shed a few tears, I no longer felt like going out on a wild boozy night in the Old town, so I walked soberly back to the hotel and played word games with Anna and Sunny in reception. Back in my room I

got a call from Lisa and we had a long talk about our deceased friend, it was a very sad evening.

Day 73

I got up quite late next morning still reeling from shock about our friend. Hopefully at least I will get home in time to be able to attend his funeral and pay my respects, which Peter tells me will be a big affair. I felt quite numb and I was very upset.

You go through life, moving through each day and no-one can ever predict what is around the corner, whether that be an illness, divorce, early death of a loved one or something else that is life changing. There are only two certain facts in life, you are born and then you die, you just do not know when.
I remember when I was 18, I did not even think about getting old or dying, I had my whole life stretched out ahead of me, and what did I go and do? Get married at 20, what a total disaster that was. It is probably the one thing in my life that I truly and deeply regret and I have buried most of those hideous memories in my sub-conscious. That marriage prevented me from doing anything exciting with my life, I don't blame him, I was young, easily led and I was manipulated into doing something that looking back I didn't really understand at the time. My parents marriage was going through a rocky patch then and it looked like an escape route away from their misery. I am not particularly clever or well educated but I know I could have done a lot better than working in an office for the rest of my life.

After that first marital tragedy I then went ahead and married a man 20 years older than me with 2 teenage children who lived with us. I would NEVER EVER advise anyone to live with someone else's children unless you really love them. I was 22 years old at the time and it was bloody awful. Just because your partner loves his kids it doesn't mean you do or ever will. We never had five minutes together in the house without one of them being there or wanting something.
The relationship between us was good at first, he basically saved me from the shipwreck of my first marriage and for that I will always be grateful. Ultimately as we aged we both wanted different things, I wanted to have a baby while he wanted to take early retirement. So that marriage ended up in divorce too (though this time it was amicable) He was living out his retirement dream in the Egyptian desert in Luxor when he got up one morning five years ago, and dropped dead after a massive heart attack. This was a man who was never ill in all the time I knew him, I reiterate my point: you just don't know when your time will be up.

It was really only when I got into my thirties that I started to think more about the future. I bought my own house and lived on my own for four years, I refused to let my then boyfriend move in with me. I am so glad I stuck to my guns with him as I would never have got away from him otherwise. I had to have the police remove him from my house one night when he broke the door down, as he just would not leave me alone when I called time on the relationship. He lives in America now and still stalks me on the internet. Living on my own was the making of me and I learned a lot about myself, which is why it is so disturbing that the menopause now seems to be stealing all my strength and vitality. Everything has become a chore and getting out of bed some days is almost impossible.

I think about dying, A LOT. I know it sounds morbid but if I am lucky I maybe have 20 years left before it is Game Over and it is constantly on my mind. I feel that there is so much more to see and experience in life and I panic inside that I may not achieve everything I want to.

After another hot day lounging around at the beach, for the evening I went up to the Irish Bar where I had seen the strange Leprechaun on Paddy's Day. There was a quiz on tonight and some of the expats and myself made up a team, we didn't win but we didn't come last either. It was good fun and I had a really good laugh which totally lifted my spirits, I also seemed to know most of the answers, they were totally hopeless unless the question was about sport.

Day 74

The following day was my 55th Birthday. We are not big on Birthdays in my family, no-one really celebrates them so it wasn't particularly upsetting to be on my own, I had spent the day on my own before several times when I lived alone. Peter sent me a sweet message but I heard nothing from anyone else, out of sight out of mind I suppose.

After another hot and sweaty cycle ride through the countryside, I got showered and changed - I was meeting Danny for lunch. I had mentioned last night that it was my birthday and he had sweetly insisted that he take me out .

We went to a beautiful restaurant out in the countryside, it was really pretty and quite upmarket. There was a cool terrace overlooking the river which was surrounded by lush greenery, palm trees, lovely plants and the food was absolutely divine. I had big fat juicy prawns cooked with sea salt wrapped in a banana leaf and a couple of beers.

Despite the lovely surroundings and the good company, I did feel a bit awkward at being out with another man on my birthday, even though it was completely innocent, it just did not sit right with me.

When I got back to the hotel, Anna and the reception staff presented me with another bunch of red roses and a small blue and white iced cake. This made me laugh out loud, written on it was 'Happy Birthday Janice Coulson'. They are the sweetest people, I love them all to bits.

I lounged around in my room all afternoon doing some washing and personal grooming. I eventually received lots of messages from my friends, I should have known they wouldn't forget, there was a 6 hour time difference remember. I wanted to get the bus into town this evening to go and buy myself a Birthday present as nobody else had.

Who else should be on the bus when I got on? Den. We ended up going for a proper Indian curry together, strangely enough it did not bother me going out to dinner with him.
In town there is a small restaurant called 'Ganesh' where the food was out of this world, it was very popular and the place was packed to the rafters. Den started off questioning me about my day and it turned into another session of why was a beautiful woman like me on my own on my birthday. Yeah yeah, I had heard it all before. I turned the conversation on its head with a comment that he was actually the second man I had spent my day with so far, which made him chuckle knowingly.

I bet he was a complete lady killer when he was younger, he certainly knew how to say all the right things. He was hilarious with the young waitresses and had them eating out of his hand, nothing was too much trouble for them and he had them running back and forth the whole time, I did notice that he left them a more than generous tip. He related fascinating stories of his life in the East End, it was a bit like a Guy Ritchie film script. He came from proper working class stock, his dad was a market trader (like Del-boy from Only Fools & Horses) and his mother was a char lady (also like Del-boy), they were very poor and there was not a lot of money to go round. He left school at 14 trying his hand at several jobs, including the market stall and also in a butchers shop. I bet that's where he got his menacing side and learnt a few knife skills. He started working as a beer delivery boy to some of the clubs and was offered a job by one of the owners. The rest they say is history. By the sound of it nothing phased him and he has grafted all his life to end up very well off. Whether it was all strictly legal and above board or not I could not possibly comment.

The Old Town was absolutely heaving, it was the busiest I had ever seen it. It turned out that it was a National Holiday and all the Vietnamese were dressed up and out on the town. There were families, cars and motorbikes everywhere and it was total chaos, more than usual. There was even a traffic jam in the middle of the pedestrian area, how the vehicles had even got in there was a mystery.

There were huge groups of them prancing and clowning around in front of the cameras all the way along the river, fingers and hands wildly gesticulating. They were quite funny in that some of them were all dressed in the same clothes, or were wearing the same colour, one group were all wearing flowered light up head dresses (a bit like weird bridesmaids). Why they feel that they all have do these ridiculous poses, I will never know.

I left Den to wander off alone to wherever and went for a look around the shops with a view to buying myself something nice. I never got tired of the town at night or the shops, I always seemed to spot something I had not seen before. Tonight I bought myself a gorgeous white cotton top with blue embellishments, I haggled hard for it and in the end she came down to my price (£7) as I told her it was my birthday. She must have felt sorry for the old bird!

I was also out on another assignation, I had arranged to meet Danny in a wine bar but I didn't dare tell Den, he might have slit my throat. In the smelly, dark, rat infested market there are a set of steps that lead up to a stylish wine bar, I would never have spotted it if it hadn't been pointed out to me. As I went up the steps I saw several furry creatures running along the eaves of the roof, but it was actually quite nice once I got inside. After few glasses of decent South African wine, which tasted like nectar after the Dalat red, I headed for the taxi rank whilst Danny went off to a late night bar to go schmoozing and chatting up any mature single ladies who might be around which was a favourite hobby of his.

It had been a very pleasant day, not the best birthday ever but it had been OK. I was now 55 years old and would be decidedly richer when my two pension lump sums paid out when I got home.

Day 75

The beauty of being here for this long was that I got the chance to see the rice ripen and get harvested. In Vietnam they grow 3 rice harvests per year, in Laos they can only manage one although that is probably because they can't be bothered. When I first arrived the paddies were lush and dark green, now the fields were golden with the flower heads drooping under the weight of the rice seeds. They have some small machines to assist them with the harvest but all the bagging up is done by hand.

Most of the cycle paths up to the beach were covered in tarpaulins and the rice was laid out to dry before being bagged up and sent to market. It was a bit disconcerting as any motorcycles or bikes on the paths just drove straight through the middle of the drying rice, it felt a bit rude but there was no way around it. This was actually quite a difficult thing to do on a push bike as it was like cycling through quicksand. All the adult members of the families were involved in the process including the elderly relatives and I watched several senior citizens still wearing their pyjamas bagging up and measuring out the rice, it was fascinating to watch. I don't know how they managed to work all day under the full sun and in the mega heat.

The heat was really getting to me today. The temperature had ramped up again and it was so humid there was no relief from it anywhere. It did not help that I had cycled to the beach which got my blood racing around my body and heated me up to start with. I sat underneath an umbrella all day but it didn't really make any difference, it was boiling. In other countries if you sit out of the sun you can usually cool down, here it makes little difference to your body temperature in the shade or out of it. I sat watching the Vietnamese sales ladies on the beach, one of them was lying on a sun bed underneath an umbrella wearing denim jeans, hoodie, woolly gloves & socks, a Ninja face mask and sunglasses, I was only wearing a bikini and I was baking, how did she do it?

Let me explain to the uninitiated what happens when you have a hot flush. You are absolutely fine one minute going about your business as normal, when you begin to have this strange feeling start to creep over you, coming up from your abdomen. It crawls slowly up through your chest and bursts into your face, you almost feel like you are going to combust because of the heat your body is suddenly generating. I am fortunate in that I do not go bright red, break out in beads of sweat along my forehead or soak my hair, but my skin feels very hot to the touch and at night my chest actually feels wet. Yes I know YUK! At that exact moment you will do anything to cool down, I usually end up stripping off (I always wear cardigans which come on and off all day long) and I now carry a fan everywhere. I can no longer wear jumpers or anything long sleeved that I can't roll up, tights are a particular no go area and so is anything tightly fitting or heavily lined with viscose. I am probably the only person in the world known to strip off on a bus during a freezing Winter in Norway when it was -19C . The flush may only last two or three minutes but if you are having these all day long it can be quite debilitating and it wears you out.

A night sweat is a similar sort of thing except that starts from your feet going upwards to your face. I spend all night pulling the duvet on and off.

In the winter, Peter has started to wear pyjamas and socks to bed, he would wear a hat as well if he could. I have tried every natural remedy on the market, Holland and Barrett made a small fortune out of me - none of it really helped. I have cool pillows which don't work, a 4.5 tog duvet on the bed all year round, the windows are always open and I have a ceiling fan continuously whirring around. Last year Peter gave in and bought us an air conditioning unit for the bedroom which I have on ice cold when it is really hot. I never have the central heating on in the bedroom and I sneak around turning all the radiators down during the winter months, mind you I don't put the heating on until late November and turn it off again in March. Hot flushes are a hideous sensation and along with all the other menopausal symptoms they cause pure misery.

Day 76

The following day I did not feel great, I think it was the heat getting to me. I decided not to cycle anywhere today and just mooched around by the pool. I went up the road to the nail technician to get my toenails gelled for the last time before I leave and she did another brilliant job.

Peter rang me with the date of our friends funeral, I will just be home in time to attend. I am glad I can go but it's not want you really want to do when you get home from your holiday.

In the early evening I went into town on the bus again, I still did not feel too good. I decided to eat at a small restaurant a bit outside the main drag that I had spotted when passing on the bus. I entered in and took a seat at a table, I was given the menu and then completely ignored whilst the French waitress chatted to two fella's at the bar. This place only had 6 tables and two of them were free. I waited 25 minutes to be served and in the end I got up and walked out and they did not even notice. This gave me the right hump, I cannot stand bad service, they weren't even busy. I then got assailed by some woman trying to sell me something and for the first time I snapped back. I then get mobbed by people trying to get me to go out on their boats and again I snap at them. I was in a really bad mood by now and to finish the perfect evening off, when I got back to the hotel the swimming pool was full of very loud French guests who made so much noise that I could still hear them up on the fourth floor.
An emergency glass of Dalat red was called for and I slowly unwound in the coolness of my room.

Day 77

The following morning the weather had changed again. Today it was still hot but the humidity had dropped and there was a good wind blowing which kept the temperature at a bearable rate. I cycled to the beach and stayed lounging around all day. On the way back I cycled along to see Greenie and Eric who were both fine, but they said that their new hotel is much busier as they get lots more independent guests who all need their attention whereas there were more organised groups at my hotel that came with a tour leader who sorted out all of their transportation and trips.

Hurrah, the good news from Kayla back at my hotel is that I do not have to move out after all, the overbooked tour group arriving is not as big as previously thought. I was so pleased as it saved me a lot of hassle.

I had my dinner next door at the laundry ladies house. I had been trying to get hold of Peter for two hours and he was not picking up. My mind had gone into manic overdrive and I started to imagine all sorts of catastrophes and accidents. I texted him and whatsapped him but he still didn't answer. I was beginning to feel so sick now that I thought my dinner might reappear and I rang my sister to see if she could get hold of him. Of course eventually he rings me, he had been driving from Manchester on his motorbike and obviously could not use his phone. He told me off as I had got my sister all stressed out and worried as well. Feeling a bit stupid I went back into the hotel, who should be sitting up at the bar? Den. "Come and have a drink gorgeous" he shouts across reception, I have to say he looked like he had already had a few. So I spend the rest of the evening fighting off Den's outrageous flirting and lurid suggestions of what he could to do with a woman as beautiful as me. It was such a load of shit, are there really women out there who would fall for this?
He was as subtle as a brick, but he did make me laugh !

Day 78

I woke up at 1:45AM feeling very ill and experiencing weird sensations throughout my body. The room was spinning around so fast I could not open my eyes properly. I had pains in my chest and I seriously wondered if I was about to have a heart attack. What on earth could have caused this? OMG a dreadful thought suddenly dawned on me, I hope Den didn't slip something in my drink, he wouldn't would he? He certainly would have access to those sort of substances living where he lives. The room continued to rotate at an alarming speed, I switched on the light which helped me to focus a bit and propped myself up on the pillows. I stayed sitting bolt upright like this for the rest of the night, I daren't close my eyes, the pain in my chest did not abate and I was truly terrified that I was about to die. I was also freezing cold and physically trembling, I had to snuggle up

165

under the covers, something was definitely wrong. At some point past 5.30am I eventually fell into a deep sleep. When I woke up later all the symptoms had disappeared and I almost thought I had imagined it.

I laid low all day on the beach hiding underneath my charming Vietcong hat, trying to avoid Den, who I could see lurking around further up the shore line. I went for my weekly massage and Linh made me eat two whole mangoes before she released me and dropped me at the expat bar on her bike. I had a few beers and something light to eat but resisted the invitation to go out on the town with the boys, last night had scared me a bit, and anyway I desperately needed some sleep.

Day 79

At breakfast the next day there were two new guests who I got into conversation with. They were sisters from Dublin and were spending a month travelling the length of Vietnam. They wanted to go to Hidden Beach and I offered to take them there on bikes via the cycle paths. Now these two ladies were both in their early sixties and had not been on bikes in years, with all the rice laying out on the paths they found the journey a bit hairy in places, the dodgy bikes probably didn't help. By now I was a bit blasé about everything here and hadn't give it a thought, they were both mighty glad when we arrived. Both Den and Danny were on the beach and we all had such a laugh, the girls were really feisty and along with Den's deadpan humour and Danny's naughty charm we had a really fun day together.

After a pizza for tea I met up with Danny in the wine bar for a few glasses of decent wine. He was not my type at all, I always go for slim, tall, dark haired men and as I got older the occasional silver fox, but I did find him very amusing and enjoyed his company immensely. He made me laugh a lot and it was nice to get chatted up. I had really thought it was all over and I was invisible to men now, but as this trip had proved so far: it's never over (that's a line from The Best Marigold Hotel) I know that if I had given him the green card things might have taken a different turn, but my guard was firmly up and I managed to keep him at arms length the whole time. I have to say he was a proper gentleman and never tried to laid a finger on me. I left him to go catting around the late night bars to see what middle aged woman he could charm the pants off that evening and got the bus back to the hotel.
Back in my room my nephew had sent me a long video of himself, telling me what he had been up to recently, as I played it back it brought tears to my eyes.

Day 80

Blimey it was Easter Sunday today, there were no chocolate eggs for me this year. I was off to visit Danang. I had been driven through the city about 10 times but have actually never set foot in it, so today was the day. I had booked a car through the hotel and we set off. The driver made Miss Daisy look like another Formula 1 racing driver, I think we would have gone faster if I had got out and pushed. We trundled along at a sedate 25 miles an hour, I thought we would never get there.

First stop was the 'Fifth Military Museum' which has remnants of the countries tumultuous past fighting against the French and the Americans. This was an enormous place and I at first thought it was closed as there seemed to be no-one around. I was beckoned into a small kiosk near the gate and a very officious tiny man filled out a form, stamped it and proceeded to hand me a ticket, this cost me about £3. He waved me in the vague direction of the building and went back to watching what looked like the Vietnamese equivalent of 'Britains got Talent' on an old TV - It sounded like a right old load of crap.

Inside the museum was a lot of historical stuff about Ho Chi Minh. Hundreds of photos adorned the walls and there were glass cases full of his letters and personal items. There was also a mock up of his modest house, the original is in Hanoi. He died in 1969 but is still revered by the older Vietnamese and there was always a queue to get into his mausoleum in Hanoi, where his body lies embalmed in a glass coffin for all to see surrounded by an armed guard. I saw it when I visited Hanoi, apart from a bit of a waxy sheen he could have just been sleeping.
I wandered around this enormous museum and only saw four other visitors, maybe they will eventually knock it down and build a huge karaoke bar, it would certainly be much busier and make more money for the economy. There were some thought provoking pictures of soldiers, dead bodies, political prisoners and myriads of pictures of people who just disappeared, never to be seen again, but it was all old, a bit worn out, unloved and not in the best state.

Out of the front of the museum in a manicured garden were a large selection of helicopters, fighter jets, rocket launchers, tanks and cannons, all left over from the war with America. They were in a slightly better state than the ones in Hue and were displayed well, but to be honest they gave me the willies. I felt distinctly uncomfortable when I walked under one of the enormous guns on a tank, at that point I felt that I had seen enough and went to look for my driver outside. He was parked up outside with his feet up on the dash board and was fast asleep.

I had asked Kayla when I booked the car to tell the driver that I specifically wanted to visit the Pham Lam Pagoda. Now I am quite sure that is not where I went next and I still do not know where it was but it was very pleasant! I shall explain.

My driver dropped me off in a tiny side street outside the gated entrance to a temple. It was in the middle of a neighbourhood, the pagoda I actually wanted to visit was in a more open space. In the grounds were some brightly painted effigies and a very fat golden Buddha, this told me it was in fact probably a Chinese temple. The pagoda was surrounded on all four sides by local houses, I think it was the local neighbourhood temple, a bit like your Parish church at home. Anyway as I was there I climbed up the steps, at the top were lots of satchels, shoes and hats laying around abandoned in the courtyard. Inside the temple the temperature must have been hitting 45C, I had arrived during a child's prayer session, probably a bit like Sunday school. I sat on the floor to one side and watched them, I loved the tranquility of the place and the children were really getting into it, bowing their heads and chanting along with the monks. Most of them were well behaved but one or two tiny little mites were getting a bit bored, went rogue and had to be brought back in line by the teachers. No-one even looked in my direction, I was of no interest to anyone.

I sat there for about 20 minutes with the perspiration pouring off me, when I attempted to get up, the marble floor was so slippery underneath me with my sweat that I could not get a grip in my bare feet and I couldn't stand up. Very ungraciously but silently, I had to crawl across the floor on my hands and knees to the entrance and pull myself upright on the door frame, no-one took any notice whatsoever. I cannot imagine that happening in our local village church without the whole congregation watching and wondering what the hell I was playing at.

After the strange pagoda experience we went to the Han market. This is a huge two floor undercover wholesale market in the centre of Danang next to the Han River. The whole place was busy with tourists and locals alike. The aisles were only as wide as the Vietnamese, so if you are a Westerner with a big bum it was quite difficult to navigate without banging into things. There were hundreds of stalls, downstairs it was mainly food and souvenirs but upstairs was full of clothing, shoes and bags. This is where the shop keepers in Hoi An come to buy their stock and it was really cheap, I imagine they get it cheaper still if they buy in bulk and there was a fair bit of heavy duty haggling going on. All around the edges of the top floor were sewing machines with ladies whipping up elephant trousers, cheap dresses, matching floral unisex shorts and shirts which you see all over Hoi An, the Koreans particularly like to dress the same as their partners, and all sorts of other cheap clothing. I stood and watched one women, she ran up a pair of trousers on her old fashioned Singer machine in 3 minutes flat, chucked them in a basket and two minutes later they were on a stall for sale at £2.

There were some lovely stalls selling traditional Vietnamese dresses, called the Ao Dai. These consist of a pair of floaty trousers with a long sleeved tight fitting dress split to the thigh, usually topped off by a conical hat. You need to be very slim with no love handles to pull this look off and the Asians always look beautiful but it's not something that any shapely or buxom Westerner can do easily. Several of the stalls will make you a Ao Dai to fit your shape and there were European ladies of all heights and shapes being measured up. They had fabulous colours and fabrics, I would secretly have loved one but I know I would look a bit stupid when I tried wearing it in Bedford.

Fortunately there were ceiling fans whirring overhead to keep the temperature down otherwise there would be no breeze at all squashed between the tight stalls and the sweaty bodies. There was no hard sell here, no-one kept stopping me to sell me anything, the real money to be made lies with the Hoi An shop keepers. At least they didn't laugh when I asked if they had any pineapple shorts to fit me, just mumbled something unintelligible and walked off!

I purchased a dress which cost me £3 and actually fitted my larger figure. I then perused the cheap plastic shoes, they would give Peter nightmares and keep him awake at night. I came across the handbags, unlike the nasty cheap shoes these Fake bags were of excellent quality. I toyed with the idea of buying a gorgeous black leather lap top bag which they wanted £18 for. At home something like this would cost £200 easily. I then spotted a small dark green leather bag on a silver chain, it was love at first sight, just my taste and I bought it for £12.

I fought my way through the crowds to the busy road outside, this was lined with more wholesale shops mainly selling hats and baskets. In one of these I purchased a Panama hat for the grand total of £1.75. I had seen one in Monsoon before I left the UK and I still do not know why I didn't buy it, it was a bit late now but it would do for future adventures.
I set off walking along the river, taking in the view of the new skyscrapers and the Dragon Bridge. This bridge has been built in the shape of a huge dragon which breathes smoke and flashes it's eyes, it is quite a spectacle, especially at night. You get the feeling that this city is really taking off and I imagine in a few years it will easily compete with some of the other Asian powerhouse cities.

Whilst I was minding my own business I was stopped by a group of Viet students who wanted to interview me to practice their English. This was very amusing, they led me to a bench where they surrounded me on four sides, pushed a microphone in my face and jotted down notes in their books regarding my replies. They were very sweet and polite, they wanted to know why I was here, how long I was staying, had I been here before, what did I think of Danang etc etc. I felt a bit like an ageing film star and they all wanted to shake hands with me when the interview was over. I could see my driver parked out on the road watching over me and he found this is all very amusing.

All along the waterfront were restaurants and bars, a bit like the Thames - NOT. I came across a Baskin Robbins ice-cream parlour, not what I was expecting here, and I emerged with a giant cornet which I snaffled as I walk along the river. It was a lovely afternoon and the sun was starting to go down as I made my way back to my car. I had enjoyed my afternoon here and would like to see more of the city, it is after all the third largest in the country and there must be a lot to see.

On the way back we passed China beach, which is a wonderful expanse of soft white sand and rolling surf. It was nicknamed China beach by the American GI's who came here for a bit of R&R during the war. The locals call it My Khe beach and apparently it is owned entirely by the Vietnamese army. Further on we passed some enormous 5 star resorts, Furama, Hyatt, Sheraton & Pullman, I counted 24 luxury beach resorts and 7 building sites before we even cleared Danang. There were several professional golf courses along here as well, most people wouldn't even imagine they have such a thing in Vietnam, they are all top notch and beautifully maintained. There were also some very nice looking apartments for sale along here, I wonder who can afford to own one, certainly not the Vietnamese

Miss Daisy eventually dropped me off at the hotel. After a quick shower and change I headed downstairs to meet the Irish girls, they had invited me to show them around the town and have dinner with them. They were sitting in reception already having had a few colourful cocktails by the look of the array of empty glasses on the table, off we traipsed into town on the bus. They instantly loved the place and I led them around the tiny streets and showed them where the three night markets were. I introduced them to my secret little cheap clothes shop and they had a good old browse before deciding (like me) that there was nothing that would fit them. The shop keeper came to the rescue, measured them up and offered to make them two dresses by tomorrow for around the cost of £14.00. I pointed out where the livelier bars were, there was another Irish pub in the town centre which they wanted to try out. We ate dinner at Cuisine Dannan where we got treated like visiting royalty. Tania and I had a fabulous meal but Mary's was not that great and she's not backward in coming forward, if you know what I mean. We finished the evening up in my secret wine bar where they could not believe how cheap a glass of wine was compared to Dublin, after a few glasses we headed back to the hotel where I slept like a log all night long.

Day 81

The next day the weather was gorgeous, just right with a strong cooling breeze. My tan looked amazing and I was starting to go really dark, I hardly recognised myself in the mirror, I looked like a different woman .

I met the girls at the beach, they arrived in a taxi this time, I went on my bike, cycling through all the drying rice on the cycle paths. All the farmers were out in their fields harvesting the rice and they had also started to burn some of the stubble, so I had ridden through huge plumes of black smoke and smelled like a kipper when I finally arrived at Hidden beach.
I found the girls lolling under an umbrella and joined them. They were really good company, both widows, Mary had only just lost her husband at Christmas. We nattered all day long discussing in lengthy detail men, marriage & sex, it was the perfect girlie way to spend some time.

Later on back at the hotel whilst talking to the reception staff we realised that no-one had seen Den since last night, he had yet to make breakfast since he had been here, so no one was unduly worried. We were a bit concerned he might be ill or had even snuffed it and no-one had found him, so we drew lots to go and knock on his door to investigate. In the end Tania went to find him, he was just sleeping off a lot of booze from the night before and was raring to go out again.

I was now at the point where I realised I would have to go home to reality in 5 days and I was starting to panic big time. The logical part of me said it was time to go, you can only sunbathe and lounge around for so long. The other part of me did not know how I was ever going to drag myself away from this wonderful place and how would I ever be able to say goodbye to all my girls.

After we discovered that Den was alive and well, I was informed by Kayla that the hotel management would be paying for all the reception staff and myself to go out for a farewell lunch (no karaoke this time - phew) together on Friday and they were also going to pay for my car to the airport. This was all because I had been the best guest they had ever had staying there, well the longest staying guest at least!

The following day I sat out by the pool in the morning before a bit of an adventure in the afternoon. Danny picked me up to take me on the long awaited tour of his building site and erection process. I had already seen it several times from afar but when we got closer you could see exactly what an enormous project it was. On a pristine piece of beach about 8 miles outside Hoi An they were building an entire leisure city with Chinese money - 4.2 billion dollars worth. It will consist of hotels, casino's, shops, restaurants and a premier golf course. There are over 2000 workers on site and up close it was an impressive undertaking.

We drove around the site, it was far too big to walk, and I was open mouthed at the money being spent here. Inside the offices was a model of the proposed site which could take up to 10 years to complete. They are only on Phase one at the moment, there are at least twelve more luxury apartment blocks to be built along with all the roads and infrastructure once the hotels are finished. They had been told the hotels should be open for the new season but that looks a long way off to me, but then look at the hotel near the lighthouse, that was just a building site last year, they may very well achieve their target.

There is also talk of building another airport out here, oh dear, I don't know what to make of that bit of information. Yes, it will bring in lots of jobs and more money for the local people but it will also bring thousands more visitors into the Old Town, how will it ever cope, it is mobbed most nights as it is.

I was handed a stylish (Not) white hard hat and climbed aboard a golf buggy for a bumpy tour of the golf course. The grass had already been laid and there were sprinklers everywhere keeping it green and lush, we rode through some of the spray and I ended up looking like I was in a Miss Wet T-shirt contest. I found the whole thing absolutely fascinating, I used to work for a building company and always found the process from bare land to the finished product an interesting journey. We drove all over the golf course where there were women tending to the grass and shrubs, in fact 10% of the work force here were women, and I was reliably informed that they are very hard grafters. Of course they are, I wouldn't expect anything less of the modern Viet woman.

After the site visit we sat in an Irish bar drinking Magners cider for the rest of the afternoon, I am not sure if Danny actually does any work, he always seems far too busy guiding his harem of lady friends around the town.

It was early evening and there was a bit of a panic going on in reception. Apparently one of the guests had asked Toby Hot Boy if he would arrange to hire a motorbike for him so that he and his wife could ride the Hai Van Pass. Apparently on the way back down the brakes had failed, and with the driver being relatively inexperienced they had had to crash into a tree to stop themselves and were now both allegedly injured. It was dark now, there would be very little passing traffic up there, there were no street lights and it was a very dangerous road at the best of times let alone in the dark. It was the first time I had seen Toby in a bit of a sweat and he was frantically ringing around trying to get someone to rescue this stranded couple from the mountain.

I headed into town with the girls and Den in tow, he wanted to show us a restaurant he tried last night which he said was fabulous. Tania was going back to do some charity work in Thailand after this trip and had Den's number, they might meet up. Somehow I think even an experienced ladies man like himself might actually come a cropper with her, she would eat him for breakfast. Again we all had a superb meal except for Mary, it was another culinary disappointment for her. For the second night in a row we ended up in the wine bar, these two girls certainly know how to drink. I offered to split the drinks bill but I was told in no uncertain terms to 'Feck off' I was too scared to argue.

Days 83-84

The next two days passed in a similar vein, we went to the beach (them in a taxi and me on my knackered bike which I was now very fond of), met up with Den, lounged around all day and then returned to the hotel. We went into town both nights for dinner, I introduced the girls to the 'Banana Leaf' restaurant and miracle of miracles Mary got a dinner to her liking. We drank buckets of cocktails at 'The Red Snapper' and slurped down copious amounts of red wine at the various wine bars. I am a bit of a light weight drinker at home but in Vietnam I had turned into a hardened drinker, my current companions did not help the situation.

I set off one morning on a complex shopping trip to try and buy some thank you cards. This was harder than I originally thought it would be. I ended up in three different shops buying all different cards with strange spellings on them, I had really wanted them to be all the same. I sat and wrote them out, I have to say I felt quite emotional whilst doing so, slipping sterling notes inside each one, ready to give to the girls and Eric.

I took Tania and Mary along with me for my last massage at Linhs. We three buxom women lay practically naked in a row whilst Linh and her assistants kneaded and pummelled us all into submission. I said my goodbyes to Linh, I would not be seeing her again before I left, we had a huge hug and I promised to look up her new salon if I visited again.

I had spoken to Peter every other day but he was now deeply preoccupied. Luton Town FC were possibly going to get promoted to the Championship next season and he could not really focus his mind on anything else.
It had been nearly three months and I still had not heard from my mother, but I had spoken regularly to all of my friends, my sister and Maureen. In fact I think we had all spoken more than we do when I am at home. I will be pleased to see them all but I had a continuous nagging doubt, would I be able to tear myself away from this magical place?

I spoke to the injured couple at the hotel (fortunately they only had cuts and bruises), they were going to try seeking compensation, there is no such thing here, good luck with that! Why don't people read their guide books or heed advice on the internet - **DO NOT** hire a motorbike of any description here unless it is from an approved dealer and you are a very experienced rider. I later found out that Toby was being made to pay for the vehicle recovery costs out of his wages by the management.
Fortunately because of all the tips he gets, Toby probably earns more than the hotel manager. He always seems to have wads of cash.

The hotel tonight was full of Russians, they are the rudest people on the planet and so full of themselves. They pushed the three of us ladies out of the way to get on the bus, and conversed with each other over the tops of our heads in their harsh voices all the way into town. Mary could not stand them and we had to pull her away to stop her having a go at them.
Tonight we just had a light meal and a few drinks, we were all strangely tired. I secretly think we were permanently hung over, and we all opted for a relatively early night.

There was another very amusing moment as we left town, again with a taxi driver. I was so blasé now about the bad driving that I sort of expected it all the time, but Mary & Tania were still relatively new to it. The driver this evening obviously did not want to take our fare but was pushed into it by the taxi supervisor. I sat in the front holding on for dear life, weirdly it did not even cross my mind to put my seatbelt on, the girls were literally screaming in the back. He drove like a man possessed, weaving in and out of all the other vehicles on the wrong side of the road all the way up the Cua Dai Road. He barely stopped to let us get out and virtually tipped us out of the car at the hotel. Mary had had enough and she blew her top at him, she stood in front of the car totally blocking him in, he would have to run her over to get out. She screamed at him at the top of her voice ' you are a Feckin loony, you Feckin bastard'. After a few more choice words were tossed in his direction the taxi driver actually was beginning to look scared and I was starting to feel sorry for him. With one last bang of her fist on his bonnet Mary at last let him go. Toby Hot Boy and the other concierges were all watching amusedly from the safety of the security hut, it was a very funny incident.

Day 85

I had another funny turn during the night with more chest pains and weird sensations going down my body. It was quite frightening laying there on my own in the dark and I had to switch the lights on again. I think it was possibly the stress of knowing I had to go home back to real life after being cocooned here for so long, I know I would have to pay dearly for having three months off somewhere along the line.

As the trip came to an end I had mixed feelings. I had missed Peter (but not clearing up after him) and I felt that I was ready to go home to start my new job but I knew it was going to be so hard to leave. I am not a complete airhead and I was fully aware that living here full time would probably end up being a bit boring, unless you had a job, not any easy thing to get here for a Westerner. It is a harsh climate to live in, the humidity is constantly high and in the Winter months it rains torrentially from September to November. But I had totally loved being here, fully embraced the experience and really felt like I had properly connected with the place. I had fallen totally in love with all my 'girls' (and the boys). I no longer batted an eyelid at the traffic, I cycled across huge traffic junctions and it did not faze me. I had covered every inch of Hoi An on that battered old bike with no gears and dodgy brakes. I had felt little fear of doing anything on my own for the whole trip. I hadn't been ill and apart from a few days I had coped fairly well with the heat and humidity considering my menopausal state. At 55 I did not feel entirely invisible anymore, I had been chatted up so many times, I felt that maybe I still had it, whatever IT was, and men still found me attractive.
I had not spent all of my money and was going home with £300, that would go towards my next trip. Most of my clothes and shoes were only fit for the rubbish, I looked thinner and healthier, I had a suntan to die for and probably skin like an elephant.
All in All it had been a truly magical experience.

Day 86

On the Friday morning I arose early and surprised the hell out of the restaurant staff again. I felt a bit ropey this morning after the bad night and I lounged around the pool all morning before getting dressed for my lunch with the staff. They had told me to look beautiful so I decided to wear a shortish sundress which turned out to be a big mistake. I was driven to the restaurant on the back of Misa's motorbike which caused a breeze that whipped the skirt up and everyone on the Cua Dai Road saw my knickers, several times.

The restaurant was nothing like the one we went to on our anniversary, this place was dog rough. It was out near the beach, a firm favourite of the locals, and served fresh seafood, Kayla said the food was always amazing. There were dirty glass tanks full of sea life and as you can well imagine the restaurant stunk of fish, not in a pleasant way. The chairs and table were made of red plastic and it was full of noisy Vietnamese women chucking all their rubbish everywhere. There was no alcohol served and only bottled water to drink.

All my girls were in there along with Greenie, Eric and the Customer Services Manager, Jenny. Kayla was in charge of the budget and of ordering the food. I have to say it was horrible, I normally love fish but everything we had tasted like the sea - salty. I was seriously worried that I might be seeing it again later, though I noticed that they all tucked in with glee and cleared every single plate.

There was obviously lots of gossip going on amongst them, just like at any normal office party. Greenie was winding Kayla up about her tiny waist and said she was worried that Kayla didn't eat enough, Kayla got all indignant at this point and woofed a whole plate of slimy squid to prove the point. They both did the same job and were on the same pay grade, I think they needled each other a bit. Anna was quieter than usual, maybe she was suffering from a bit of morning sickness, she certainly looked a little pale, but I watched her closely as she snaffled a bowlful of chip chips (clams) so I think she was OK. There was lots of hilarity, I had absolutely no idea what they were talking about but strangely it didn't matter, I still felt included.

Jenny gave a lovely speech about how I had been a wonderful guest and please would I come back again. She also told me that she would give me a special rate if I did. There were lots of toasts with our bottles of water and Yo Yo's all round. I tried not to cry but I welled up and they all got a bit flustered and upset as I was crying again. I managed a little speech back and handed out my thank you cards. There was a lot of laughter that Greenie and Eric only got tiny cards and the others got bigger ones. I couldn't help it, they were all I could get.

We then had the ubiquitous selfies taken and they took a load more photos outside the restaurant before they all went back to work. I have one hilarious photo of the six girls wearing their motorbike apparel, completely covered head to toe, looking like six tiny Ninja's and there is me in the middle wearing a short skimpy sundress and flip flops.

Back at the hotel I felt really queasy all afternoon, I was almost sure my dinner was going to make a reappearance. They had all been so sweet and kind at the restaurant and I felt so sad as I made a half hearted attempt to start packing up my stuff, it seemed like a Herculean task. In the end I left it half finished and went to bed for the rest of the afternoon.

That evening I took Tania and Mary up to the ex-pat bar to meet all the fella's. We sat up at the bar all evening having a right laugh. I thought Mary was going to cause a riot when she was served a very small vodka in a tiny glass. I cannot imagine anyone brave enough to argue with her, apart from the Kiwi landlady, and a larger glass was sought immediately. I spent most of the evening talking to Danny and drinking refrigerated red wine which was completely tasteless but not as bad as my favourite tipple of Dalat Red. I would not be seeing Danny again either as he was off to Ho Chi Minh City in the morning for a boys weekend. The mind boggled as I tried to imagine what they might get up to in the fleshpots of HCMC. I felt very sad when we said goodbye, he had been really good fun, great company and had behaved like a gentleman, he had never put one foot out of line with me - I liked him enormously.
There were big hugs all round with everyone in the bar, it was the start of Goodbye Vietnam.

Day 87

On my final day I took my last solo cycle ride out through the paddies to Hidden beach. I would not be seeing the stunning beauty of the paddy fields every morning and it was a deeply sad feeling, I wanted to imprint the image on my brain. I knew I would now be spending most of my mornings sitting in a traffic jam on the A1 at Stevenage, not the most scenic of places. The weather was not perfect today and it clouded over dark and ominous in the early afternoon, a bit like my mood. I finished most of my packing and then went into town for a farewell dinner with Tania and Mary. We went to the Banana Leaf for fat juicy prawns and shared a bottle of decent wine whilst sitting on the balcony breathing in the atmosphere for one last time. Afterwards they went off to the Irish bar but I went straight back to the hotel, I needed to get some sleep. It would be a long journey home.

Day 88

In the morning after a surprisingly decent nights sleep, I officially checked out of my residence after nine idyllic weeks and left a massive wedge of sterling notes in the tip box, the biggest tip I have ever left anywhere. Toby Hot Boy arranged all my luggage for me and loaded it all into the car.

It then got really heavy and emotional. All the staff came out to say goodbye, the other guests must have wondered what was going on, there were so many people in the lobby. Eric turned up as well as Greenie and all of her family. Even the staff who's day off it was came along to say goodbye. Anna was there wearing a tiny little black dress with tears rolling down her face. Tania and Mary also came down to see me off. I was bombarded with presents and completely overwhelmed by it all. When the time came to get in the car I broke down entirely, I could hardly breathe I was sobbing so hard. I will never forget that last sight of their faces as the car pulled away and I cried my heart out all the way to Danang. The poor driver was getting really concerned about me and I tried in vain to pull myself together, but it wasn't easy.

On the way to the airport we passed the beach, there is a small green sign pointing the way:

'Hidden Beach - the end of the road'

Yes, it was all over, I had had the best months of my entire life and I will never forget one second of it.

7 HOLIDAY FALLOUT

As you can imagine the long journey home was absolute hell for me.

I robotically checked in at Danang airport all the way through to London, my luggage weighed 28.5 kg. I have absolutely no recollection of being in the departure lounge or the flight to Singapore, let alone if I ate or drank anything, I was in a complete emotional fog. I was so out of touch with the real world it was a bit of a culture shock when I got to the hustle and bustle of Singapore airport, to see all the designer shops, tourists and business men rushing around to catch their flights.
I couldn't even figure out the simplest method of connecting to the Wifi - I had to ask a smartly dressed young assistant to help me, he looked down at me as if I was some sort of alien - I know I certainly felt like one. I had eight hours to kill here and had planned to do one of the of the free city tours that you can do if you have more than 5 hours to wait, but they were all fully booked up (book in advance if you want to do this). I had no other option than to find a comfy chair, sit and wait out the 8 hours until my late night flight. Fortunately I had a decent book, and armed with a sandwich and bottle of water I stayed in the same place all day. The cleaners even started hoovering around me at one point but I was totally oblivious to everyone.

Of course it was sods law, the flight was running 45 minutes late, so that extended my stopover even longer. The departure lounge was overflowing, there were 7 International flights going out of the crowded Satellite terminal within the same time frame. I just wanted to get home, I wasn't even panicking about the flight at this point. Everyone wanted to embark the plane to get settled down for the night and all the children were starting to get a bit cranky and whingy.

When my flight was eventually called we were squashed in like sardines, there were no spare seats at all. I was sat on the back row of a section in front of the galley, next to a very large lady who seemed to continually encroach into my personal space, normally this would annoy me but I couldn't have cared less. The other thing I noticed was that everyone in my part of the plane were wearing long sleeved hoodies. After half an hour into the flight I realised why, it was freezing cold in this part of the cabin. I ended up wearing the silly little socks they give you and wrapped myself up in the thin airline blanket, but I was still cold. I had sent my thick cardigan home with Peter and I was just wearing a T-shirt, jeans and flip flops. As soon as dinner was finished, I have no idea what I ate, all the lights went out, the staff disappeared and it was pitch dark in the cabin.

I had drunk two bottles of red wine with my dinner which numbed my senses a bit and then I watched four films: Widows (OK), A Star Is Born (I didn't like it), Aquaman (totally daft but Jason Momoa was well worth watching) and The Girl in the Spiders Web (very good).
I must have dozed at some point for all of 10 minutes, the flight was fairly smooth, I don't remember any turbulence, every passenger was fast asleep except for me, for the whole time. I really hated them all.

We landed at Heathrow around 5.30am to a grey and leaden sky. As we were one of the first flights in there was not too much of a queue at immigration and my case appeared very quickly on the carousel. I brushed my teeth, combed my hair and layered on some mascara and lippy. I emerged through the double doors into the arrivals hall but I could not see Peter anywhere, he suddenly appeared in a bit of a fluster, he had not expected me to be through so quickly and was having a quick coffee in Costa.

The journey home was uneventful, the M25 at least was kind to us, the weather was bland and all the traffic seemed to be moving at lightening speed. Usually when you come home from a holiday it sometimes feels like you have never been away, I felt like I had landed on another planet in a far off galaxy.

Peter dropped me off at home and then left me alone to go out on a job for work, this was a really bad idea of his. Wandering around the house, I cannot describe the huge sense of loss that flooded over me. It took me all day to unpack my case and the other one Peter had brought home. With the washing machine going I started slowly to put everything away. Full marks to him that he had cleaned the place which I was very grateful for, at least I had not come home to a dirty house and a huge pile of his washing. There was not a scrap of food in the house though so I had to venture out to

Asda, which felt like I had actually arrived in Hades, I really could of done without that the first day back.

When Peter got home that evening we opened a bottle of decent wine with dinner to celebrate my home coming. This became a worrying pattern that then followed practically everyday for the next 4 months, I had had an alcoholic drink virtually everyday for the last 13 weeks and I kept repeating to anyone who would listen that I had come home with a drink problem! Who knows how many bottles of wine and gin we went through that Summer.

That first week back was a total physical killer. Over the next four days (96 hours) I only managed to get 13 hours sleep, I do not know how I functioned or got through it. I could not remember how to get into the house and had to ring Peter for the code, he pointed out that I had a fob on my key ring! I remembered how to drive but kept forgetting to change gear and couldn't remember in which direction to go round a roundabout as I approached it. In retrospect I should not have been driving, I was too spaced out.

I scooped up a load of loose change off the kitchen counter that had been sitting there since Christmas and paid to have my car washed with it. Peter went ballistic when he found out, one of the £2 coins was a rare one and was worth £50. My head felt like it was full of cotton wool and I just could not think straight, I was so tired. My body was back in the UK but my slow fuzzy brain was still in Asia. We went out to a Toyah concert in Harpenden on the first Friday back, it was a freezing cold night and poured with rain and I had to wear a big thick puffa jacket. I dozed fitfully through most of her set whilst Peter jiggled around by the stage in front of his idol.

I looked amazing though, even if I do say so myself, I did not recognise myself in the bedroom mirror when I got up in the mornings. Slim, darkly tanned with fantastic platinum hair, beautiful nails and for the first time in a very long time I actually liked what I could see. It never lasts though does it, within 6 weeks the tan had faded, all my nails broke and I put all the weight back on, the booze every night didn't help with the size of my fat arse.

Oddly Peter never once said that he had missed me, just repeated that he had kept himself busy, filling the time whilst I was away. This bothered me more than you can imagine and still does. He seemed really bad tempered with me, but mind you I was behaving like a mad woman, I was completely off the end of the scale and every movement I made felt like I was wading slowly through thick treacle all the time. The final straw with Peter came when I unthinkingly threw away a piece of paper of his, I was in the middle of a meeting and had to leave early to come home and look for it whilst he went absolutely berserk at me.

As the weeks went on I felt him retreating further and further away from me and then I realised that he had just disappeared altogether. All summer long he went out leaving me on my own with just the dog for company, and she doesn't even like me, she only has eyes for him. As the months went on I really struggled, all the menopausal symptoms were back on full throttle, I felt like I was losing my marbles and I got quite introverted which isn't like me at all. I lost interest in things that I had once enjoyed, clothes, sex, shopping, food, my garden & the house. I didn't watch TV for 5 months, it was only when Strictly restarted in September that I took an interest. I didn't pick up a book until October, I had no concentration long enough to read. I couldn't cope with all the rooms and possessions we had in our house, I felt totally suffocated with it all - I had really enjoyed the simpler life.
I couldn't be bothered to do any house work, cooking became a complete bore, I stopped visiting my friends and family regularly, the only people I really saw were work people. I also went down with a nasty chest infection that took three weeks to go away and left me feeling drained.
Even Luton Town getting promoted to the Championship didn't lift my spirits much, and that was a true gift to any hardened football fan.

What is it with people? I had been on this amazing trip and no-one was really interested. My friends didn't even ring me when I got home, I had to ring them to let them know I was back and still alive. My mother behaved as if I had been away for a long weekend. Peter didn't even bother to look through my photographs with me, he fell asleep half way through, mind you there were 4000 of them. My sister and Maureen were the only ones interested enough to look through my pictures. I had had this huge life changing experience and there was really no-one to share it with. The only person who had an inkling of what I had been through was Tracey at work. And thank god for work, on the surface I was still immaculately dressed and made up but it was the only reason to get out of bed every day, otherwise I may have stayed underneath the duvet forever.

Initially my only saving grace was speaking to the friends I had met along the way. Derek and Ivan emailed me often with their news. Anna sent me all the pictures of her wedding in May and then a few months later sent me the complete wedding album (that really made me cry). She kept me up to date weekly with her baby news, and she was actually started to looked quite podgy in the face, even if she only looked like she had a small melon up her jumper. One evening she was out on a girlie night with Sunny, Kayla and Misa and I ended up being passed around the restaurant so that I could see and speak to them all (that made me cry as well). Greenie sent me lovely little messages and pictures of herself and her children, Danny usually sent me something rude. I spoke to the Irish lasses regularly and I even went to the South of France to stay with Mary in her holiday home which really lifted my spirits.

I will never know if keeping in touch was a good or a bad thing, but it kept my adventure alive for me for several months whilst I was having trouble coping with the reality of normal life. I yearned to be back in Vietnam every single day, what I actually thought I was going to do there I do not know. I even toyed with the idea of doing a Shirley Valentine, I told no-one about this thought so they will be a bit shocked when they read it.

I think most people just thought I had the holiday blues and I would get over it, but it was more than that. Looking back now I think I was seriously depressed, not helped at all by the menopausal symptoms. You would think I would have been bad at first and gradually got better, but it worked in complete reverse. At first I was glad to be home but as the months went on I missed the excitement of travelling more and more. On the surface I still looked and acted normally but I was having a total meltdown inside and no-one noticed. I did visit the Doctors for a chat about HRT but she put me off again when she said it could mess up my thyroid, another episode of Graves disease at this point was all I needed.

8 IN RETROSPECT

So like women the world over who are having a menopausal crisis, I just got on with life as best I could.
And Peter just like men the world over kept out of the way of his mad menopausal wife by disappearing for the whole summer.

We booked a cruise later in the year with some friends to the Emirates that was cancelled due to the looming problems in the Gulf. We then booked with Thomas Cook to go to Mexico and that also got cancelled leaving me with a deficit of £3500 in my bank account. At the time of writing this I still don't know when I will get it back. We finally booked to go to the Caribbean which was very nice but a bit boring for my intrepid taste, at least we had lovely weather and a nice rest.

We attended some very high profile events during the summer, I was at Lord's when England won the Cricket World Cup, what an atmosphere, it was amazing.

We spent two weeks helping to organise a large country fair at Hatfield House in July, it was a massive International event and the volunteers pulled it off with aplomb. We also worked at the Clacton airshow in August and spent a very interesting night moving equipment around in the middle of the early hours to prevent it being stolen but that is another story!

I went to our friends funeral the week I got back. The turn out was overwhelming. It was a sad service but good to know it was exactly as he wanted it. I bawled my eyes out through the whole thing.

I made the decision to take our house off of the market in May, there was just no interest, nothing in our area was selling, the public fear over Brexit had seen to that and the housing market was dead. At the time Brexit had been postponed again and who knows what will happen to house prices when it eventually happens. In retrospect if we had managed to sell our house I would at least of had a project to be working on and may not have got so wrapped up in myself.

Happy 55th Birthday. Two letters were waiting for me: please come for a cervical smear and a bowel cancer screening test.
As most women know a smear test is a bit of an undignified procedure that we all have to go through. They tell you to open your legs, go floppy and relax whilst they shove a metal willy inside you, screw it open as far as it will go, then delve around inside your private parts with an ice lolly stick.
The bowel screening made the smear test look like a day in the park, I don't even want to describe it. I lay on a bed wearing a pair of hideous green paper knickers with a huge slit up the back whilst a nurse inserted a camera up my rectum, which we then watched the progress of on a huge TV screen, along with the other three nurses in the room. I don't think I will ever get a Bafta for that performance.
It was worth it though, as both tests confirmed that there was currently nothing nasty lurking in my nether regions.

The good news from Burma in July was that Bagan at last got granted Unesco Heritage status . That was indeed good news as it will come under their protection now and no-one can mess around with it.

Anna got married on 11th May to her Physical Education Teacher, as she described him to me. She had three different white wedding dresses and also a bright red Ao Dai for the traditional ceremony, she looked beautiful except they had plastered her in make up and she looked very different! The baby arrived by emergency C section on the 4th November. I could tell by her messages and voice that she was completely traumatised by the whole event. We desperately want to see each other but she has been advised not to go out or do anything for three months so she has asked me to go out in February when she will be allowed out and I can see the baby who's English name is La Vie.

The Vietnamese hotel I stayed in shut down on 1st August for a complete refit. They also let all of the staff go, so when it reopened in November all the staff were brand new except for the senior management. All my girls had got new jobs in other hotels and home stays and are not returning. Just because everything is shiny and new does not mean that future guests will have the amazing time that I had, I hope the management realise that the staff were what made it so special not the fixtures and fittings. They have a huge job on their hands to improve on my experience with their new workforce.

I went to France to stay with Mary in October, I have never been to Cannes or Nice and I loved it. The weather was amazing and we had a good catchup, she is still dealing with the unexpected death of her husband but is looking onwards and upwards. Hopefully I will also meet up with her and Tania in Dublin some time next year. The strange thing about both of the flights to France and the Caribbean was that I was not scared or nervous, I think my sub conscious knows now that I have to get on a plane to go somewhere exciting and I will just have to accept it.

Strictly Come Dancing started again and at last I began feeling some avid interest in something (saddo that I am). I was glued to the TV every night and just loving it (Kelvin or Karim for the winner).

Peter and I went through a very difficult few months where I think we lost each other. Probably most marriages go through a rocky patch, it's whether you can work it out or not. Sometimes you both need a bit of a rocket up your arse to make you realise what you really want from a relationship. Currently we are trying our best to make things right again, like they used to be. I know we cannot go backwards and have to move on with life, but we are both making an effort to do more things together whilst still having our own space. We still love each other very much so that is a good starting point.

The menopause is unfortunately a fact of life for every woman. It affects everyone differently but we all have to go through the hormonal change at some point. It is currently a hot topic for discussion, but I still do not think men will ever understand the madness of it all nor do they have any real inclination of how we feel. Whatever the hype, most men are definitely not in touch with their feminine side and have no idea how much we are suffering. We all know that if they went through it there would be some sort of cure for it by now.

As we go into the winter, the hot flushes have ramped up a bit, that is purely down to the central heating being on at work and in the house. Last week I asked for the heating to be turned down in the office as I was only wearing a bra, knickers and a sleeveless dress and was still overheating. When someone complained that they were cold I justified it by explaining that I as was currently only wearing three items of clothing and could not remove anything else, unless they wanted me to walk around the office in my underwear I suggested they get a woolly vest.

To prove to myself I am not over the hill I have purchased the tightest black leather jeans, I don't care what anyone thinks, they look fab and I intend to wear them everywhere.

My sleep pattern is still up and down, I have good nights and then bad ones. My mood has lifted though I still have decidedly dodgy days when I could just jump on a plane going anywhere. As Christmas approaches I am being the biggest humbug, I just cannot get enthusiastic over the commercial hype but I look forward to all the parties.
Thanks to the guys at work for covering my desk in tinsel whilst I had a day off!!!! I really appreciate it - NOT.

If I knew back then what I know now would I do it again? Would I advise anyone else to do it? Was it the best time of my whole life?
The answer is unequivocally YES, YES, YES. Travelling to foreign places and cultures makes you see the world through different eyes, it makes you evaluate your own life. Doing it on your own makes it such a big adventure, you learn things about yourself that you didn't know before and it also means you have no-one else to please but yourself.

'Make it happen, girl. Shock everyone'

'Pour yourself a drink, put on some lipstick, and pull yourself together' - Elizabeth Taylor

ABOUT THE AUTHOR

Jan lives in a village in Bedfordshire, she has always travelled around the world despite unliking flying. For many years she has wanted to do a big travel adventure and the opportunity arose in 2019 for this to happen. Married to Peter for 19 years and already working on a follow up book.

Printed in Great Britain
by Amazon

65962482R00116